WHY YOU SHOULDN'T SHOW THE SOLES OF YOUR FEET IN SAUDI ARABIA, OR SAY "NO" TO A THAI . . .

WHY YOU SHOULDN'T TALK BUSINESS AT LUNCH IN PARIS, OR FIRE A WORKER IN BALI . . .

WHY YOU SHOULDN'T BE LONG-WINDED IN LONDON, OR SHORT SPOKEN IN JAPAN . . .

These are a few of the reasons why, if you have business abroad, you should have this book.

"Literally hundreds of the nuances of international trade in a single volume . . . a fine job."

—George J. Stathakis,
President and CEO,
General Electric Trading Company,
and Director, National Foreign Trade Council

"This book does an excellent job of showing Americans how to deal with foreign trade."

—Kenn George, Director General, U.S. and
Foreign Commercial Service of the
Department of Commerce

LENNIE COPELAND grew up in the Middle East and England, and has degrees from Vassar, Boston University, and Stanford's Graduate School of Business. She has headed her own consulting firm, with clients that included General Electric and Sony.

LEWIS GRIGGS has degrees from Amherst and Stanford's Graduate School of Business. He has successfully started up several small companies, and has taught negotiation skills to employees of many major American corporations. Currently he is Ms. Copeland's partner in a San Francisco-based film production and consulting firm, where the authors were responsible for the highly a̶ series.

GOING INTERNATIONAL

How to Make Friends
and Deal Effectively
in the Global Marketplace

*Lennie Copeland and
Lewis Griggs*

A PLUME BOOK

PLUME
Published by the Penguin Group
Penguin Books USA Inc., 375 Hudson Street, New York, New York 10014, U.S.A.
Penguin Books Ltd, 27 Wrights Lane, London W8 5TZ, England
Penguin Books Australia Ltd, Ringwood, Victoria, Australia
Penguin Books Canada Ltd, 2801 John Street, Markham, Ontario, Canada L3R 1B4
Penguin Books (N.Z.) Ltd, 182-190 Wairau Road, Auckland 10, New Zealand

Penguin Books Ltd, Registered Offices: Harmondsworth, Middlesex, England

Published by Plume, an imprint of New American Library,
a division of Penguin Books USA Inc.

PUBLISHER'S NOTE

Grateful acknowledgment is made to the following for permission to reprint previously published material:

Business Week: excerpt from "The Japanese Manager Meets the Americans Worker," *Business Week,* August 20, 1984.
Directories International, Inc.: quotations from the following *Advertising World* Magazine articles: "Media Notes and Quotes" (July 1984); "London, Eye-View of Ad-Placement Skills" (April/May 1984).
Forbes: excerpt from "Back-Patting Clapping," *Forbes,* June 18, 1984. Reprinted by permission of *Forbes* Magazine, © Forbes Inc., 1984.
Foreign Affairs: quote from "Foreign Policy and the American Character," by Arthur Schlesinger, Jr., *Foreign Affairs,* Fall 1983, p. 7. Reprinted by permission of *Foreign Affairs,* Copyright 1983 by Arthur Schlesinger, Jr.
Fortune: quote from "Ad Biz Gloms Onto Global," *Fortune* Magazine, November 12, 1984.
Harvard Business Review: The following material reprinted from *Harvard Business Review:* excerpt from "Made In America" (Under Japanese Management)," by Richard Pascale and William Ouchi (September/October 1974). Copyright © 1974 by the President and Fellows of Harvard College; excerpt from "Doing Business in Islamic Markets," by Peter Wright (January/February 1981). Copyright © 1981 by the President and Fellows of Harvard College; excerpt from "Developing Managers in Developing Countries," by J. Lee (November/December 1968). Copyright © 1968 by the President and Fellows of Harvard College; excerpt from "The Honorable Picnic," by Dudley Miller (November/December 1961). Copyright © 1961 by the President and Fellows of Harvard College. All excerpts reprinted by permission of *Harvard Business Review.* All rights reserved.
The New York Times Company; excerpt from "Ventures in the China Trade," by Christopher Wren, April 3, 1983. Copyright © 1983 by The New York Times Company. Reprinted by permission.

(The following page constitutes an extension of this copyright page.)

Published by arrangement with Random House, Inc.

 REG. TRADEMARK—MARCA REGISTRADA

Library of Congress Cataloging-in-Publication Data

Copeland, Lennie.
  Going international.

Originally published: New York : Random House,
c1985.
  Includes bibliographical references and index.
    1. International business enterprises—Management.
2. Business etiquette.   3. National characteristics.
4. Ethnopsychology.   I. Griggs, Lewis.   II. Title.
HD62.4.C66   1986   658'.049   86-8554.
ISBN 0-452-25864-2

First Plume Printing, November, 1986

9 10 11 12 13 14

PRINTED IN THE UNITED STATES OF AMERICA

To Ashley

Preface

It is an axiom among American management consultants that those companies which need them the least are always first in line for their services. This has certainly been our experience. When our series of training films, *Going International*, became available, the companies that were losing millions in foreign operations were not the first to buy. Rather, it was the more successful multinational corporations that immediately recognized the benefit of using these films to help prepare their international personnel. Not surprisingly, America's "excellent" companies were among the first: IBM, Hewlett-Packard, Levi Strauss, Procter & Gamble, Raychem, Caterpillar, 3M, Bechtel, Amoco, Hughes, PepsiCo and Digital Equipment. Several companies ordered thirty to forty films to have on hand at their various locations. The United Nations, Peace Corps, CIA, Air Force, Small Business Administration, as well as schools of business, also bought in the first few months. Films were sold in Australia, Canada, England, Finland, France, Japan and Saudi Arabia, among others.

The *Going International* films challenge one's complacence about what it takes to do business abroad and show ways in which international travelers must change if they want to succeed. This book strives to do more than that. We will provide the fundamental intelligence required for successful international transactions, whether buying, selling, negotiating, getting information, paper pushing, supervising employees, engineering, administering aid programs, soldiering, preaching, training or representing a government. In addition to many specifics, we will provide universal truths and rules of thumb that apply virtually anywhere and in almost any situation.

Going International, the book, is intended for the following audiences:

- International travelers, whatever the nature of their work abroad.
- Employees (and families) living abroad for extended periods.
- "Armchair travelers," all those who are involved in international business without personally going anywhere. This group includes anyone who has direct contact with people of foreign cultures (hosting foreigners here, telephone, telex, mail), those who have indirect contact (advertising copy, product design), and those with responsibility affecting international operations (strategic planning, staffing, consulting, and so on).
- Educators, government personnel and policy makers, as well as officials of religious and philanthropic enterprises.

This book is for the novice *and* the seasoned traveler. After interviewing hundreds of business travelers and residents abroad, we can say this: knowledge about other cultures does not automatically come from experience. The traveler can remain ignorant after many trips abroad because foreigners are unlikely to give feedback. Someone unfamiliar with different communications styles is likely to miss the subtle clues indicating that something is wrong.

Every book has its point of view, and ours is distinctly American. Therefore, throughout the book, the authors use certain words which some readers may object to, but which we must use to avoid cumbersome synonyms. We use "Americans" to apply solely to citizens of the United States. Some cross-cultural experts advise against this, but in our experience people from the other Americas typically call themselves Canadian, Brazilian, Venezuelan, Mexican, and so on, *not* American. Canadians and South Americans may complain that we have usurped the word "American," but in most conversations, even they are likely to call us that for want of another word.

Throughout the book we use the word "expatriates." Purists insist (correctly) that the word means those who are banished or who withdraw from their own country. In this book—and in contemporary usage among Americans abroad and personnel administrators here—"expatriates" applies to any American citizens who live overseas. We also use the word "foreigner" when we speak about people of other cultures. To an American, a foreigner is any non-American; the word has no pejorative connotation. It makes a big difference *where* you use the word, however. Understandably, foreigners object to being called foreigners in their own country. When overseas, Americans have to accept that *they* are the foreigners.

Acknowledgments

During production of the *Going International* films and while writing this book, we talked with hundreds of people about their international business. Only a few are named in the book, but we are indebted to them all for their open and frank sharing of experiences, insights and ideas. We want to thank specially those experts who have helped us from the beginning (Clifford Clarke, Price Cobbs, Nessa Loewenthal, Fanchon Silberstein, George Renwick and Tom Rohlen), as well as the international business travelers who appeared in the films and upon whom we continue to call (John and Margaret Toppel, Bob and Jan Rix, Tim and Lauri Dorman, Lewis and Rinda Burleigh, Eric and Lynn Brown, and Mimi Murphy).

We can't thank enough those who read the long first draft and sent it back with comments, corrections and more anecdotes: Hubert Johnson of the U.S. Air Force, Mike Copeland at Procter & Gamble, Phillip Grub of George Washington University, André Rude at Hewlett-Packard, Richard McElheny at Price Waterhouse, Ron Boring at Apple Computer, Deidra Deamer at Unison Corporation, Brad Mills of Tradex International, Alison Lanier of the *International American*, Noel Slocomb and Rita Morrow of International Relocation Resources, Virgil Brown at Goodyear International, Ron Nagle at General Electric, Judy Esterquest at Booz Allen Hamilton, Margie Goldman at Baxter Travenol Labs, and Joan Mincy at Westin Hotels. Nancy Adler of McGill University is especially thanked for her help with the appendix on "Women in International Business."

We are also grateful to our agent, Rafe Sagalyn, and our Random House editor, Derek Johns, for making our entrée into book publishing so easy and enjoyable. Derek's own international sensitivities added immeasurably to his artful editing and enthusiasm.

Finally, we thank Sheldon and Lisa of Robinson Word Processing in San Francisco for many, many hours of extra effort on our behalf.

Contents

CHAPTER 5
Communicating: How Do I Talk with These People? 99

How to give and get good information. Patterns of communication. The meanings of "yes" and "no." Reading between the lines. Learning the language. Interpreters and translations. Making presentations.

CHAPTER 6
Managing People: Getting the Best Performance 119

Managers, power and decision making. Work ethic, motivation and incentive systems. Supervision and evaluation. Hiring and firing.

CHAPTER 7
Skills Transfer and Training 139

Obstacles to skills and technology transfer. Preparing for the transfer of knowledge. Teaching and training in a foreign culture.

CHAPTER 8
Business and Social Etiquette 156

Form over substance. Showing respect. Greetings, titles and business cards. Pitfalls in conversation. Entertaining and protocol. Gift giving.

CHAPTER 9
Getting Things Done: Making the Machinery Work 173

Negotiating the rules. Who you know. The omnipresence of government. Bribery. Business supports.

CHAPTER 10
Dealing with Headquarters; Dealing with the Field 184

The two realities. Problems of distance, isolation and autonomy. Visiting firemen. Information flow, both ways. Doing the job without going native.

CHAPTER 11
Managing Personal and Family Life 193

The frequent traveler: tips for the road. The expatriate family, the single abroad, and culture shock. Preparing for a move. Coping: the special ordeal of the spouse. The shock of reentry.

CHAPTER 12
The Road to Success: What It Takes to Be a Winner 209

Are you internationable? Success traits. Rules of thumb for all occasions. Now it's up to you: homework.

INTRODUCTION

❖ ❖

*American business
is international*

American business is international business.

We have to face it. We are no longer economically self-sufficient or capable of commercial isolation. International commerce is vital to American prosperity. Roughly a third of U.S. corporate profits are generated by international business. American competitiveness abroad has a tremendous direct effect on domestic employment levels and on the economic health of entire industrial sectors and regions, and ultimately on the entire nation. Every billion dollar's worth of exports creates about 25,000 new jobs. In the past five years, nearly 5 million new jobs created in manufacturing were export-related. At present, one out of every six manufacturing jobs is directly dependent on foreign trade, and one out of three acres of American farmland is harvested for export.

Most business leaders believe that the growth potential of the domestic U.S. market is leveling off and that any growth we can expect from 1985 onwards will be through greater participation in world commerce. In a 1981 congressional study of U.S. industrial competitiveness, the Office of Technology Assessment reported that "where a global market exists, firms operating on a worldwide basis may have advantages over those that restrict themselves to a domestic market, even one as large as that of the United States." Major multinational companies plan to invest heavily abroad in the coming years, mainly to get access to markets but also to take advantage of lower wage rates and cheaper goods and services, as well as to reduce vulnerability to protectionist trade moves by foreign governments.

American performance is weakening.

The global marketplace has become highly competitive. The United States is losing out not only to Japan but to South Korea, Taiwan, Brazil, Mexico and a host of other nations. Our share of world exports declined from 15.4

In 1985, the following companies derived over 35 percent of their revenues from overseas operations.

COMPANY	% OF SALES	COMPANY	% OF SALES
Pan Am	74	AMP	43
Exxon	71	Emhart	42
Schlumberger	68	Pfizer	42
Ocean Drilling	67	Schering-Plough	42
Mobil	59	Polaroid	42
Gillette	57	Foster Wheeler	41
CPC International	56	Warner-Lambert	41
American Brands	56	Black & Decker	40
American Family	55	F.W. Woolworth	40
Dow Chemical	55	Norton	40
Phibro-Salomon	54	American International	39
Lafarge	54	McDermott	39
Mattel	54	Baker International	38
Colgate-Palmolive	52	Johnson & Johnson	38
CBI Industries	50	Coca-Cola	38
NL Industries	47	Sterling Drug	37
Lubrizoil	47	Crown Cork & Seal	37
Texaco	47	ITT	37
NCR	46	Avon Products	36
Merck	45	Squibb	36
Trans World Airlines	44	Xerox	36
Burroughs	44	Castle & Cooke	35
IBM	43	Intel	35
Hewlett-Packard	43	Hughes Tool	35

SOURCE. *BusinessWeek*, "International 150," April 18, 1986

percent in 1970 to below 12 percent in 1984. According to RCA's Robert Frederick, chairman of the National Foreign Trade Council, 80 percent of our industry now faces international competition. No longer do we consistently have the best goods at the best prices, as we did in the years after World War II. No longer are we the "only game in town." Now when our foreign customers or partners are dissatisfied, they can turn to French, Germans, Japanese, Brazilians and any of a dozen others. Of the world's 100 largest industrial corporations, 46 were American in 1984, down from 67 in 1963.

In 1985, U.S. foreign trade produced a record deficit of 148.5 billion, up some 20 percent over the 1984 figure of $123.3 billion. Hewlett-Packard's John Young, chairman of the President's Commission on Industrial Competitiveness, reports that America's drop in share of world trade between 1960 and 1980 represented a loss of $150 billion to the U.S. economy, with losses mounting as the value of the dollar soared. Some economists estimate that the trade imbalance in 1984 cost America 2.5 million jobs.

U.S. dominance in world agricultural trade has decreased since 1980 by over 10 percent in several grains; construction-equipment exports dropped 63 percent between 1981 and 1983; machine-tool shipments went down 60 percent. Even our lead in high tech is being chipped away. Between 1965 and early 1985, seven out of ten U.S. high-technology industries lost world market share.

The United States faces competition in service industries as well. In advertising, Japan's Dentsu is the number one agency in the world, and Britain's Saachi & Saachi has taken over two American companies and is a major challenger to the U.S. advertising giants. In software, foreign programmers are recapturing their national markets. British, French, Brazilian and Indian software companies are now strong exporters. Korea's Daiwoo, Gold Star and Hyundai conglomerates are entering the fray. In space telecommunications the French-led consortium Arianspace is challenging NASA for a share of the $10 billion market over the next ten years. By 1990, Japan is expected to have its own space program.

In the Middle East, the United States is losing ground in services ranging from health care to construction. Whittaker Corporation recently lost its exclusive $1.4 billion hospital-management contract in Saudi Arabia. The new American embassy in Riyadh is being built by a Korean company. In France, Motorola lost out to the Japanese when France's Thomson group chose Oki Electric Industry Company to expand the French company's semiconductor business. After working with Motorola for six years, a Thomson group executive said: "We may just have more in common with the Japanese than we do with the Americans." He explained, "We both attach great importance to form and style."[1] Western shipping has been lost to Taiwan's Evergreen Marine Corporation, which is likely to become the world's largest container line by 1986. In real estate, Canada's Olympia and York Development Ltd. has become the world's largest developer. Even Hollywood is feeling the pinch of increasing competition from abroad: foreign countries are showing a growing preference for films of their own culture and shunning American-made movies.

Foreign firms are also invading America's domestic market.

"International" no longer means "outside the country." So many foreign firms operate here that "foreign" is as close as across the hallway.

For the first time a non-U.S. company, Germany's KNU subsidiary of Siemens, has won a contract to manage a U.S. nuclear plant. We are buying Japanese cars and electronics, Korean ships, Philippine underwear, Hong Kong watches, Taiwan clothing and Malaysian calculators. No black-and-white television sets sold in the United States are made in the United States.

Foreigners now own such American symbols as Howard Johnson's, Baskin-Robbins Ice Cream, Saks Fifth Avenue, Alka-Seltzer, Chesterfield cigarettes, Bantam Books and the *Village Voice*. A Saudi Arab owns a majority interest in the National Bank of Georgia and Mainbank of Houston. Australians have bought Utah International. Kuwaitis own Santa Fe International. A Canadian company owns Paul Masson wines. Swiss Nestlé's acquired Libby and Stouffer Foods, and more recently doubled its presence in the United States by buying Carnation. A French firm owns a major portion of the A&P food chain.

America's fourth largest exporter, after General Motors, Ford Motor Company and General Electric, is a Japanese company.

Mitsui USA is our fourth largest exporter. The Japanese parent has invested over $540 million in around forty American subsidiaries and joint ventures in thirty-three states. Its industries include wood products, sugar, chemicals, grains, hospital supplies and leisure.

U.S. MERCHANDISE TRADE BY AREA			
	EXPORTS F.S.S.	IMPORTS C.I.F.	BALANCE F.A.S./C.I.F.*
	(Billions of dollars, annual rates)		
Western Europe			
1984	58.0	74.9	-16.9
1985	56.8	84.2	-27.4
Japan			
1984	23.6	60.4	-36.8
1985	22.6	72.4	-49.8
Canada			
1984	46.5	66.9	-20.4
1985	47.3	69.4	-22.2
OPEC			
1984	14.4	28.1	-13.7
1985	12.5	24.1	-11.6
Other developing countries			
1984	60.0	98.8	-38.8
1985	59.2	99.0	-39.8
Communist countries			
1984	7.2	5.7	1.5
1985	7.1	6.3	0.7

SOURCE. U.S. Department of Commerce International Trade Administration

*C.I.F.—Cost, Insurance & Freight. Includes value of product and all costs of transportation, loading, shipping, insurance, etc.
F.A.S.—Free Alongside Ship. Includes only the value of goods and cost of getting goods to dock. Does not include shipping costs from port of exit.

Many American ventures drop out of the foreign environment.

According to JETRO (Japan External Trade Organization), roughly one out of seven foreign companies retrench and pull out of Japan. Another 28 percent stick it out despite sustained business failures. And in China, according to Landy Eng, president of the Asian Business League, "for every ten businesses entering China, nine will leave with a big hole in their pocket."

Failure rate for individuals assigned abroad is high too.

It is virtually impossible to get statistics from international companies, and the limited research on this subject has produced statistics which vary widely. Data suggest that somewhere between 20 and 50 percent of international relocations end with premature return. In developing countries the failure rate has been as high as 70 percent.

Bob Kohls, director of Washington International Center, says that without international training, only 20 percent of the Americans sent abroad can be expected to do well, and 40 to 60 percent will quit the assignment early or function far below their abilities. He calculates that 10,000 overseas Americans can be expected to give up and come home early each year, for many reasons. (These reasons will be discussed in Chapter II.)

Direct costs of failure can run, in the most extreme cases, well over $200,000 for an overseas employee and family returned home prematurely. If Bob Kohls' estimates of the number of returnees are correct, American companies are losing $2 billion a year in direct costs. There is no figure for costs of lost business and damaged company reputation caused by these expatriates or by the millions of international travelers and armchair travelers involved in but inadequately prepared for international business. We can assume the figures to be frightening.

"Before we invested in predeparture training, we had a very high return rate of people from Great Britain and the US involved in technology transfer in Venezuela. After we conducted workshops, the early failure attrition dropped to zero . . ."

SOURCE: Vice president of a U.S. aluminum company, a client of Moran, Stahl & Boyer.

The costs of international business are tremendous.

Americans made over 5 million business trips abroad in 1984, up from 2.3 million in 1977. Two million Americans live overseas (not including Canada or Mexico), about twice as many as in 1968. The figures are hardly surprising considering that 93,000 American firms are involved in international trade and 25 percent of them maintain offices abroad. Horwath & Horwath, a British consulting company, recently reported that 280 million international travelers now spend $95 billion a year on air fares, hotels, food and other travel expenses. Only 30 percent of all international travel is tourism.

Corporations and other international organizations spend several billion dollars each year on plane tickets alone. Companies are unwilling to reveal details regarding their travel expenditures, but one can make estimates. For example, in 1983, Bechtel employees just from the San Francisco headquarters made 3,000 trips abroad, many of them going to the farthest reaches of the earth. If you add in the Bechtel employees who travel from other domestic and foreign locations, total travel costs can be assumed to be the millions yearly.

Already high, travel costs are rising (42 percent from 1980 to 1984), and corporate America has increased its travel at an even higher rate. Runzheimer International's preliminary figures reveal that 84 percent of U.S. companies sent employees abroad on business trips in 1985, up from 75 percent in 1984 and almost 67 percent in 1982. The median annual cost of business travel per firm has risen from $330,000 in 1980 to $557,000 in 1984 (74.8 percent). Organization Resources Counselors, Inc., reports April 1986 per diem rates to be as high as $231 in Abu Dhabi, $292 in Tokyo, $210 in Lagos and $243 in London. Transportation plus per diem allowances make the financial investment in international travel costly.

Notwithstanding high costs and high risks, frequent travel is a minimum requirement for success in the international marketplace.

Savvy traders say, "If you want the competitive edge, you've got to get overseas frequently and let your foreign customers and partners know you care about them." As a Commerce Department spokesman puts it: "You can't do it by remote control." Others agree that if you cannot travel, constant communication is a must.

More and more heads of international operations are becoming aware that it is a mistake to send people abroad or assign international responsibilities to people who will not be effective working with people of a foreign culture. The cost of training is inconsequential compared to the risk of involving people who do not have the required skills and sensitivities.

Meeting the international challenge is not simply a matter of improving products, protectionist trade laws, or tax breaks.

Our ability to remain in the world economic major league will depend on the competence of our players, the managers and personnel we send to the front line of international business. And competence must now be defined in terms of cultural savvy as well as business skills.

Trend watchers predict a worldwide revival of cultural assertiveness. As

John Naisbitt says in his book *Megatrends:* "The Swedes will become more Swedish, the Chinese more Chinese. And the French, God help us, more French."[2] The message is clear: study and be prepared to adjust to the foreign culture or stay out of international business.

American success abroad is hindered by failure to understand how cultures differ.

Failure overseas rarely results from technical or professional incompetence. Multinationals take their international business seriously and typically send abroad high achievers who have proven skills and expertise. But their success is usually in the United States, where their skills, style and attitude may be exactly the opposite of what will work overseas. Employees' ignorance of or inability to adjust to foreign ways are usually what cause problems.

In the United States we know in vivid detail the colors, designs and sounds that appeal to various customer groups. We know what people dream about. Careerists climbing the corporate ladder study intently the values and norms that characterize their company's "culture" so that they can maneuver successfully toward the top. Negotiators approach the bargaining table with a rich understanding of what motivates their adversaries. When it comes to foreigners, however, we see only silhouettes. Overseas, many U.S. companies approach their customers, colleagues and employees with an ignorance that would be unthinkable on home ground. We are willing to transact business with foreigners without understanding who they are, what makes them tick, how they view the world and (with the exception of our fascination with Japan) how their corporations work. Because we do not look behind the foreign mask, our approach to international business is often like shadowboxing. We are dealing with imaginary targets.

Becoming an expert on one country will not be enough in the future.

Most international activity now demands a cadre of personnel capable of operating easily with people from a variety of cultures. As personnel manager for Bank of America's Asia Division, Tim Dorman was based in Tokyo but he traveled all over Asia and had repeated contact with at least fifteen countries under his responsibility. It quickly became clear to him that all Asians are not alike; social and business customs vary greatly. Bob Rix, assigned by Bechtel to run staffing operations in Abcaiq and Jubail, Saudi Arabia, had to deal with a labor pool of Malays, Filipinos, Koreans, Jordanians, Saudis and Americans. Sensitivity to national pride, values, and even tastes in food was essential to maintain peace and productivity.

Why are we innocents abroad?

Fewer than 8 percent of U.S. colleges and universities require knowledge of a foreign language for entrance. Fewer than 5 percent of America's prospective teachers take any courses in international subjects as part of their professional training. Some years ago a UNESCO study in nine countries placed American students next-to-last in their comprehension of foreign cultures. Only a few years ago, 40 percent of high school seniors in a national poll thought Israel was an Arab nation.

America's labor and management pool is critically deficient in skills required for competence today. Only 3.4 percent of MBAs major in international business, and worse, 61 percent of business schools offer no international courses. Curricula have not been internationalized to provide American graduates with the knowledge today's manager needs to maintain a competitive edge in the international arena. Nor are multinational organizations bringing managers up through the international divisions. Nearly two thirds of the presidents and chairmen of the largest international firms are guiding those companies without having had any experience in the international divisions or overseas.

Meanwhile, other nationalities tend to be better informed about Americans. Mitsubishi has 650 to 800 employees in New York simply for the purpose of gathering information about American rivals and markets. One of the Japanese businessmen in the *Going International* films had been sent by his company to St. Louis to do *nothing* for the first few years but learn to understand Americans.

Peter Thigpen, now president of Levi Strauss, The Jeans Company, ran the Brussels office for many years. He worked regularly with personnel from practically all of the European nations, and of course with the various cultural groups within Belgium.

But let's not exaggerate. Even if hated, Americans are imitated.

American business practices are respected around the world. We have excellence to be proud of. We are an inescapable cultural influence in the world. Coca-Cola is asked for in eighty languages and is served 279 million times a day. A Japanese child in Los Angeles exclaims, "Mommy, they have McDonald's in America, too!" The television show *Dallas* is broadcast in ninety countries.

Many people around the world are alert to our American ways and easily accommodate us. Let's not give the impression that if your first mistake is not fatal, your second one will surely be. In fact, people will overlook, tolerate and endure our gaffes, as we do theirs, for a number of reasons: economic self-interest, curiosity, political purposes or simply because the boss said so. People are willing to try, and even when the damage is severe, people are sometimes willing to forgive.

And let's not overestimate the competition.

Business analysts fall into the trap of reading foreign business activity as planned and purposeful when room should be allowed for impulsiveness, improvisation and serendipity. Foreign firms, too, have had failures outside their own boundaries; they are just as vulnerable to accident, ignorance, negligence and sheer stupidity.

Henry Kissinger's description of the Soviet and American predicament is instructive: "The superpowers often behave like two heavily armed blind men feeling their way around a room, each believing himself in mortal peril from the other, whom he assumes to have perfect vision. . . . Each tends to ascribe to the other a consistency, foresight and coherence that its own experience belies."

Naturally, that does not mean we can afford to ignore the opponent's moves. Kissinger continues: "Of course, over time, even two blind men can do enormous damage to each other, not to speak of the room."

But the point is, cultural awareness can give us great leverage.

Tom Rohlen, international management consultant and anthropologist, puts it this way: "When I was a wrestler in high school, I built up my muscles. But when I went to Japan and learned Judo, I found that you can be even stronger if you use your *opponents'* power to overwhelm them. You get in line with the direction of their effort, and you simply take advantage of it. The implications for other areas of my life were clear: if you stop trying to press on the world, pushing and shoving, and instead watch where the world is flowing and make the best of that, you gain a powerful advantage."

GOING INTERNATIONAL

CHAPTER I

THE AMERICAN WAY

❊ ❊

I F AMERICANS TRAVELING ABROAD have just one experience in common, it is the chagrin they feel watching other Americans behaving badly. In hundreds of interviews with business travelers and expatriates, virtually everyone had an anecdote to tell about some other Americans, and their response was predictable. "I felt so embarrassed to be from the same country," they complained. "I cringed behind the bookstand and tried to look French or English, or anything but American." Even people who probably had made many *faux pas* themselves had something to say about the behavior of other Americans.

People all around the world know that Americans are sensitive to being thought of as insensitive. We take great pains, with varying success, not to be "Ugly Americans." A Lebanese taxi driver once told a CIA agent, "There is nothing more ugly than an American trying to be an Arab. America is a good country. You must be proud." So before exploring the ways to do better internationally, we want to make one thing clear: this book is written on the premise that the international traveler is not handicapped by nationality but rather brings special traits and know-how to the international marketplace. We are not going to suggest that Americans become Chinese or British or anything else.

Americans abroad must never forget that they are Americans. They should not flaunt it, of course, but without disrespecting other cultures, they need make no secret of being proud of being American. We stress this because we don't want our readers to go overboard when they take the advice of this book. Some Americans, in trying to ingratiate themselves with local populations, become so sympathetic to local customs and attitudes that they fail to accomplish the objectives of their assignment. For diplomats and businesspeople alike, the major part of any job is not only communication of local interests to headquarters, but more important, the reverse —getting the host-country people to understand the employer's position. It is essential for the American abroad to understand what is involved in doing business with the Malaysian, for example, but it is equally essential for the Malaysian to understand what it means to be doing business with an American.

The traveler who "goes native" loses his employer's trust as well as the trust of locals. Many foreigners find Americans dynamic and likable. We should not abandon wholesale our values and methods; if we completely conform, we have vastly less to offer. Worse than that, as one British executive told us, "When you imitate us, you so exaggerate that it is embarrassing. Like a transvestite dressing in women's clothes, it just does not work." In short, "When in Rome, do as the Romans do" is an axiom that should be applied only with caution and good sense.

"I attended a counselor's workshop in Hong Kong with a group of about fifteen British counselors. We were asked to volunteer for a role play and be graded on our warmth and naturalness with the client. I decided to use British expressions for fear they might critique my American familiarity and friendliness. I scored very low and was criticized for being stilted and artificial. I did another role play and was my old American self. Then I scored at the top! I learned my lesson."
Rita Morrow, International Relocation Resources, Chicago.

The American abroad steps off the airplane with a mark on the forehead that says "Made in USA, by Americans," and that is what people will react to. Until we establish ourselves as individuals, we had best appreciate that most foreigners have a complex of love-hate feelings toward Americans. In cities where "Yanqui go home" is scrawled on walls, American pop music blares from radios carried by youths wearing Levis and drinking Pepsi. But the international traveler cannot take this American clutter to be a sign of westernization. It rarely means what it seems to mean. In fact, some of our most avid imitators are "revolutionary" youths who went to American universities—those students who occupied the American embassy in Iran in 1980, for example. Conversely, even in countries where Americans are hated the most, an individual American can be respected and even liked. An American archaeologist who had lived in Lebanon for many years later returned and was accosted by an excited young Palestinian soldier who happily exclaimed, "Remember me, madame? I am Skandar, son of Soraya." Soraya had been the family maid, and both she and her son felt great affection for their American employer.

In trying to explain the ambivalence foreigners feel toward Americans, a former CIA official comments: "When Rome was the center of the world, those who were born elsewhere blamed their parents and their gods for such an onerous accident of birth. In the days of the Roman Empire one was supposed to be Roman. Nothing else would do. In the last century and in the early part of this one, the same kind of latent resentment was directed toward the British by peoples of the world who had the misfortune to be born anything else. And now the Nigerian, the Dane, the Uruguayan and even the Englishman, to an extent he doesn't realize, resents not being an American." Perhaps the next generation will wish it were born Japanese. Already, Americans are beginning to feel the same ambivalence toward the Japanese that for so many years other peoples have felt toward us.

Americans who have the greatest success in doing business abroad are those who have learned how to strike a balance between capitalizing upon the strengths and advantages they enjoy as Americans and showing a credible appreciation and understanding of those with whom they do business. They are *genuinely* respectful of the local cultures, not patronizing; they are *genuinely* sympathetic to positions taken by those on the other side of the negotiating table, while at the same time holding as firmly to theirs as is appropriate in the particular situations. In short, they know how to make the most of their Americanness without going too far.

The first step to understanding another culture is understanding your own.

Much is being said these days about corporate culture; there is a Procter & Gamble culture, an IBM culture and a State Department culture. But whatever the culture of the individual organization, it is only a variation upon and operates within the culture that unites all American enterprise: the American way of doing business.

There is an American way that is quite distinct from the way business is done in every other country. It is made up of all the habitual ways Americans behave at work and do their job. It is shaped by common attitudes and assumptions about work, the workplace and markets. And it is supported by common ways of thinking about life and other values more or less directly related to work. Certain behaviors are expected and rewarded here. Others are considered antisocial, unprofessional or counterproductive. The bundle of expectations we have about the way things are or should be make up a frame of reference or lens through which we view the world. When we look through our own cultural lens at home, we generally know how to interpret and evaluate what we see. But when we look at foreign situations through our own American frame of reference, we may come to the wrong conclusions.

You can't leave home without your frame of reference and value system. Nor should you. But if you want to really understand what's going on and to be effective in a foreign situation, you need to understand your own assumptions and know how different they are from those of the rest of the world.

Some cross-cultural educators like to debate whether we are basically different from or similar to foreigners. Whatever the answer, social psychological research illustrates that people tend to be attracted to others who believe the same things they do and people whom they perceive to be most similar to themselves. When we are in ambiguous situations, we assume similarity where there may be none in order to avoid the threat of differences. By only seeing the similarities, we operate with a severe disadvantage: we interact with a mirror of ourselves and not the real person. Americans are different from most other peoples in several outstanding areas, and it is in those areas that we often experience our greatest frustrations, fears or failures. This book is not going to present an anthropological thesis about American culture, but will highlight the American traits that get us into the most serious trouble.

Two qualifications are in order: first, the American culture described here is the majority culture. Members of ethnic minorities will nonetheless see their particular American subcultures represented because as international travelers, they are primarily American and only secondarily anything else. According to Price Cobbs, author of *Black Rage*, members of minority groups that have had to learn to accommodate themselves to white culture may have an easier time adapting abroad. He says, however, that "whether we are minorities or not, once leaving the shores of the United States, we are Americans. We are going to run into the same cultural barriers that any other Americans do, unless we take time to learn about and understand the culture."

Second, many generalizations about cultural norms will appear in the pages that follow. Every country has a national character, meaning that members of that nation have a shared system of values and common behavior. It is these commonalities that make cultural generalizations possible. Generalizations can aid understanding. However, generalizations are simplifications. Foreign nationalities are made up of diverse groups and individuals who conform to cultural norms in varying degrees.

The traveler can make big mistakes assuming that all individuals fit the norm. A traveler is wrong to assume, for example, that all Asians are formal and reserved in business situations. Japanese tend to be formal and correct, but Koreans are informal and outgoing. A Korean saleswoman might spontaneously put her hand on a customer's shoulder, while the Japanese is very unlikely to touch. Japanese will refrain from argument; Koreans are more likely to argue vociferously. Arabs from Morocco, Yemen, Iraq, Syria and Saudi Arabia differ greatly in attitudes and mores. Scandinavians have much in common, but there are differences between Swedes and Norwegians. Australians and New Zealanders are quite different in a number of ways.

Generalizations are less useful in countries where there are diverse cultures, such as in Israel. Sumatra, just one island in Indonesia, has at least six different cultures with radically different traditions. And in any country, there may be tremendous differences among socioeconomic groups as well as regional differences. City people in contact with multinational organizations and foreign cultures are quite different from the populations of rural hinterlands, where people are unaffected by outside influences. Even in the cities, cultural differences exist, especially in the Third World, where traditional value systems compete with value systems more like our own. Sweeping generalizations may cause us to mistake the "ideal" culture for the "real" culture.

In order to render generalizations throughout this book useful, the reader must always keep in mind that a generalization does not explain the individual. An international traveler must constantly distinguish the normal expectation from what is actually at hand.

Cultures are not right or wrong, better or worse, just different.

People around the world feel as strongly about their culture as we do about ours, even if they do occasionally feel ambivalence. It is pointless to argue whether a culture is "good" or "bad": every nationality thinks its culture is the best. For every foreign peculiarity that amuses us, there is an American peculiarity that amuses others. The Chinese tell American dog jokes, reflecting their amazement that a space-age people could feel the way we do about an animal that the Chinese consider better for eating than petting. Yet we are astonished by the French penchant for taking their dogs to the finest restaurants, where they may be served at the table.

Cultures have their own logic. Anthropologists say cultures are different because various peoples had to deal with diverse circumstances to meet their common human needs: different climates, different resources, different terrain. Just as animal species evolved differently to adapt to different conditions, so mankind evolved diverse solutions to life's problems. Over the years the complex array of solutions to problems (many of which disappeared long ago) created a confusion of cultural behaviors. But there *are* patterns, and one can begin to understand them by considering the different past, present and future of the cultures of the world.

Cultures are changing.

Cultures, on the surface, are changing every day in momentous ways. People are buying different kinds of clothing, using different products, watching different media, and so forth. But people in foreign countries who eat fast foods are no more "Westernized" than the New Yorker who eats sushi and drives a Toyota is "Easternized." Deep down, the fundamentals of culture change at a glacial pace. People believe and feel the way they have for generations, even when they know better. Ali Naimi, Aramco's Saudi president, spent his first eight years with his mother's Bedouin tribe. One of his jobs was to take care of the baby sheep, and one rule was never to stray out of sight of the home tent. Ali Naimi's subsequent Lehigh and Stanford degrees could not eradicate the influence of his childhood—he simply cannot view the world in the same way as David Rockefeller, Harold Geneen or Lee Iacocca.

There are many examples of business people who dress or behave one way at the office and go home to change and relax and behave in the traditional ways. We try to ignore these differences and to assume a "world business culture." To a certain degree there is uniformity in business around the world, but when you get down to working with people abroad, the most profound things you should pay attention to are the differences. In some countries, such as England, Australia and Canada, the differences may appear to be slight, but the nuances can be enormously important.

What follows are the most outstanding differences that seem to separate Americans from most of the rest of the world.

Problems of pace: "Time is money."

The American is always on the go. To many foreigners, we seem always to be in pursuit of something just beyond our grasp, always in a hurry, rarely stopping to enjoy the present. We come across as harried and jittery, slaves to the clock. And our clocks "run"; in other countries, a clock does not run, it "walks." Many have observed that we treat time as a valuable, tangible and limited resource. Like money, we save time, waste it, give it, take it, make it, spend it, run out of it and budget it. We certainly account and charge for it. We are always aware of how much time we have, as a relentless clock ticks away in our inner ear. Because time is so valuable to us, we try to use it productively and we compartmentalize it into efficient intervals of activity on our daily calendars. In many ways we rank time: earlier is better than later, first better than last, faster better than slower.

How we value time affects our business conduct. We operate according to hundreds of conscious and unconscious rules about how we move with the march of time. We even use time as a form of communication, an unspoken language that is understood loud and clear within our own culture. Consider a typical appointment in America. Whether it is a job inter-

In some places, language doesn't allow precision regarding time. In Mexico the dictionary meaning of *mañana* is "tomorrow," but *mañana* really means only "soon." In Arabic, *bukara* means "tomorrow" or "some time in the future."

view, sales call, or any other kind of business meeting, the visitor will be on time. To arrive early, however, would suggest that the visitor is anxious, overly eager, or has time to spare, an impression one would wish to avoid.

A visitor in America will be kept waiting only briefly. A longer wait would communicate lack of interest or disrespect, or an extreme disparity in status. Presidents can keep janitors waiting, but peers cannot be kept waiting. After only a few pleasantries, if any, the people meeting will get straight to the purpose of the visit. Both parties expect the business to be accomplished within an allotted twenty, thirty, or sixty minutes, and they move directly and unhaltingly toward that objective. If the meeting is interrupted by phone calls or other distractions, the visitor will resent the loss of time that had been implicitly promised. If the objective of the meeting is not accomplished near the end of the appointment, panic may set in. Decisions may be rushed and disappointment may be felt. But if the meeting proceeds on schedule, a conclusion will be reached and all involved will feel a sense of accomplishment.

Meetings are likely to progress this crisply in Australia, Israel, Germany, Switzerland, or Scandinavia. But in many parts of the world, time is flexible. People come late to appointments or don't show up at all. Signs of impatience or indignation would astonish the Arab, South American and some Asians. In many countries, meetings begin with extended social acquaintance and the establishment of social rapport over many cups of coffee or tea. "Extended social acquaintance" does not mean five or ten minutes; it may mean hours, perhaps even several meetings during which the business objective is not mentioned. Evaluation of how the time is spent is different. For instance, Arabs consider the drinking of coffee and chatting as "doing something," whereas the American sees it as "doing nothing." The American who resents the "waste of time" needs to know that during the apparently aimless conversations, important progress is made toward establishing credibility and rapport, which are fundamental to the conduct of future business. The American who rushes into business will not find efficiency rewarded.

Americans are also frustrated by how meetings progress once they start. In Saudi Arabia, the visitor is likely to find that the appointment is not a private affair. Many people may be in the room at the same time (including competitors) and the Saudi may "do the rounds," circulating around the room, stopping to chat with each of his visitors. In answer to the American who asks, "Couldn't we speak privately?" the Arab will simply lean closer. Meetings may frustrate Westerners even in countries where promptness and efficiency are important. Clifford Clarke, President of Intercultural Relations Institute, south of San Francisco, says that a typical American outburst in Japan might be, "Look, there were just eight items on the agenda, we should have been on the third item by ten-thirty, but we're always going off on tangents that don't make any sense. I just can't get them to move along on the agenda. We never get through."

Americans work by schedules. Given a deadline, we race to beat it. Giving a task a deadline heightens its importance and creates a sense of urgency. But deadlines elsewhere may produce opposite results. An Arab may take a deadline as an insult; the American insisting on needing something by a certain time is sabotaging the likelihood of getting that thing when needed. In Ethiopia, prestige is attached to things which take a long time. Westerners are often mystified to find that government officials will delay the most important jobs. In Japan, a delay means something quite different: Japanese organizations involve many people and invest much research and analysis in a decision. But once a decision has been made, it is carried out more readily than in the United States, precisely because so much preparation and consensus building went into the decision. In Russia and China, delays are caused by bureaucratic routines beyond the control of individual parties.

How soon is one day soon?

A Chinese official matter-of-factly informed an ARCO manager that China would one day be the number one nation in the world. The American said he did not doubt it, considering the size of the country and its population, and the tremendous technological progress that will be made, but he asked, "When do you think that China will become number one?" The Chinese responded, "Oh, in four or five hundred years."

Unfortunately, many foreigners have a double standard about time. While they are habitually late for meetings, for example, they know that in our value system, promptness is important, and they expect the American to be punctual. Often some clarity can be gained by specifying tactfully, for example, whether a meeting is to be on "Brazilian time" or "American time." However, patience is paramount. An American who has been working successfully with the Saudis for many years says he has learned to take plenty of things to do when he travels. His Saudi client not once but repeatedly has flown him to some major city or exotic resort for a meeting, only to delay for days. The American inevitably spends one to five days waiting in his hotel until the Saudi is ready to see him. Of course he is paid for his time and expenses, but he has to master his indignation at being kept waiting.

Problems of conduct: Form over substance.

In Japan's early history, a serious disregard for manners could be punishable by death, and any samurai could kill any common person who failed to show him proper respect. The Japanese were required to behave in precisely prescribed ways—wearing permitted clothing, walking only a certain way, sleeping with their heads pointing in a certain direction and legs arranged a particular way. Eating, greeting, gesturing with hands, opening doors and many work tasks had to be done in assigned ways without deviation. Conduct became a measure of morality, and virtue in manners was visible for all to see. Even today, the code of conduct plays a significant role in the lives of the Japanese.

Many societies, not Japan alone, have a prescribed form and manner for every familiar situation that might arise. Unforeseen situations can cause intense embarrassment or discomfort. Throughout East Asia, actions are judged by the manner in which they are performed. More important than the accomplishment of a task is the question of how someone went about trying to complete the task: Did he act sincerely? More important than winning the race is the grace of the runner. More important than expertise is the way one gets along with others. More important than profits is harmony. In contrast, Westerners and particularly Americans are more concerned with the principles of things, hard "measures" and objective facts. Although rules of ethics are extremely important, we are more goal-oriented than method-conscious; we say "a good loser is a loser." Some peoples consider us boorish.

One aspect of form is the concept of "face." Much has been written about "face-saving" in Japan and China, but face-saving is important absolutely everywhere, the United States included. The difference is only a matter of degree and nuance. Where an American might feel a little guilty or inadequate, an Asian, Arab or South American may feel deep shame and humiliation. What an American might see as a little honest and constructive criticism, the foreigner may take as a devastating blow to pride and dignity. A foreigner is likely to be sensitive to feelings of others in transactions that an American would consider strictly impersonal, such as returning a defective product or switching hair dressers. The traveler simply must be more conscious of saying things or behaving in ways that cannot be taken as disrespect, criticism or humiliation. In some countries it seems just about anything can be taken personally, even such indirect affronts as not taking your shoes off in a mosque or complaining about the heat.

Harmony with the environment can be as important as sensitivity to people in some cultures. In Japan a woman wears a soft pastel dress to a flower show so as not to take away from the beauty of the flowers. In countries where people believe in reincarnation they are careful about all forms of life. In India, for example, people are careful not to swallow gnats or step on ants—one might be a relative.

Problems of communication: What is truth and does it matter?

Americans tend to speak directly and openly. We try to say what we mean, and are uncomfortable with silence. We want the truth, and we want it now. We are suspicious when we think someone is being evasive. We need contracts to be very specific, detailed and, most important, in writing. The person who seeks a job or sale or raise will *ask* for it. The adept American will sum up a meeting, pinpointing agreements or progress made toward an objective that was defined when the meeting began. We distrust the person who is suspected of having a "hidden agenda" and who "plays the cards close to the chest."

The American who proceeds in the direct American style in a business meeting will not be particularly effective in some countries. He or she will be on a different wave length than the foreigner because our style of communicating is very different from that of others. Consequently, misinterpretations result even when translation is perfect. In many cultures, directness comes across as abrupt and demanding or intrusive. An open person may be seen as weak and untrustworthy, incapable of appropriate restraint. Giving details and specifics may insult one's intelligence. To some, written contracts imply that a person's word is not good.

Every job involves communication, and skill in giving and getting information is so important that we are devoting an entire chapter to this subject. (See Chapter 5.)

Problems of work attitudes: "If there's a will, there's a way."

American parents from New Canaan to San Diego read *The Little Engine That Could* to their two-year-olds. We get the message from infancy that if you just try harder, you can do anything, even the impossible. Underlying much of American enterprise is the conviction that individuals and organizations can substantially influence the future, that we are masters of our destiny, that we can make things better and that we get what we deserve,

> "An Italian air force officer gave me his impressions of Germans. He likes Germany, but found the Germans very *lineare,* meaning direct, purposeful and efficient. *'Lineare'* is not a compliment. It characterizes a one-dimensional person, while Italians feel it is important to develop the whole person, not just the work side. I said I thought the Americans were probably just as bad as the Germans, but he shook his head and grinned. 'Worse,' he said, 'much worse.' "

i.e., hard work will be rewarded. Throughout our career, we make what we perceive to be "life choices."

Self-determination is a concept almost outside the comprehension of many peoples. In Moslem countries from Libya and Turkey to Indonesia, the will of Allah influences every detail of life and many feel it is irreligious to plan for the future. Although many Moslem executives do think in terms of strategy and plans, even they will regard their efforts in the context of what God wills. Workers hold even less faith that what they do affects the future, and that very much influences their approach to work. Striving in the American sense is uncommon in Southeast Asia, where Buddhists believe that suffering is caused by desire for possessions and selfish enjoyment. Whether Moslem or Buddhist, the fatalist individual looks around and sees forces beyond human control: fate, gods, or people with more influence. Hard work seems futile. And hard work *is* futile in countries where the way to get ahead is more a matter of currying favor with the right persons.

Perhaps because of our Puritan work ethic and basic belief in cause and effect, we take pride in our work; we conduct business at social functions and we take work home with us. Beer and chewing-gum commercials show the happy middle-class American couple painting their house or washing their car; we enjoy as leisure what other people consider manual labor—gardening or tinkering in the workshop, for example. Work gives us identity; we often define ourselves and others by what we do; elsewhere identity often stems from religion, family and village.

Other people find us "workaholics." A British manager asked recently, "Why do you work so hard?" Few other cultures have such a devotion to work as the Americans. Overseas, work is generally something that must be done out of necessity; it is not an all-consuming drive and certainly not appreciated for its own sake. In some countries, hard work is considered unmanly. Even in Australia, where we sense a more compatible work ethic, there is an admiration for the "bludger," a person who manages to appear to be working hard but actually does very little.

One common objection to the American enterprise overseas is that it is efficient, purposeful, direct, single-minded and materialistic. We may be proud of these traits, which helped make America dominant in world enterprise, but they clash with ethical and esthetic values in many parts of the world. In South American culture, business is just one aspect of life; it is integrated with the family, the *compadre* relation, friendships and the Church. Business is done among friends in a leisurely and sympathetic way. Hiring of relatives is widely practiced around the world. We call it nepotism. But often it makes more sense to hire relatives who can be trusted than strangers who feel no family obligations. Cooperation rather than competition is the mode of conduct in many places, particularly in Japan, where workers are encouraged to work in teams, and singling people out either for criticism or for praise can cause great embarrassment. Competition involves losing as well as winning, and thus is destructive of group harmony.

Differences in work values have a strong impact on motivations, job satisfaction and promotional systems. Money is not an incentive everywhere —it may be accepted gladly, but will not automatically improve performance. Honor, dignity and family may be much more important. Imposing the American style of merit system may be an outrageous blow to a respected and established seniority system. Merit is defined differently: "May the best person win" can mean "the most popular person" or "the person from the most aristocratic family."

Every international job, somewhere along the line, involves getting a good work performance out of people in a foreign culture. Because it is so critical to understand deeply and clearly the differences in work attitudes and practices in any foreign activity, we will discuss the management of people in detail in Chapter 6.

When a rich vein of ore was found in the Andes, Americans rushed in to develop the mining. But it was hard to get workers. Although the Americans offered all kinds of perquisites—good meals, hot water, housing, movies, and so on—the workers flocked to the French, who seemed to offer them nothing. The workers for the French lived in the roughest housing, had no movies, none of the comforts offered by the Americans. Baffled, the U.S. company sent in a stream of senior executives and conducted a series of studies, and eventually figured out what was happening. The French offered no perks but paid workers by the hour. The people of the Andes cared more about their time off; it was important for them to be able to come and go without question. When the Americans switched to an hourly basis they were able to lure the workers.

Problems of relationships: Individualism versus the group.

Girl Scout cookie boxes recently were imprinted with a picture of a smiling girl and the caption "I'm not like anyone else." In the United States, great value is attached to individualism and the freedom to "do your own thing." We are an extremely mobile society, free to move far from family and roots, quick to make and leave friendships or jobs, and unhampered by the complex of obligations that are so characteristic of foreign societies. The ethic of self-fulfillment generated in the 1960s swept the country in the 1970s. For those who suffered self-doubt, pop psychology reassuringly cooed, "Just remember, no one is better at being you than you."

Daniel Yankelovich and other social trend watchers in the 1980s see in Americans a growing need for interpersonal relationships and stronger "ethic of commitment" to society. However, Americans continue to rank "self-respect" highest (followed by "freedom") among their personal goals, and "ambition" near the top of their valued code of conduct. Independence is more valued than helpfulness.[1] We are a far cry from what former Ambassador to China Leonard Woodcock describes as the "individualistic collectivism" of the Chinese or the "collectivist individualism" of the Japanese.

In other countries, American self-reliance and independence are seen as anathema to family and community responsibility. Around the world, friends and family, and in some places the tribe or employer, are institutions of social insurance not to be taken lightly. Dependence among members of a group is reinforced by a system of rights and expectations. And dependency is nothing to hide; in many places people gain status from their group affiliations.

Americans like to think of themselves as friendly. Yet others find us impersonal and rushed. We come on too strong too fast; we are intimidating to some foreigners. We then fail to fulfill the implicitly promised friendship; we seem phony. In most parts of the world, friendships are slow to form, requiring tremendous commitment and attention over the long term. Anything less than the gradual and deliberate approach may be seen as insincerity, and *is* insincerity compared to the seriousness with which friendships are taken elsewhere. Once formed, many foreign friendships are virtually permanent. And with the friendship come obligations, not only to help in emergencies, but to help in a number of ways the average American would consider entirely unreasonable.

The importance of relationships strongly affects the conduct of business. The foreigner needs to assess any business associate and most likely will make a deal not purely on the basis of the best price or product but rather on personal estimation—are you *simpático* and trustworthy? From Italy to China, extra personal involvement is important; many foreigners feel that if both parties can be friends, than business between them will flow naturally and smoothly.

Typically, a business partner is more desirable if well connected to a respectable family or network of friends and influence. One who is connected to others of any status is better than one who is a loner. The Chinese have a phrase, *"mei guanxi,"* which means "It doesn't matter" or "It's not important." Literally it means "not related to anything," "not connected." Cross-cultural expert George Renwick, president of Renwick and Associates in Carefree, Arizona, describes the person of substance abroad as someone who "carries his scenery with him," meaning someone who enables others to see his background, to see him in context, to understand him. In most countries of the world, Americans should try to bring their scenery with them.

Problems in use of space: My space or yours?

The way we use space "talks" as expressively as the way we use time, and the language of space varies around the world. International travelers are disoriented when spatial cues and relationships are different. One consultant said, "I've seen it time and again. The American managers walk into a Japanese workplace and the first thing they want to do is put up office structures so everybody can have their own individual rooms—so they can *think*. They can't imagine how anybody can work in a place with so much noise and people so crowded."

American treatment of space is remarkably similar to American treatment of time. It is regarded as a resource to be carefully compartmentalized and used. Space, like time, indicates status—more important people have more space. Americans who are moved to smaller offices or who are crowded together worry about their status in an organization. When a company moves into a new building, the power play for the larger offices, higher up, and in the corners would be outside the comprehension of a foreigner. While window offices are high-status in the United States, the Japanese expression "sitting near the window" refers to employees who are being retired.

Office configurations are different abroad, and we cannot rely on our customary spatial clues to organizational structure. The French are likely to place a supervisor at the center, where subordinates can be kept under control. Space will be laid out in a network of related activities or areas of influence. In Japan, everything is open. Supervisors sit at one end of a room, possibly at the head of a giant table, from where they can see and hear everything that is going on in the room. Other spatial clues vary too: what we perceive as a small or crowded office the South American or Arab may consider as spacious. What we see as a bare room will be cozy to the Japanese—a Japanese room typically has most of the furniture in the middle of the room, while we place furniture and room décor around the walls.

How we move in personal space varies too. When our space is invaded, we become perplexed and back off to regain it. Conversely, when we feel people are too far for us to comfortably communicate, we will move closer. Americans are most comfortable when standing a little over an arm's length apart. The next time you are talking to an American, you will probably be able to stretch out your arm and find your thumb pointing into an ear. (Try it!) On the other hand, Arabs or South Americans are comfortable much closer, so close that an American may become extremely uncomfortable. Chinese women often touch foreign women in business to express close feelings, although they would certainly not touch a foreign man. The American who backs off, as he or she inevitably will, may perplex the foreigner, who will sense the backing away as rejection.

Problems of power: Who's in charge here?

In America, leadership qualities are highly valued. However, "followship" qualities are not: in one study, obedience was on the bottom of a list of behavior values. Without realizing the hostility we arouse, we barge into foreign situations with a take-charge attitude that makes the foreigner bristle. In a country with a history of colonialism, the people may be especially sensitive about appearing weak or subservient to an American visitor. This extreme sensitivity to the nuances of power is hard for many Americans to understand—it should not be mistaken for megalomania, lack of intelligence, or Communism.

How people get, display and exercise power in a culture is influenced by local attitudes about autonomy, authority, equality and hierarchy. The rules for what is appropriate between peers and what is appropriate between subordinates and superiors vary from culture to culture. In Latin America the distance between those with power (an employer, teacher, the rich, a leader) and those without (employee, student, the poor) is much greater than in the United States, and the distance is marked by a great respect shown to charismatic leaders and authority figures, a love of ceremonials, a terrific sensitivity to criticism, and the importance of pride. High-status people do not take off their jackets and roll up their sleeves; low-status people do not argue with supervisors.[2]

Of course Americans, too, have rules that define customary behavior between people in different positions of power; we tend to make greater distinctions than the Austrians or Scandinavians, for example, but we certainly do not encourage what appears to us as the obsequious Latin or Asian respect for hierarchy. Americans invest emotionally in the concept of equality. In most situations, fairness demands that everybody be treated the same, but in other countries efforts to treat all people as equal are contrary to the value system and can be counterproductive. The Japanese value hierarchical relationships and place tremendous emphasis on one's occupying the proper place, performing a role corresponding to one's position or status. South Americans have a strong sense of individuality, but it is defined differently than in the United States. The Latin finds distasteful and untrue the notion that each person is just as good as the next. All South American employees know that they are not the company president's equal, but they also know that they are not the equals of anyone else. The Latin prefers to be a distinct individual "equal" to none, and derives a feeling of great dignity from this. North American managers run into problems when they try to impose their brand of individuality and egalitarianism on people who feel differently about their place in the social order.

Given the same problem to solve, ten different nationalities are capable of producing ten radically different solutions.

We have mentioned only a few of the major themes that reappear in the tasks that international businesspeople face. It is essential to keep in mind that people around the world just do not see things the same way; our ways of thinking are at odds with much of the rest of the world. Take the following question, for example: "On a sea voyage, you are traveling with your wife, your child, and your mother. The ship develops problems and starts to sink. Of your family, you are the only one who can swim and you can save only one other individual. Whom do you save?" In Western countries, 60 percent of those responding would save the child, and 40 percent would save the wife. None saves the mother. In Eastern countries, 100 percent would save the mother. The Eastern rationale is that you can always remarry and have more children, but you can never have another mother.

The next ten chapters examine the effects of cultural differences on functions that characterize most international business activities. We use this structure, rather than a country-by-country organization, because we think it is more responsive to the traveler's need for comprehension and strategy in approaching international business. A country-by-country approach runs the risk of being used like a book of etiquette, a search for rules rather than understanding. Fanchon Silberstein, former director of the State Department's Overseas Briefing Center says: "I'd sooner send someone over who has no knowledge of a country but who knows how to look and listen in a foreign place rather than someone who speaks the language and knows the rules but has the wrong attitude."

Summary

The first step to understanding another culture is understanding your own.
Cultures are not right or wrong, just different.
Cultures are changing—at a glacial pace.
Outstanding differences separate Americans from the rest of the world and
    cause us problems, including:
  Problems of pace: "Time is money."
  Problems of conduct: Form over substance.
  Problems of communication: What is truth and does it matter?
  Problems of work attitudes: "If there's a will, there's a way."
  Problems of relationships: Individualism versus the group.
  Problems in use of space: My space or yours?
  Problems of power: Who's in charge here?
Given the same problem to solve, ten different nationalities are capable of
producing ten radically different solutions.

CHAPTER 2

GETTING STARTED

❂ ❂

*What do
I do first?*

FOREIGN COUNTRIES WANT OUR BUSINESS. Every week another country —Israel, Ireland, Brazil, Germany—takes out colorful ten- to twenty-page ads in *Business Week* and *Fortune* magazines extolling their industries, trade potential and the benefits of doing business there. To support China's tremendous modernization programs, Beijing promised to sign over $1 billion worth of contracts for advanced Western technology in 1984 alone. Japan, Germany, Canada and other countries provide outstanding assistance to encourage local investment. Yet megacorporation and entrepreneur alike need beware. Tellingly, the bar in one of China's hotels frequented by Westerners was nicknamed "Hall of Broken Dreams."

The novice can be devastated by the unexpected cost of a foreign venture. One businessman learned the hard way. When the Saudi government announced that it was going to invest several million dollars in modern communications technology, he went to Riyadh to "get something going." His plane fare and expenses for a week were projected to be $3,700. He arrived on a Monday, checked into his hotel and began making phone calls to the "obvious points of contact." To his surprise, he could not track down anyone to see regarding his business. By Wednesday he discovered that most offices were closed on Thursday afternoon and on Friday, the Islamic day of communal prayer. There was nothing he could do but extend his stay and hope for better luck next week.

Eventually he made several appointments, but no one seemed impressed by his company's credentials. In each case he was frustrated by hour-or-more waits, interrupted meetings, endless cups of coffee, and instructions to "come back another day." He was particularly unsettled by the Arab habit of straying from the subject. His lack of progress led his colleagues back home to become suspicious about his activities. After a month he ran into an old Army buddy who introduced him to the basic rules of Saudi etiquette and how to do business with the Arabs. He was horrified to discover that he had repeatedly insulted his contacts by his thinly disguised impatience, refusal to take coffee, rush to talk business, aggressive selling, occasional swearing, exposing the sole of his shoe when sitting on the floor, and even when he conversationally asked an Arab official about his wife. By now his trip had cost well over $13,000 and he had only established himself as an arrogant, rude and untrustworthy American. He learned too late the three secrets to successful business in Saudi Arabia: patience, relationship building, and respect for the Arab and his ways.

Each foreign venture begins with a first contact and the process of opening doors. Doors can be solidly closed to the individual who starts off improperly, and tremendous costs can be incurred by misdirected efforts to get business going. Whether selling a product, negotiating a deal, teaching technology to company employees, running a hospital, news reporting or saving disappearing species, nothing is quick or easy in international business. Going international successfully requires commitment and knowledge.

Step 1: Reconnoiter before you go.

People do not read maps until they are lost. And then when they need one, there is no map around. Needless to say, people who do study maps before setting out are less likely to get lost, waste much less time and effort finding their way, and are more likely to have a map with them in case they need it. The necessary first step to getting started in any overseas venture is to "study the map" and learn as much as possible about the target country and culture well before going there. As one adviser puts it: "It is a lot cheaper to do your homework at home than sitting in the Farangistan Hilton at a hundred dollars a day, plus per diem and lost time from work. You don't have to travel to Farangistan to learn their laws. You can learn the laws here, then travel there to see how they are actually applied, enforced, ignored or circumvented."

Many people feel they have a "map" when all they really have are some fragments of information and anecdotes. Stanford's Richard Pascale says: "A lot of people who think they're smart and have done their homework on Japan get creamed. *Real* effort is more like thirty hours of intensive study, not just cocktail conversation." Research material is available for every country of the world, so there is no excuse for entering international business unprepared.

The first stop for any organization or individual venturing into a new country should be the U.S. and Foreign Commercial Service (US&FCS),

part of the International Trade Administration of the Department of Commerce. The US&FCS is the only government agency with a global outreach capability. Its mission is to promote U.S. export trade by helping American businesses make sales. It does this through its vast domestic and foreign field operation that includes offices in seventy cities throughout the United States and 120 offices in 63 countries overseas. The US&FCS is staffed with international business men and women who have significant business experience overseas, and who speak foreign languages, understand local customs and regulations, and know how to make the connections that are necessary to getting any business going. Your local or nearby district office is the best place to start: ask to meet with a trade specialist who can counsel you on the best markets for your business. As in many large organizations, the quality of service appears to be uneven, but many trade specialists are extremely knowledgeable and helpful. It is an easy, cheap and potentially very productive contact to make. We consider the US&FCS services to be so valuable that we have described them in Appendix III.

After the Commerce Department, the foreign embassy can be very helpful. Virtually every country has an embassy in Washington, D.C., and some countries have consulates in major cities across the USA. Most consulates can at least provide you with written information pertinent to doing business in their countries, and all embassies will have a commercial officer who can give some guidance or refer you to another knowledgeable person. Every country and every field has its experts. By asking around, you will easily find the resources you need right here in the United States.

Your reconnaissance must continue after you leave the United States. For the American overseas, whether in the beginning stages or already operating abroad, our own government provides services that can be extremely valuable. In the past, the U. S. diplomatic service has not been as strong as the Japanese diplomatic service, which pull out all stops to help their international businesses, or the British diplomatic service, which will support a British company's efforts in bidding on contracts in the foreign country. However, great strides have been made since 1979, when Congress mandated that American commercial interests overseas be given top priority. The U.S. commercial officer in our embassies overseas, the foreign side of the US&FCS, is a resource that should not be overlooked.

The commercial officer has two objectives. The first is to give your company its best chance for succeeding in the country, partly by keeping you informed about potential contracts, agents or distributors, but also by going to bat for you if your firm seems to be locked out of bidding. Commercial officers are often in the position of promoting an American company's credentials so that the firm's bid will not be overlooked. The second objective is to help you bridge the culture gap. The commercial officer is supposed to be an expert on the country, able to steer you through the cultural shoals of local business. Of course some are better than others, and if you suspect you are not getting the best of help or want a second opinion, it might be useful to meet with the commercial attaché from another government. If there is an American Chamber of Commerce in the foreign country, its personnel can also help you make contacts and explain subtleties of local trade. Finally, other Americans living and working in the country may be willing to help, particularly if they have a vested interest in your success. Some travelers have found the banks to be helpful.

The commercial officer has a third objective, which can be in conflict with your best interests, although consistent with the best interests of the United States. When two or more American companies are competing in any country, our government does not play favorites. (The British, by contrast, are more likely to decide which British company has the best chance of winning against the American competition and to put all support behind that one company.) A commercial officer will also want to avoid favoritism among the host nationals, such as when recommending a local agent to the American firm. The international business person will have to size up any agent and decide whether or not to accept the officer's recommendation. Diplomacy is vital—offended local officials or agents can directly or indirectly sabotage your efforts.

Step 2: Find out who is dealing the cards and learn the rules.

Government influences all foreign business, although with varying degrees of control. Whether you are doing business in one of the 24 member countries of the Organization for Economic Cooperation and Development (OECD), such as Japan, or the countries of Western Europe, or trading in non-OECD countries, such as Mexico, Korea or Taiwan, your business abroad will be affected by the country's trade structure. Just as at home, business practices are restricted by law. You must play by a different set of rules, and it is your job to know the restrictions.

In the USSR, East European countries and the People's Republic of China, you must find out from the Ministry of Foreign Trade which commodity group includes your product and which foreign trade organization (FTO) is responsible. Foreign trade is a function of a state monopoly, and contracts are negotiated with foreign trade organizations (FTOs) or foreign trade corporations (FTCs), legal entities assigned by the state to serve as intermediaries between foreign and domestic organizations. The FTO or FTC is not an unbiased intermediary; it represents the domestic operation in negotiations and may act as its purchasing agent. The FTO or FTC is primarily responsible for evaluating the commercial aspects of a potential import—price, quality, quantity, delivery times and payment terms—while the technical evaluations will usually be made by the end-user.

In the USSR, the German Democratic Republic (East Germany), Bulgaria, Czechoslovakia and Rumania, an American firm is unlikely to have any direct access to the foreign company. Elsewhere, such as in the People's Republic of China, Poland, and Hungary, decision making has become somewhat more decentralized as a result of economic reform. This does not mean one may completely by-pass FTOs or FTCs, but it does mean that contact with the end-user can be more direct once initial contact is made with the FTO.

In a centralized business environment it is best to establish how much authority any individual or department really has before wasting too much energy "barking up the wrong tree." And the more centralized the decision making (as in Russia but less so in China), the more negotiations or promotional techniques must be carefully adapted to the audience of decision makers and may even ignore the actual end-user or supplier. Once business is under way, promotion, market research and conduct of business in general will continue to be restricted.

There can be stringent restrictions in "free" economies too.

More than ever, international business requires outsiders to work directly with local people. In many countries you can no longer send your employees from home to run a company or to fill all the professional jobs, nor can you entirely own a foreign enterprise. Growing nationalism and economic protectionism around the world are forcing international enterprises to accept more demanding requirements for local participation. In Nigeria, for example, smaller department stores, garment manufacturing, blending and bottling of alcoholic beverages, commercial transportation and many kinds of distribution agencies must have 100 percent Nigerian participation. Another group of enterprises, such as construction, fertilizer production, clearing and forwarding agencies, and the manufacture of rubber products must have at least 60 percent Nigerian participation. All other enterprises must have at least 40 percent equity held by Nigerians. The Saudis require that 30 percent of monies going to contractors be turned back to Saudi subcontractors. Latin American countries are among the most restrictive in the world, with very stringent demands for contribution to national development goals. Foreign countries are now demanding and getting more than a percentage of short-term profits. They are getting more control, equity, training, jobs, capital, technology, housing, hospitals, schools, bigger shares of profit, and more.

Step 3: Before going anywhere, communicate in writing.

Written communications with foreigners can be extremely frustrating, depending on the degree of red tape, the language barrier, availability of translators, familiarity with international trade practices, and mail systems. Business is very paper-oriented in European countries, such as France, Germany and England, where a steady stream of correspondence is the comfortable way of leading up to meetings and negotiations. In Japan, preliminary letters can be important to establishing a company as being "known" or connected, otherwise the company is likely to be ignored. In other countries, paperwork is anathema and correspondence is a weak way to get oneself going in business. In India, for example, mail is totally unreliable—letters are lost or simply remain unanswered. As a general rule, however, you should write letters before venturing overseas, and several copies should be sent if you want to be sure that at least one gets through.

Wherever the correspondence, several rules apply. First, writing must always be simple, and straightforward. Detailed technical information should be included as an attachment, so as not to divert from the intended thrust of the letter. Second, if the foreigner's ability to read your language is questionable (and it *is* questionable until proven otherwise) a translation by your own translator is a good idea. A translated letter will more certainly be read, read by the right person, read sooner, and interpreted more faithfully to your intentions. Many subordinate personnel in foreign companies file mail they cannot read rather than lose face by admitting inability to read English. Most Americans are too impatient, lazy or unconvinced of the importance of translations, but they should think for a moment about how seriously they would take a letter written to them in Chinese or Urdu, assuming the unlikely event that such a letter would make it to their office.

Addressing foreign correspondence is a challenge too. Letterheads can be misleading; one of our secretaries almost addressed a letter to our foreign client's board of directors. Their names appeared on the letterhead in the area where we would normally expect an address. Very often it is hard to distinguish the return address from the Telex information or promotional statements. Needless to say, the problem exists in reverse, and the American firm doing business abroad should have stationery and business cards that will be intelligible to foreigners.

Job titles are important. U.S. companies' international personnel should have titles that have local meaning, and they must understand the significance of titles in the local culture. Since the designation for the same position may vary around the world, getting the title right can be tricky. In England, for example, a "managing director" is often what Americans call the chief executive officer or president, and a British "deputy" is the equivalent of a vice president in the States. In France, responsibilities are assigned to individuals without regard to titles or organizational clarity. In China, "project manager" has local meaning, while "sales manager" may not.

To make matters worse, individuals in some countries sign correspondence without their names typed below. The Germans, for example, say that employees represent the company, and emphasis of their personal names would be inappropriate. German letters often have two signatures because some individuals may act only in concert with someone else, or two individuals are assigned to a job. When signatures are illegible, the names of the signators can be found out by writing the company, alluding to the reference numbers or initials that will normally appear on a well-executed German letter.

Letters from foreign companies may be hand-written because of a lack of typewriters. They should not be treated as informal. And no answer does not necessarily mean no interest. David Chang, an executive at Nike, tells of a letter received in 1981 that began, "In response to your Telex of 1978 . . ." In the United States, failure to answer a letter is either an insult or sloppy business, but elsewhere, failure to answer a letter may be insignificant, resulting from communication problems, a complex decision-making process or other priorities. Most foreigners from Japan to South America to the Arab world prefer face-to-face contact and may "respond" to a letter by waiting for further contact.

How to read a foreign letterhead

One way to find a sender firm's name, amid the mystery of logo and foreign words, is to look for the initials that indicate the firm's status, such as:

INITIALS	COUNTRY	MEANING
AB	Sweden	Incorporated (Aktiebolag)
AG	Germany	Incorporated (Aktiengesellschaft)
A/S	Norway	Incorporated (Aksjeselskap)
Cie.	France	Company (Compagnie)
GmbH	Germany	Limited Liability Company (Gesellschaft mit beschränkter Haftung)
KK	Japan	Joint Stock Corporation (Kabushiki Kaisha)
Ltda.	Latin countries	Limited Liability Company (Limitada)
NV	Netherlands	Incorporated (Naamlose Vennootschap)
Oy	Finland	Incorporated (Osakeyhtiot)
PLC or Ltd	Britain	Public Limited Company
P.T.	Indonesia	Limited Company (Perusahaan Terbatas)
SA	France, *et al.*	Incorporated (Société Anonyme)
S.A.R.L.	Brazil, *et al.*	Incorporated (Sociedad Anonima de Responsabilidade Limitada)
SpA	Italy	Incorporated (Societa per Azioni)

Normally the address you see on the letterhead or envelope from your foreign contact shows the form you should use to address a return letter. The order may be different from what we are used to, as shown below. Whenever writing a U.S. government office abroad, you may use its American post office address.

Blaubach 13	Street address
Postfach 10 80 07	Post-office box
D-5000 Köln 1	District and city
Federal Republic of Germany	Country
24/31 Grosvenor Square	Street address
London, W1A 1AE	City, zip code
England	Country
10- 1, Akasaka 1-chome	Building and block address
Minato-ku 107	District and postal service
Tokyo	City
Japan	Country
19/21/23	Building number
Ulitsa Chaykovskogo	Street
Moscow	City and zip code
USSR	Country

Step 4: Find out who the right person is and make an appointment, always.

Appointments are necessary all over the world. For some reason, Americans who wouldn't think of dropping in on a company at home will arrive in a foreign city and call from the hotel for an appointment that day, or simply drop in. "I'm in town only for two days" sometimes does work to give the appointment some urgency, but it is a foolish way to do business. Without prior scheduling, the right people are unlikely to be available, and even if they are available, the business traveler will be handicapped. Establishing credentials and getting acceptance require time. Americans may appreciate the impromptu and spontaneous; however, many other cultures equate this behavior with instability, opportunism and aggression.

A proper appointment should be made by a local go-between in many places, especially Asian countries, unless you are willing to risk time and money on a shot in the dark, or unless you have established yourself through a previous contact. Where an intermediary is unnecessary, the best way to ask for an appointment is by mail. Telex is not elegant enough for getting across the right image for the newcomer but may be necessary if the mail system is unreliable, as in India and Indonesia. Telephone service is unreliable in most places; even the French themselves joke about their phone system: "Half the population is waiting to have a telephone installed, the other half is waiting for a dial tone."

Any trip abroad may turn up leads that should be followed up while you are still in the country. In that case you should apologize and ask for a meeting just for introductory purposes, *not* to accomplish a business deal. Face the fact that you are going to have to make another trip, maybe several trips, if you want to do business.

See the right person at the right time.

The time of year when you travel can make a big difference in how much you can accomplish abroad. France is on vacation in August—no one should try to do business then. Many German firms observe *Betriebsferien,* a period when an entire enterprise shuts down. All of China closes for the seven to ten days of Spring Festival, which occurs at different times each year. The Arab world is largely closed for business during the month-long fast of Ramadan (a moveable fast!), during which no food or drink is taken in the day, and feasting occurs through the night. Offices are open but people work at half speed. During summer months, Swedes leave work early on Fridays to drive to their summer cottages; many Israelis take Friday off throughout the year. Whenever planning a trip abroad, inquire about holidays or differing definitions of "weekend."

You can't unlock a door with the wrong key, and you will have a hard time getting started abroad if you see the wrong people. It is a delicate but serious task to make the right first contact: the visitor must go high enough in the hierarchy to reach a decision maker but low enough to create a solid, realistic foothold for entry. If sights are set too high, early rejection will be final or delegation may land your company or proposal in a department that is strategically weak for you.

In most countries, the best idea is to have the highest manager that would be appropriate at home approach the foreign company at an equal level. In general, senior people should not only open contract but also make the first visit, perhaps accompanied by subordinates who will pick up responsibility. In many countries, from Mexico to the USSR, people are so status-conscious that a low-level expert should never be the one to initiate contact, even if the most qualified. Low status of a representative will cause offense and imply that the meeting is not serious. In Japan it makes sense to initiate contact at several levels because of the consensus style of Japanese decision making.

Before initiating communications, you can research the person you wish to contact by discreetly questioning other members of the organization either in other branches or in other locations. It is a waste of time to try to send "Dear Sir" letters to a company or department of a company. It pays to get a direct lead to a certain name. Germany and China are exceptions: letters can be sent to the organization, not an individual.

Step 5: Get over there and meet your clients, partners, suppliers.

Anyone seriously involved in international business is going to have to travel. The advertising account executive cannot really hope to understand the marketing challenge without direct experience in the overseas market. The exporter will never really understand exporting without seeing the foreign distribution system through to the end-user. A buyer will never get the best products, prices or delivery times without making personal contact with suppliers abroad. The negotiator will never deeply understand and negotiate effectively with people he has never seen in their own territory. The personnel administrator cannot truly empathize and help expatriate or foreign personnel without insight into their situation abroad. People who maintain otherwise are deluding themselves. If you try to conduct international business entirely from home, you and your company will be severely handicapped.

Aside from improving your understanding of your international job, traveling abroad can be used to accomplish a number of important tasks that are impossible or difficult from home. Your presence will greatly improve your communications and relationships, making it a lot easier to solve problems, whether in personnel, shipping or quality control. You can personally make calls to clients, customers, suppliers, government officials, and media, and any others involved directly or indirectly in your business. You can take the opportunity to clarify objectives, provide training, make evaluations and establish procedures or do whatever is appropriate to your line of work.

Even expatriate or traveling personnel must be instructed to venture out to meet their foreign colleagues or customers. Too many people overseas cloister themselves in the expatriate community and Western hotels, avoiding the local culture and the players in the foreign market. In every major city of the world there is an "American Ghetto" in which live Americans who see little more of the culture than if they had stayed in the States. Their understanding of the local situation is in direct proportion to their interaction with the local people.

Step 6: Be prepared for your first meeting.

You must learn as much as possible about the particular culture and individual you are going to meet. Plan your approach, then take time to rehearse the kind of behavior and attitude that is effective in your destination culture. It is one thing to read about what you must do to be effective abroad, and quite another to actually do those things. When we made our first contacts with a potential Japanese distributor for the *Going International* films, we were surprised to find how awkward we felt doing what we knew was correct: formally presenting business cards, showing photographs, understating our accomplishments, asking questions indirectly and sitting straight. Fortunately, the subject of our product, cross-cultural training films, gave us a buffer zone because we could draw attention to the cultural differences during the interaction as examples of the importance of the product. It helped to understand what was going on, but we would have accomplished more and felt much better if we had rehearsed enough to develop some grace.

Being prepared for your meeting also means making sure you really have one. After checking into your hotel, your first action should be to reconfirm your appointments, ideally a day or two ahead. If you are poorly connected or seem to lack status within your own organization, you may find your appointment was never recorded or was canceled. In some places an appointment is granted only out of courtesy, with no real intention to keep it. By calling a day or so early, it may be possible to reschedule, or to call in the help of connections to salvage the trip. Even then, things can go wrong. Meetings that have been confirmed several times may still be ignored. In the Persian Gulf states, for example, a top executive acts on impulse or by directive of the head of state. When you arrive for a meeting, a minister or banker may have gone elsewhere, even out of the country, with no word of expected return. This is not meant to be an insult; the Arab is likely to feel that if you are sincere, you will wait or reschedule. (On the other hand, this same Arab executive would be terribly offended if he was not received most cordially when dropping in unexpectedly in the United States.)

When you arrive for your meeting, be prepared to wait, perhaps a long time. Bring something that you can read or do inconspicuously. One can't stress this enough: most of the world is lax about time. Scandinavia is an outstanding exception; there the rule is to arrive five or ten minutes early —a guest will sit in the car until the precise time. In Japan, where meticulous schedules are kept, Germany, Switzerland, and a few other places, you will not have to wait long. However, even in those countries, people are as busy as you are and you will be given lower priority if problems arise. So the rule still holds everywhere: plan to entertain yourself and keep calm. More important, do not overbook your time or you will have an itinerary that is impossible to keep.

The status and authority of individuals you meet may not be obvious. Business cards help, but often titles are ambiguous; everyone present might be titled "manager" or simply identified by department. In most places, you can safely assume that the older the person, the greater the status because position is usually closely related to age and seniority within a company. There are exceptions, such as in the Middle East, where many of the younger executives trained in England or the United States are given more responsibility. One trick is to watch the sequence of people entering a room or leaving an elevator: the most senior person usually goes first. However, it is best to find out beforehand who will be at a meeting and identify their positions. Your local personnel or a secretary in the foreign company can get this information for you.

Business cards are important in meetings all over the world, particularly for the visitor. Anything you can do to make yourself easier to remember should be done, including having your business cards translated for the country you are visiting. (Many hotels can easily arrange this for you.) In some countries certain other information on the card can help: in France and India, for example, add your academic credentials, identifying degrees and the disciplines they are in, even the name of the institution if it is a particularly distinguished university. The cavalier style with which Americans treat business cards should be avoided, particularly in Asian countries, where business cards are treated with formal dignity or respected as extensions of self. (Chapter 8 covers social and business etiquette in more detail.)

Step 7: Don't rush your meeting.

Most meetings begin with some small talk, a few minutes in Europe or Japan, but much longer in the Arab world, China, South America or Africa. Personal subjects (family, politics, money, religion) should be avoided, as well as particularly sensitive subjects, which vary by country. Generally the rule is to follow the lead of the host. When in doubt, it is safe to talk about weather, sports, local nonpolitical events or local sources of national pride, such as architecture. A travel agency or the embassy may provide tips on the country's conversation pieces.

In countries where friendship must come before business, initial visits may last forty-five to sixty minutes with no visible accomplishment by Western standards. The visitor in most places should initiate the leaving, since a host will not be so rude as to end a meeting. In countries such as China where the host signals the end of a meeting, you must watch for signs that it is time for you to go. The way a host hints that a meeting is over varies from country to country, so you should always inquire beforehand. Throughout a meeting, the shift from social to business topics and from business to the end of the meeting should be graceful, barely noticeable. The traveler who is afraid that progress is too slow when business is not being pushed forward must remember the old Dale Carnegie advice: keep the client always saying "yes." If you push too fast, you will get a "no" and will not be able to continue.

Wherever you are, in countries as diverse as Germany and Japan, a formal and restrained approach is advised. Slow down, lower your voice, and take it easy. The French hate salespeople—don't push or hype. Germans like well-ordered meetings—don't rush or overwhelm. Japanese are formal and distant until a decision to do business together has been made —don't be too familiar. In general, a full-throttled pitch will offend most foreigners, though the reasons vary from country to country. In most places, the key is to demonstrate your own personal integrity first, then sell your company, then present the proposal or product. Most important, talk about how things are done in the host country, *not* how they are done in America or elsewhere. Most people don't care about elsewhere.

In China the first meeting is likely to be quite different from a first meeting anywhere else in the world. Usually it will be a technical seminar, and the Chinese will expect a presentation of detail far beyond what would be expected in the United States, especially considering that the first technical seminar is merely exploratory. Americans must skillfully draw the line between providing enough information to win an invitation to do business in China while protecting proprietary information. Many leave China feeling exploited, and often they have been.

Don't rush your meetings.

"Breaking this rule can cause wanton destruction. I was present when a newly arrived office chief was taken by the outgoing office chief to meet a key contact. The hand-off was so important that I had traveled some distance to be present. The incumbent and I watched, helpless and horrified, as the new man destroyed in five seconds what the incumbent had taken a year to build. Undoubtedly the new man thought he was creating the impact of the hard-charging young executive. The problem is that this tendency in Americans is *so* strong, and it is likely to be even more pronounced in newcomers who believe they are doing the right thing to create a good first impression."
Major, U.S. Air Force.

Step 8: Start on the right foot, with the right image.

First impressions count. Whether the first contact is through mail, telephone call or meeting, it is best not to count on trial and error. A wrong move will leave a bad impression that can forever contaminate your future efforts. In so many parts of the world, business is done on the basis of evaluation of the people involved rather than on strictly business judgments, hence the presentation of self and company becomes particularly important. In countries that have a history of business involvement with the United States, you can be at a great advantage or disadvantage depending on the impressions made by your predecessors. A Filipino commercial officer says that "what counts most in the Philippines is the company you represent. There have been some sad cases where the Americans did not deliver. We know the U.S. companies, and if you don't have good company accreditations, you'd better have referrals from friends."

In order to present the right image from the start, you need to know what will enhance your image in a particular country. In many places, notably European and South American countries, academic and intellectual accomplishment make favorable impressions. One who comes from a distinguished university has a distinct advantage. With or without the right academic credentials, you should understate the self-promotion while giving evidence of good education, particularly knowledge of the host country. In France the foreigner who speaks impeccable French will be highly regarded; second best is knowledge of French history, culture or appreciation for French industrial accomplishments such as the Concorde, excellent postal service, nuclear power, and so forth. In Germany, to be cultured is to know German music, theater and literature. Facility with masses of factual, even trivial information, as well as an occasional quote from the classics, will impress. In the USSR one who is *kulturny*—familiar with art and artists, particularly Russian—is respected. In Mexico, a little familiarity with Mexican history and recognition of Mexico's contributions in art and literature help. The Westerner who speaks Chinese is such a rarity that fluency in the language is guaranteed to impress the Chinese; even a few words will go a long way.

Whether or not academic achievements confer status, host nationals will be favorably impressed by your knowledge of the world, starting with their country first, the rest of the world second, and your own country third. Many foreigners are astonished at the average American's ignorance of U.S. history, arts and literature. You will be expected to know your Mark Twain. (It goes without saying that you should know your own industry.)

A second image enhancer that seems to impress around the world is evidence of success, but of course that which is a symbol of success in one country may be in poor taste in another. Arabs appreciate signs of power and wealth and the self-confidence that comes with both. Latin Americans love to criticize the "materialism" of the United States but enjoy money and luxury as much as anyone. The USSR is much more materialistic than one might expect of a Communist country—high status comes from an apartment in a good location, a country home ("dacha"), fashionable clothes and a good car. Status is important in Germany, and the Germans themselves say they spend much time in what they call *"wichtig tun"*—acting important.

In Africa, success and status have traditionally been closely related to maturity. A younger man automatically stood lower on the status scale than an older man, who was assumed to have the wisdom of age. However, to an African, a foreign education and signs of business success will count a lot. In Japan, status depends on a series of accomplishments that can come only with age: graduation from a top institution, which makes employment in a better firm possible, and an important title from a well-known company. In many countries, from Britain to India, status is a matter of "blood," and the foreigner who can appear to be "upper class" receives respect.

In some countries, display of educational or occupational accomplishments is not so important as manifesting the proper values. Scandinavians, for example, seem unimpressed by lifestyle, material things, famous people, and other such "superficial" status symbols. They do value depth and genuineness. They are deeply concerned about one another, society, and the environment around them. Similarly, Moslem Arabs tend to respect those who value the spiritual life.

Status symbols vary among Chinese in the People's Republic of China, Hong Kong, Taiwan and Singapore, and among other "overseas Chinese." The PRC Chinese have their own set of status symbols: proper dress and elaborate banquets, for example, and other signs of prosperity and wealth. As in the USSR, high-ranking party officials live very well. In business, great value is attached to modernization. Current official policy in the PRC encourages whatever is modern and efficient, so the visitor who comes across as crisp, professional and progressive will have an advantage. With competition for trade in China so fierce, firms aiming to do business there must impress groups of Chinese negotiators with their business team's technical, marketing and finance expertise, as well as decision-making authority. A good impression will not be made if the firm sends only a decision maker who lacks the necessary technical expertise.

In most countries what will *not* impress is an air of superiority, comparisons to the United States, political or religious argument, dogmatic statements, a loud voice, and any behavior causing embarrassment or loss of face. In some places, notably Germany, people appreciate a detached attitude—not too ebullient, friendly or pushy.

Step 9: Make the right connections.

Americans are proud of being "self-made" in their field of endeavor, and want to keep it quiet if they get too much help from family or friends. Quite in contrast, people in most other countries are proud to have powerful connections and derive special status from receiving help from the right quarters. In India, the visitor without an introduction is an unknown, and not likely to get very far. In South American and Arab countries, everybody accepts the fact that business simply will not move ahead without the right access to public or private decision makers. In some places more than connections are necessary; business may stall until military officials or their family are put on the company's staff.

Even where connections are not essential to the conduct of ordinary business, it still helps to be associated with the Old Boy network, such as in England and Australia. Introductions provide an invaluable entree, and where the bureaucracy is cumbersome, can be very helpful in cutting through red tape. In Japan it is always possible to arrange meetings with officials or businessmen, but discussions are more productive if another Japanese introduces you, describes your company and explains the purpose of your visit. In China, connections are not necessarily needed to get started, but they are critical to getting anything done.

An organized systematic search among customers, banks, suppliers or diplomatic offices should produce a beginning group of relationships that can be nurtured into useful connections. Of course, what makes for the best contact depends on the industry and the country. The most prestigious connections are ones tied to family status (especially in South America), money (in the Middle East), schooling (in France) or corporate affiliation (in Japan). (See Chapter 9 for more on the art of using connections and "getting things done.")

Step 10: Get a good local representative.

Whether you or your company enters a country via acquisition, joint venture, capital investment, franchise or distributor arrangement, a local partner is often required by law. It is always advisable to seek out local representation and expertise even if none are required.

The local representative should be a native of that country; it is not enough to be from a neighboring culture. Even assurances of personal connections with high-level individuals are not enough to make it work. A *Fortune* 500 multinational that had been successful in Saudi Arabia and Kuwait wanted to bid on a major project in Jordan. The company's very successful contact was a Middle East prince, but he was not Jordanian. The company failed simply because it did not have the right local partner.

An agent should be a cultural go-between as well as a doer—someone who can help with the countless details and procedures in regulatory matters, and with other problems that often prove a source of tremendous frustration everywhere. The agent can show you the ropes or handle the ropes for you. Selecting the right agent is a critical matter. Since the agent is likely to work without much supervision, you must be confident that your trust is well placed.

Working in the cross-cultural dark, it is hard to know how to evaluate foreign representatives. Ethnic differences make your own criteria marginally useful. At best, you can try to ascertain how successful the individuals are within their own country, and second, how successful in relating to you and other outsiders. You must check local references, but it will be difficult to get meaningful feedback. If you watch faces carefully for the reaction when you first mention a representative's name, you may get some indication of the candidate's reputation. Don't stop at checking references, and don't be taken in by hospitality or personal charm. Some people may overwhelm you with service, entertainment, introductions to their family, or other attempts to get close. Don't get carried away by words; go to the office, look at the operation, and know the agent's background before becoming partners.

If you just don't seem to click with the agent you selected, try another right away. It will be more difficult to switch as time passes, and if you do switch, take pains not to offend. A rejected agent can make life **very** difficult for you. In many places everything is personalized and you must be careful to maintain loyalty or suffer disastrous consequences.

In some countries there is no choice about using an agent—for example, most of the Persian Gulf states, Bulgaria and the German Democratic Republic. All of the East European countries have local state-owned agencies for representation of foreign firms. Rumania is an exception and recently has begun helping Western firms set up their own representation. A major problem with Communist-country agents is that they are paid a set

---

Agent or Distributor?

Agents' responsibilities vary from country to country, and are usually negotiable. In most places agents are responsible for introductions, consulting about market strategies for their market, arrangements for exhibition at fairs, and general promotional activities. They generally help in the negotiations and final sale of the product, and then perform support services, helping with the continuing problems with quotations, financing, import regulations, permits, keeping supplies on hand, and collections.

Distributors are independent merchants who buy your goods for resale (wholesale or retail). A distributor performs more functions than an agent, including stocking inventories, promotion, extending customer credit, processing orders, shipping, and product maintenance and repair. While agents are paid a fee or royalty based on sales, the distributor's compensation is the profit margin. Most distributorships are on an exclusive basis for the entire country, at least for particular product lines.

Other popular alternatives are licensing, franchising, partnerships and joint ventures. All are highly specialized activities, beyond the scope of this book.

fee. Trips to the United States to see the plant or learn new product developments have been found to be good substitutes for monetary incentives.

Step 11: Don't count on your local representative for everything.

Relations with your agents must be managed with the same care given to employees. They are your eyes and ears, and their loyalty is crucial. They must be nurtured. But don't make unreasonable demands or expect them to take over your role.

Few overseas businesses can be initiated and successfully completed through a representative alone. Contracts are usually secured through leads obtained from officials or business contacts in the countries. The agent can help with these, but at some point the outsider must make direct contact. Business in most parts of the world is done person-to-person, and contacts must be repeated. Telephone or Telex is not enough.

Step 12: Travel smart.

It is so easy to book a ticket to anywhere in the world that many business travelers don't think about a visa. Unless you know for sure, you should ask about what visas or sponsorships are necessary. In Saudi Arabia, a Saudi company or individual must sponsor an application for a business visa. Travelers who want to visit relatives in Saudi Arabia must have the relatives' Saudi sponsor sponsor them, too. Employment visas permit only managers and professionals to bring their families into Saudi Arabia. They are given residence permits, and cannot leave the country under any circumstances without the permission of the Saudi sponsor and issuance of an exit visa.

Leave enough time to get your visas. A visa problem in one place can foul up your whole itinerary. And make sure you get the right visa. One American executive arriving in Beijing was sent back to the United States because he had a visa for the Republic of China (Taiwan), not the People's Republic of China. The American ticketing agent had not noticed and had permitted him to board.

Not to be overlooked is the importance of your passport. Keep it valid. It is proof of your identity and citizenship and it is the single most important document you will carry with you. In many places you must have a passport on you at all times. In some countries you will be asked to hand it in when you register in the hotel, and it will be checked and returned within twenty-four hours. (In China it may be kept for the duration of your stay.) This is one of the few instances where you should let your passport out of your hands for longer than a few minutes. If you are traveling between countries that are not on friendly political terms, you should check to see if having the visa of one country in your passport will make it difficult to enter

Steps to Selecting Your Foreign Agent.

1. Your agent should be a national of the country where you aim to do business, and should have experience in your industry or product line. (Some exceptional Americans have accomplished wonders as agents abroad, especially if teamed with a national; look for a track record.)

2. The agent should not be involved with a competing company or product, but could be representing a complementary line.

3. Do your own checking of references. Have your banker check your agent's bank references. Another source of data is the Commerce Department's World Traders Data Report (see Appendix III).

4. Where credit is an issue, get a credit report from a local credit agency. The U.S. Department of Commerce has a booklet called "Sources of Credit Information in Foreign Countries."

5. Check at least five or six of the agent's references: clients, customers or other business contacts relevant to your business.

6. Visit your prospective agent in the foreign country and ask to come along on customer calls. Watch carefully how clients, secretaries, and purchasing agents respond to the agent.

7. Since the personal relationship is so important in business abroad, the contact person must be someone who can negotiate for your company and who has authority to sign a contract on the spot.

8. Make sure responsibilities are clear. The agent is typically responsible for promoting your interests and product, but it is no standard procedure as to who pays for what. For example, the agent can design local advertising and pay for it, or bill you, or, conversely, you must provide advertising.

9. If possible, make the written contract with your agent short-term and nonexclusive so that you have a safety valve. However, it is essential for you to treat it as an exclusive arrangement and to establish a strong mutual long-term commitment. Many agents will not consider a contract that is not exclusive or that does not continue for several years.

10. Consult a local attorney before making any commitment to a national. It is difficult to get out of an agent agreement, so terms of termination and other "outs" should be established in the beginning. Agency laws in foreign countries are changing rapidly and legal problems arising from small mistakes can put you out of the market permanently.

another, such as travel from Israel to some of the Arab nations, and between China and Taiwan. In this case, the visa can be attached separately and removed from the passport when entering the hostile country. Some people carry two passports for this reason.

Your plane ticket has the cash value of the travel listed on it, so it is an object of theft in many places. Safeguard a $500 ticket as you would $500 in cash, and record the ticket number in a separate place. If the ticket is stolen or lost, you may be able to replace it, though not easily. And you can speed things up if you remember precisely how your name appears on the ticket, including any misspelling, because the computer will not make corrections. On the subject of plane tickets: many frequent travelers say economy or business class is perfectly comfortable for international flights; on long trips during which you have decided to sleep and forgo the amenities, flying first class is a waste of money. However, when you are traveling within an area overseas on smaller local airlines, economy class can be a "scramble." It pays to go first class if only because your reservations and connecting flights will be more secure and you can avoid the mobs in countries where people don't line up but push and shove to board a flight.

Immunization requirements are certainly not what they used to be when travelers had to be inoculated against a variety of exotic diseases. Still, disease is a problem and certificates of inoculation are required for some countries. Check with the consulate or any hospital about present requirements, or better yet, call the World Health Organization in Washington, D.C., the Center for Disease Control in Atlanta, Georgia, or the Worldwide Health Forecast Hotline (800) 368-3531. The information is updated constantly.

In some countries, customs clearance is formal, lengthy and thorough. A full search of every piece of luggage may be made. Travelers should be aware of the customs regulations and sure not to be importing or exporting food, alcohol, firearms (even toy guns or knives) or other prohibited items. In Islamic countries, some personal religious items may be confiscated, and printed or video materials that may be deemed pornographic by strict Islamic standards are forbidden. Some prescription and nonprescription drugs may be illegal in one country even if legal elsewhere. Prescription drugs should cause no problem if they are clearly marked with the doctor's name, patient's name, pharmacy, contents, and so on. Otherwise one can land in jail for trafficking in drugs. Even doctors have been challenged going through foreign customs. If the amounts are large, repercussions may be severe.

You should also check baggage restrictions if you plan to travel within a foreign country. Limits on the number, size or weight of bags can vary, and domestic flights are usually more stringent than overseas flights. Sometimes no exceptions are allowed.

Traveling smart also means preparing for jet lag. A diet and sleep

Traveling with Portable Computers

If you plan to bring a computer, inquire about the country's voltage and any restrictions about transporting data. In some countries, strict limitations can be a problem. Make backup copies of all data and leave copies at home. When using the computer abroad, save and back up your data frequently because power-outs are common.

Do not walk through the metal detector with your disks. The microwaves may produce a field large enough to scramble your data. And do not pack your disks (or any media) in the baggage you plan to check because the cold of the storage area during flight may cause the mylar to shrink. It will not hurt to pass your data along the conveyer belt, but repeated exposures to X rays can damage any media.

Contrary to some advertisements, it is unlawful to use portable computers on an aircraft. The radio emissions from the machine disrupt the plane's navigational systems. The same goes for electronic games or FM radios.

SOURCE: Dysan technical services.

regimen developed by the U.S. Department of Energy's Argonne Laboratories actually seems to work. It is available to the general public through a paperback entitled *Overcoming Jet Lag* by Dr. Charles F. Ehret and Lynne Waller Scanlon, published by Berkeley Books in New York. It provides a three-step program that varies depending on the direction of travel and number of time zones crossed.

It is important to be well rested and alert when doing business abroad. Don't schedule big receptions each night; give yourself a chance to rest. Some foreigners are notorious for meeting travelers at the airport, wining and dining them until all hours, then beginning business at seven or eight o'clock the following morning. Whether this entertaining is out of obligation to take care of the guest or purely part of a strategy, the travelers are put at a great disadvantage. Try to allow time to do additional sleuthing of the competition or territory, as well as overcome exhaustion. Some experienced travelers recommend giving the Japanese or Korean host the wrong date of arrival, then coming a few days earlier, only announcing your arrival once you are well rested. In countries where dates must be specified for visa purposes, you can schedule your meetings to allow time for yourself.

Fear of Flying

Twenty-five million adults in America, about one in eight, have a fear of flying. Studies show that they tend to be nervous people with a vivid imagination, perfectionists and people who place a premium on self-control. It is hard to pinpoint the causes, but like other phobias, fear of flying seems to appear at a turning point in one's life: a birth, death, marriage, divorce; the beginnings and endings of things.

A retired Pan American pilot, T. W. Cummings, runs a program called "Freedom from Fear of Flying." His seminars around the country involve classroom discussion and a graduation flight. He also provides a home-study tape cassette and booklet that give basic information about airplanes and flying. The tape takes the victim through an imaginary flight using relaxation exercises. Call (305) 261-7042 or write Captain T. W. Cummings, 2021 Country Club Prado, Coral Gables, Florida 33134.

Step 13: Don't go into foreign business for the wrong reasons.

The wrong reasons for entering a market include: large population, cheap labor, and "Everyone else is going there." Population does not necessarily mean consumers or a skilled work force, and even a large consumer base does not mean there is an established market. A terrific investment in education and the establishment of an infrastructure for the conduct of business, whether manufacturing or marketing, may be necessary. Companies rushing into China, for example, are not going to find it easy or profitable for a long time. Thrilled to have a "deal" with the Chinese, some companies have overlooked how badly they have actually done in negotiations, and do not fully understand the implications of their concessions, such as long-term warranties in a country that lacks the technical know-how to properly maintain equipment. One overseas operations manager says, "You laugh with tears in your eyes over the problems." A Nike executive says, "After four years there, management is still asking if it is worth it." Some groups have already pulled out.

Some markets may be too small to support the cost of doing business. Dick Alberding, executive vice president of Hewlett-Packard's international business, says: "It is critical to enter only these markets where we can serve customers to their satisfaction and according to HP's standards. An inadequate understanding of products due to degree of technical sophistication and language barriers may require special attention to adapt documentation, training and support to the market and customer." Many apparently small markets can be surprisingly active. Asked how there could possibly be enough business in Cameroon to warrant a recent trip there, Apple Computer's Ron Boring replied with a list of foreign-aid agencies, religious relief organizations, and even a few multinationals.

Step 14: Try to avoid setting up shop from scratch.

Setting up an office abroad should involve a reliable adviser. Many legal and procedural nuisances can be avoided by using an experienced local who can cut corners. The adviser can be a national or an expatriate who has been around long enough to know the ropes. Often the adviser should be physically present when you negotiate for space, staffing, training, sales promotions, and so on. Do not rely on contracts—wording can be ambiguous even when seemingly specific. For example, a lease for office space in lots of countries can be ended abruptly even though it defines a specific number of months or suggests that it is "forever."

Office space is scarce everywhere, particularly offices equipped with telephone lines and Telex. From Egypt to Venezuela it can take *years* to get a phone installed. The best trick is to capture space being vacated by another firm and take over all furniture and equipment, and even personnel. Obtaining these things in most places will take an inordinate amount of time. Do make sure, however, that any equipment you buy is in good shape or that maintenance can be provided in that country.

Business services are virtually unavailable in many places, and the traveler should not count on being able to pop down to a copier or secretarial service. Hotels that offer them are often backlogged for months, and services whose ad you once read may have long ago gone out of business. You will have to ask at the embassy, schools and elsewhere to develop a list of temporary services, and it is a good idea to do this early so that in an emergency you will have backup. In some places, such as China, the only solution is to take a typist and a word processor with you, making sure your machine will run on 220 V/50Hz.

Hiring of personnel can be a difficult problem because of local union and job market peculiarities. In many places, lack of mobility in business life and inadequate supply of educated and trained personnel make for a small labor pool, especially in the middle- or upper-management levels. Headhunting firms have not been very successful in recruiting foreign executives or managers, since most higher level employees are committed for their working lives, although sometimes one may lure away an older worker who is about to be "retired" into a lower position in his company. One should always be somewhat suspicious of the young, bright, aggressive managers who are willing to leave their companies to join a U.S. firm, especially in Japan, where they will be giving up fantastic benefits and prestige to join the outsider. (Chapter 5 will go into detail about hiring and personnel.)

Step 15: Make sure you can get your money out of the country.

Some experienced international people say the hardest part of working with foreigners is getting paid. When it is time to pay an outsider's salary or the bill, the foreigner may be forgetful, unavailable or even hostile. When an operation starts to pay off its high-risk investment, the country wants to renegotiate the deal. One executive complains that the Arabs "never, never pay salaries on time. You have to beg; even the secretaries have to ask to get paid. Sure, they pay outrageously well and take wonderful care of you. If you are not well, you will be put in the best hospital, all expenses paid. But they act like everything they give, including your hard-earned salary, is their charity. You have to take so much humiliation."

The American in a foreign land is vulnerable. In many places there is no honor system or enforceable laws to protect the outsider, or where there are laws, they are half-heartedly enforced. The American business person or firm is not linked to the local scene by anything more than a desire to make a profit, and the American players are often unable to develop a relationship that would give them leverage or power. Economic development specialist Brad Mills has found that in most places, "When problems arise, locals feel little stigma attached to trashing a foreign company. In many ways, it can be seen as an act of national honor. At the first sign of trouble, trust and commitment can disappear very quickly."

Foreign companies are highly visible symbols that often serve as a focal point for all the frustrations the local people feel about their poverty, lack of political autonomy, cultural dilution, diminished world standing or whatever it is that bothers them. The perception that U.S. companies are making huge profits and sending them out of the country is profoundly irritating to most people, even the employees of the company. One result is that people tend to feel the Americans don't deserve to keep an equity position or make a reasonable return on investment. As soon as there is a conflict, people start grumbling, "This is my country. You come here, invest a little money; we do all the work, and you take most of the profits. What's in it for us?"

Further complicating matters of money are differences in budgeting and accounting practices and generally how money and payment are handled. Serious and mutual distrust may build, and cooperation may wobble until the working relationship deteriorates too far to be salvaged. (Japanese corporations, for example, make use of debt that would be staggering to an American: four dollars of debt to one of shareholder equity on the balance sheet.)

Commercial credit arrangements are particularly tricky in foreign countries. Credit is often one of the last points on an agenda because nobody wants to talk about it, but it is also usually one of the most important issues in closing a sale or getting a contract. Denying credit, imposing conditions or requiring security can offend by suggesting distrust or insufficient commitment. Just getting adequate references is usually a long and painful procedure because there are few reliable sources of credit information overseas, and reporting rules are much more lax (if they exist at all).

The first rule to making sure you can get your money is to make no assumptions about how, when or by whom you will be paid. And do not assume that the foreigner will have a great commitment to making things work out. Whatever the rhetoric at start-up, you should not assume you are wanted or needed in the foreign country. Work out all financial arrangements in detail. Especially when providing intangible services such as consulting or research, make sure your employer or client agrees to its cash value. Some cultures (as in some of the Persian Gulf countries) may not recognize certain kinds of service as legitimate work.

Some seasoned travelers say the only solution to foreigner's resentment at bill-paying time is to downplay your "outsiderness" and try to blend into the woodwork as much as possible with logo, advertising, and so on. Some companies have successfully created a local national image, and hence are not so ready a target for hostilities. Even so, you should not become financially involved abroad unless you think the risk is worth it, and you must maintain enough flexibility so that you can extricate yourself from the business rapidly if necessary. In areas marked by political tensions, according to one executive, "Your investment will go out the window if you are tied to the wrong guy and there is a coup d'état. You have to be able to walk across the street and do business with the opposition, or move to another location. Otherwise, stick to politically stable countries."

Another rule for making money abroad is to think creatively about the form in which you require your payments. Always structure a deal so that you get most of your returns early; hence if business relations sour, you can walk away without too great a loss. Or work with a bank that is in a position to take the risk. Bartering is becoming a significant method of trade in a number of countries. However, bartering is a very tricky business, and in virtually every case, it will be better to have cash. Get expert help if bartering becomes necessary.

The issues involved in making money and getting money legally out of a country are too complex to do justice to in a few paragraphs, and much beyond the scope of this book. If in doubt, inquire at the Department of Commerce, international banks, or the foreign country's embassy in the United States.

Summary of Rules for Getting Started

Doing business abroad is like doing business anywhere at home, but more so. More care, more detail and more finesse is required for successful international business. If it's tough in Denver, it is a hundred times tougher in Seoul or Lagos.

STEP 1: Reconnoiter before you go.
STEP 2: Find out who is dealing the cards and learn the rules of the game.
STEP 3: Before going anywhere, communicate in writing.
STEP 4: Find out who the right person is and make an appointment, always.
STEP 5: Get over there and meet your clients, partners, suppliers.
STEP 6: Be prepared for your first meeting.
STEP 7: Don't rush your meeting.
STEP 8: Start on the right foot, with the right image.
STEP 9: Make the right connections.
STEP 10: Get a good local representative.
STEP 11: Don't count on your local representative for everything.
STEP 12: Travel smart.
STEP 13: Don't go into foreign business for the wrong reasons.
STEP 14: Try to avoid setting up shop from scratch.
STEP 15: Make sure you can get your money out of the country.

CHAPTER 3

MARKETING

❀ ❀

How to sell to foreigners

A FTER WEEKS filming the Tchuka tribe in the foothills of Mount Kenya, a producer sat back in his London screening room to watch the
"dailies." To his horror, his authentic Tchuka warriors, with their stretched
ear lobes, stunning beads and body paint, were wearing running shoes,
Nike's probably. Nobody had noticed.

The evidence is everywhere: in spite of setbacks, the United States has
been enormously successful in marketing its products to all corners of the
world. Coca-Cola is sold in 155 countries, Pepsi in 148. Levi jeans are worn
by England's Princess Anne, Greek fishermen and the Russian jet set. Saudi
Arabian mothers, still draped from head to toe in black robes, buy Pampers
for their babies. Attendance at Tokyo's new Disneyland exceeded 10 million
people in the first year alone. *Time* magazine is read by 31 million people
in countries all over the world.

There are several conclusions one should not draw based on the evident
spread of American products and technology. One misconception is that
people everywhere want to be or are becoming Westernized. Modernized
—maybe; Westernized—no. The Saudi who drives a Cadillac is not Westernized, he is simply rich. Japanese baseball fans are not Westernized—the
Japanese have been playing baseball for fifty years, and it's their national
sport. Princess Anne does not feel American wearing jeans—she is simply
comfortable.

Another mistake would be to think that the world's needs and desires
are becoming so homogenized that standardized products can be sold in the
same way everywhere. Some big advertising firms are now claiming exactly
that, for obvious reasons. Presumably, if the same product can be marketed
in the same way around the world, multinational companies will not need
to hire the countless small ad agencies that specialize in individual foreign
markets. "Global marketing" serves the major advertising agencies by making the small local competition redundant. The concept behind global mar-

keting is appealing because in ideal circumstances standardization brings down costs, permitting reductions in prices which should result in increased sales. The theory works if price is what counts, and indeed it often does. But international marketing is more complex than that. As Walter O'Brien, vice chairman of J. Walter Thompson, says: "Consumers don't live globally, and they don't care that you're running the same campaign in forty other countries. Ads have to talk to you on a one-to-one basis."[1]

Finally, it would be wrong to conclude that Coke, Levi and the rest could have done so well around the world if they had been less attentive to conditions and cultural differences in their diverse markets. Coca-Cola is sold everywhere, but its packaging, its channels of distribution and its advertising differ from country to country. Levi products are fitted differently for different markets, and Levi commercials around the world are distinctive, each appealing to the foreign customer's imagination: a James Dean character impresses youth in Japan; in Brazil the jeans have a European flair; in Australia the old cowboy image is what sells.

Some products and marketing campaigns travel well. Any responsible manufacturer should keep eyes open for opportunities to cut costs (and prices) by standardizing, but certainly not without regard to the impact on the customer, sales and profits. David Willoughby, general manager of Dentsu-Young & Rubicam/Los Angeles, says: "It's one thing to believe in global marketing. Many have tried it, but when faced with realities, have been unable to put it into effect. A global assignment still requires you to look at each market." For example, "If you try to take global marketing into the Third World, you run into a brick wall," says Ron Kurtz, manager of advertising services at Combustion Engineering. "You have to plan for an environment that is radically different from the American way of life."

What's good for the U.S. can be good for the world if it's adapted to local taste.

Pizza Hut, a PepsiCo subsidiary, began going international in 1979 and now operates 430 restaurants outside the U.S., in thirty-nine countries; McDonald's operates 1,625 restaurants in forty-two countries. Local management and local flavor have been the essence of the Pizza Hut strategy: jalapeño toppings in Mexico, bacon in Canada, squid in Japan. Pubs are going inside Pizza Huts in Britain; low-salt meals are offered in Korea. McDonald's has added beer in Germany, wine in France and Spain, and tea in England. Each day, three million McDonald's hamburgers are eaten outside the United States.

GENERAL PRINCIPLES

Rule 1: The fact is that ancient differences in national tastes or modes of doing business are not disappearing.

American marketing expertise is respected around the world; we have long been the marketing champion and we still have the most sophisticated tools and some of the most creative marketing people. But we do make mistakes, and a little cultural mistake can cost a big deal. Marketing lore is thick with stores of companies exporting inappropriate products, badly named, inadequately packaged, foolishly advertised, and represented by culturally inept salespeople.

Pan American World Airways recently displayed billboards showing a reclining Japanese woman wearing a kimono. There were complaints: in Japan, only prostitutes recline. Pan Am had to redo the artwork and replace the billboards, at great expense. Ironically, this incident happened in San Francisco, a thoroughfare for Japanese travelers. Any company that has seriously "gone international" has stumbled at least once. Parker Pen's slogan "Prevent embarrassment—use Parker Ink" came across like a birth-control ad in Latin America, where the Spanish word used for embarrassment, *embarazo*, actually means "pregnancy." Campbell Soup Company has had similar difficulties in a number of markets. The Brazilian housewife wants a soup starter to which she can add her own personal touch. The Japanese are anti-can (most people walk to the market and don't like to carry heavy cans). The British were not used to a condensed soup, and failing to add water, found it too strong. And people have differing tastes, particularly when it comes to tomato soup: Irish and Italians want it creamy, Germans want rice, and Colombians want spice.

Simmons had a hard time selling its quality mattresses in Japan because the Japanese prefer to sleep on futons (floor mats). Mattel had to give its Barbie dolls a more Oriental and younger look for Japan, and in Europe, Barbie's costumes needed more European styles—more lace and *haute couture*. Kellogg failed with Pop-Tarts in England simply because not enough people have toasters, something no kitchen in the United States would be without. The list of companies that have learned hard lessons abroad is endless.

Failures in marketing are not restricted to product development and advertising. Bechtel lost the Caracas Metro contract partly because American cost-conscious efficiency and aloof business style clashed with Venezuelan ways. According to a Bechtel executive, the French were better at accommodating the Latin style. A major American health-care provider built a hospital in Saudi Arabia, bringing the best of modern American medicine to the desert. The Arabs shunned it. They were offended by the cool and impersonal efficiency of American doctors, the unfamiliar meals served by American dieticians, the incomprehensible "starvation" of patients before surgery, and the "inhumane" exclusion of relatives from isolation areas. The hospital's problems were exacerbated by the fact that it housed forty-seven nationalities and five different religions, two of which were in hostile conflict. The administrator, a highly competent executive by American standards, was inadequately prepared for the particular complexities of Saudi Arabia and returned to the United States before his assignment was complete.

Rule 2: Even on a clear day, you can't see Belgium from New York.

Few people remember that the ugly American in Lederer and Burdick's best seller twenty years ago was ugly in physical appearance only. While his colleagues were rushing around Asia building roads and airports nobody needed, the American engineer went out into the boondocks to meet the people and helped villagers build irrigation systems and breed sturdier chickens. The marketing lesson was lost on Americans, however.

Business schools teach "Know your customer," yet according to Philip Kotler, professor of marketing at Northwestern University's Kellogg School of Management, the number one error made in international marketing is failure to gather insufficient knowledge of the customer. The only way to be in tune with local needs is to get overseas. As Eric Haueter, vice president, corporate commercial development of CPC International, says: "People in the local marketing unit must be steeped in the territory, and must be participants in the culture, aware of the specific tastes and wants of their consumers in order to be able to intelligently interpret and adapt concepts into specific products." Seeing is believing; for example, in England and Japan, most houses or kitchens are simply too small for many American home appliances. In many places, refrigerators are too small for large-size bottles. Only someone who has been there will really appreciate how the Arabian desert's heat and dust might affect demand for certain cars and clothing. Only by spending time in Jakarta or Brussels can you ever hope to know what the people want, what they are accustomed to, and what they are not accustomed to but might accept with open arms anyway.

If you have been to the Guangzhou (Canton) Fair, and you stayed at one of the modern hotels across the street, you have not really been to China. Many people draw mistaken conclusions about a culture when their experience is limited to the trade showcases, tourist services and people who are trained to serve outsiders. Don't stay in the exhibition world without venturing into the city and country.

Being there is essential, but "seeing it with your own eyes" does not guarantee true understanding of what exactly you saw through your own culturally filtered vision. Experts in this field talk about "self-reference criterion"—meaning, of course, our habit of seeing everything in relation to what we would want or do or feel in any situation. Self-reference criterion means "do unto others as you would have them do unto you," and produces statements such as American Ambassador Warren Austin's statement to the United Nations, "The Arabs and Israelis should settle their differences in the good Christian spirit!" The problem is that *your* interests, tastes and values are not relevant. Unless you have lived overseas or for some other reason have an affinity with a foreign culture, it is very unlikely that you will have much in common with your foreign customers.

The same market data we collect at home are important in any market overseas. The difference is that we must take a fresh look at factors that we might take for granted at home—cultural factors such as family, social and business organization, education, standard of living, materialism, technical orientation, religion, attitudes toward women, tradition and change. We have to look around. What are people doing? What is the competition doing? And just as important, what are the differences between rural and urban populations, ethnic and tribal communities, age groups and religious sectors. There is never just one culture. Combustion Engineering's Ron Kurtz reads the Koran to get a better feel for the culture. Kodak's Carlos Penalver reads the country's children's books to understand its mores and values. Sheidegger Trading's Mimi Murphy reads the local newspaper from front to back to know what is on people's minds. Whatever the approach, we need the hard facts about tastes and preferences but must also search for nuances of value and patterns of behavior.

For most international marketers, the hardest part of any analysis is to avoid culturally skewed interpretations of cause and effect, or motivation. Although the Japanese are notoriously camera-loving, for example, they will not necessarily buy any photo-related product. One U.S. company was about to try to sell desk-top photograph displays in Japan, when it learned that in Japan the executive's office is strictly for work and that family snapshots are kept at home in an album. Similarly, just because Islam is a fatalistic religion, you should not conclude that Arabs will not buy insurance. In fact, some years ago, 56 percent of Arab executives were found to have insurance and those who didn't had more than enough family wealth and pension planning. Saudi Arabia is a highly competitive insurance market now that there is much to insure.

Rule 3: Sell to the customer. (Who that is, is not always obvious.)

The decision maker abroad is not always the same as in the United States, and foreign decision makers may have quite different reasons for buying. In the United States, for example, prescription drugs are sold to patients through the pharmacies; in Mexico the government is the main buyer, since drugs are redistributed through social security programs; in Japan, doctors sell the product—they are the pharmacies. Even if the pharmaceutical industry is highly regulated in a country, the salespeople's approach and advertising must vary depending on whether they address a patient, pharmacist, doctor or government official.

Nor is the decision maker within the family always the same. Women are accepted as decision makers, authorities and spokespersons in Anglo-Saxon countries, but not in Latin countries, and especially not in conservative Islamic countries. Singer had to revise its sewing pitch in the Middle East when it learned that the husbands were the buyers and that they were not interested in saving their wives personal effort. Singer had to convince Arab men that sewing machines would make their wives more useful and better able to attend to the husbands' needs. In Japan the wife makes many decisions that are generally considered within a husband's domain in the United States.

In Japan another consideration is important. More than elsewhere, the dealer or wholesaler is king, not the customer. There are 340,000 wholesalers in Japan, one for every 323 people, twice as many as in the United States. The wholesaler is an important cog in the machinery; he makes many more deliveries than are made in America because stores (and inventories) are small. Lack of interest on the part of the wholesaler can kill a product. Hence, a certain percentage of ads should be aimed at promoting loyalty within the distribution system. These "in channel" ads are vital to marketing success and must be taken as seriously as ads directed to customers.

In Communist countries, decision making is often in the hands of the few people involved in the central planning of the economy. Trends toward decentralization of decision making are becoming more apparent in China and Hungary, so consumers are becoming more brand-conscious and industrial end-users are more involved in produce selection. Still, the more centralized the decision making, the more advertising and sales efforts should be targeted to the few who have the power to permit your product into the economy.

Rule 4: Identify national goals; promote national pride.

Despite signs of modernization around the world and growing internationalism, observers agree that nationalism is growing, not declining. More nationalities seem to be deeply concerned about preserving their history, protecting their culture and maintaining their unique identity. Not every Western product or proposal will be welcome, and the marketer must often show how national goals will be advanced. Most countries make it easy to know what is important. The *Third Development Plan for the Kingdom of Saudi Arabia, 1980–1985,* for example, clearly states: "The distinguishing mark of the Saudi approach to development is that its material and social objectives are derived from the ethical principles of Islam and the cultural values of Saudi society." In listing the main principles that underlie Saudi Arabia's long-term goals of development, the plan lists first "to maintain the religious values of Islam," followed by defense, economic growth, reduced dependency on production of crude oil, human resources development and an infrastructure for these developments. Any company planning to market its services abroad should seek out the government's plan, and respond accordingly.

Organizing a marketing effort that addresses national objectives is only half the job, simply because of local ambivalence. Although industrial development is a goal, there may be a "love-hate" reaction to the multinational corporation (or the small American entrepreneur), which is seen as an agent of change, jeopardizing traditional society. Hand in hand with great aspirations to catch up with the West is a high degree of national pride. Peoples in the Third World want to achieve a better way of life, but only through self-determination and what they describe as "equitable and mutually beneficial" trade relationships with the industrialized countries.

National pride is a powerful and pervasive influence in all international business. Says Combustion Engineering's Ron Kurtz: "Any Western company recognizing this pride and paying tribute to a country in whatever shape or form will be held in high regard by that country. I call it mutual respect." Acting on this premise, Combustion Engineering stresses equality in working relationships while working toward the country's own national goals. When some of Combustion Engineering's projects around the world were gathered into one brochure, the company thoughtfully decided not to put dots on the maps to show the locations, avoiding even a hint of colonialism.

Marketing that strikes a chord of national pride can have outstanding results. United Technologies developed a campaign for Germany, France and Great Britain complimenting local scientists who contributed to the company's technology. The program was an exceptional success. At the Hanover trade fair, United Technologies decorated its booth with five-foot posters of great German scientists captioned "Thank you, Herr Diesel" (or Kepler, Planck, Röntgen, and others). Ray D'Argenio, senior vice president of communications, says the posters attracted up to 9,000 people a day. "People actually came up to read the ads; they stood around our booth nodding and smiling."

American Motors Corporation has run full-page ads commemorating their joint venture, the Arab American Vehicles Company. The ad copy describes AAV as an excellent example of "cooperative technology transfer *between* Egypt and the United States." (Italics ours.) This kind of support can help assuage real or potential political sensitivities.

Rule 5: Don't go it alone in unfamiliar territory.

"Hire the best and most trustworthy of guides," says Joseph Coogle, president of Ketchum International, speaking about the tough job of launching an overseas agency.[2] This advice is equally sound for those retaining a local advertising agency or hiring an American "global" advertising firm. There are numerous considerations involved in selecting a marketing vehicle in any country, most of them beyond the scope of this book. Whatever firm or approach is employed, however, the people involved must be sensitive to the local needs and conditions. Numerous resources are available to help.

Whatever the relationship between the American marketer and the foreign team (independent agency, distributor, joint venture or branch-office staff, etc.), it can't be stressed enough that the poor foreign relative who does not call, write or visit will be the forgotten foreign relative. Your foreign team needs to be provided with incentives, training and whatever supports will help it do the job you want, better. (See Chapter 6 for more on managing and motivating people.)

A most important aspect of maintaining the agency or personnel relationships is to respect foreign turf as the foreigner's turf. Joe Garcia of Mattel says one of the most important lessons he learned when traveling around the world was to assume a low profile when accompanying his salespeople or agents on calls. "You have to remember it is the local person's call and the account has to feel you are not pre-empting local management." You should work out an explanation for your presence before the call. "You might be there as a resource or to talk about the company's worldwide quality program. Whatever you do," Garcia recommends, "don't dominate the meeting. Keep out of the limelight."

PERSONAL SELLING

Rule 1: Make personal contact, and lots of it.

Compared to our foreign competition, many American companies do not put nearly enough effort into direct, personal communication. Japanese success in displacing the United States as Saudi Arabia's leading supplier is instructive: Japanese exporters send small teams to meet with Saudi importers; they go to Saudi workshops, travel to secondary towns, meet with sub-agents. The Americans, on the other hand, invite all their Saudi agents together for a luncheon, do not have private meetings, do not get their hands dirty, and never travel to secondary towns—they tend to stick to the three market centers. Saudis complain that U.S. effort is misdirected: American personnel devote infinitesimal detail to making advance arrangements for visiting executives, going so far as to specify rooms overlooking a certain view from a hotel.

Japanese firms supplement their direct, personal efforts with heavy local advertising. They use gifts generously in product introductions, and warranties on Japanese consumer electronics range up to three years. To carry out this business, Japanese trading companies have large staffs of professional international marketers who have been cultivated since graduation from a Japanese international trading university, schooled in English and Arabic, and rotated world-wide as international trading specialists.

Compared to most other cultures, particularly non-Western cultures, Americans are extraordinarily preoccupied with the tangible aspects of a product. We round up all our sales agents and give a product presentation instead of putting our energies into the more important component of international marketing—people. In America and only a few other countries it is normal to do business from a distance, between strangers, by mail or telephone. The contract for this book, for instance, was agreed upon without the writers having ever met the agent, publisher or editor. This is simply not how business is done in most parts of the world.

Rule 2: Sell yourself before your products or services.

A British buyer for Marks & Spencer's, one of England's major department-store chains, says: "If you want to sell to the British, write a nice, clear, nonexaggerating letter explaining the simple facts of your business, and ask for an appointment to come over and see me. I will be busy, but British buyers, unlike American buyers, *will* see you. I will give you half an hour to persuade me, and if you are flamboyant, I will reject most of what you say. If you are not as aggressive as most Americans, I will probably take you more seriously and may even believe you. Then, of course, the final decision has to do with expected profits, not whether or not I care for you as a person." Indeed, some British companies have tried to eliminate the personal aspects of buyer-seller relations by disallowing wining and dining. Nonetheless, marketers need to sell themselves before buyers will be receptive to the product.

Just why it is so important to sell self before product became clear to us when we were going over our film-distribution contract with a Japanese company. The contract had the usual boilerplate legalese, stating the usual protections. One clause said that the distribution agreement was not to imply that the Japanese company was a "partner or agent" of Copeland Griggs Productions. The Japanese were mystified. As far as they were concerned, that was *exactly* what they were! We had to explain that the words have specific legal meanings in America and that the contract wording was intended merely to limit mutual liabilities, not minimize the relationship. This semantic knot reflected deep-seated cultural differences in how we saw the business deal: we were not just signing up a distributor; rather, we were getting into a relationship. Selling yourself is so important because people don't get into business relationships with strangers.

How you should sell yourself will vary in each country—in Africa, friendship is important before business; in Latin America, evidence of being *simpático* is important; the Japanese may be looking for reliability and commitment. With the Chinese, you should establish yourself as sincere, hard-working and even-tempered. Generally speaking, wherever the contact, the American will undergo scrutiny aimed at determining if he or she is someone with whom the foreigner can work. This is true in America but more so abroad. Mimi Murphy, an exporter working in the Pacific basin, discovered that people do their homework even before the first meeting: "The first time I went to the Philippines, I found that everywhere I went, people knew about me. I thought I was there to check out the market, but what was going on was they were checking *me*. Was I legitimate? Was I reliable? Did anybody know me?"

Basic to successful selling of self in a first meeting is to find out what the particular phasing of business is wherever you are. While the Arabs, Asians and Latins will take a great deal of time to establish a relationship, Europeans, Scandinavians and Australians will not. Germans, for example, typically avoid personal rapport lest it interfere with clear thinking and sound business judgment. Swedes are reticent and British impersonal out of respect for privacy. More and more Australians seem to be in the same rush as Americans. As a general rule, though, do *not* press for decisions, action or any form of commitment, because in so many places the first meeting is semisocial and nothing of substance will be accomplished until after several meetings. Needless to say, since relationship building is the essence of early meetings, the same person should continue to represent a company throughout.

Rule 3: Make alliances inside and outside the organization.

Informal relationships are central to the flow of business everywhere, and people in international business have to be especially skilled in using those relationships. In China a deal often begins with a Chinese leader casually mentioning during a dinner that his organization will soon be looking for a plant to buy. This hot tip will be dropped only in the lap of what the Chinese call an "old friend," someone who has been around long enough to establish the right ties.

Old hands in international business stress the importance of establishing and maintaining contact at several levels within an organization, especially where consensus characterizes the decision-making process or where it is impossible to identify any one decision maker. Joe Violette, a Bechtel executive responsible for business development in Japan for many years, says: "You can facilitate agreement throughout a Japanese company if you go in at the middle and top. Technical people work with their Japanese counterparts, while executives establish relations at higher levels." Selling to the Japanese is time-consuming, but one benefit is the number of entry points. If one Japanese contact rejects a proposal, the door stays open, whereas an American might be infuriated to find out that someone has gone around to the boss or to a subordinate. The Japanese consensus-making process allows the seller to revise a proposal and help those who support the proposal to mold a consensus in the organization. In fact, if the seller does not put in this effort, the Japanese may suspect insufficient commitment.

In many countries, government permeates commercial and daily life to a much higher degree than in the United States; consequently, relationships with government officials can make or break a business. Local bankers and leaders in the business community can also be as important as the client or customer. In Arab markets, simple problems can become insurmountable if the right "friends" have not been cultivated. On the other hand, the right Arab alliances can make easy what would be impossible in the United States. The same is true in Latin cultures, where business is done among *compadres,* or in China, where *guanxi* (connections) are critical sources of inside information. Velsicol Chemical Corporation of Chicago saved its position in the termite-control market in Japan by being able to work with various ministries when a local newspaper mistakenly reported that the chemical was banned in America. Local officials were particularly sensitive to safety concerning the chemical, and the company would have been out of business if it had not previously established close liaison with the government.

Can you ever become an "old friend"? Not really.

Some Americans have, over time, developed deep, lifelong friendships with foreigners. They are rare. The average American traveling or moving abroad is an outsider and will remain an outsider, especially when the chips are down. This is a severe disadvantage, and Americans working speculatively with foreigners tread on thin ice—chances for payoff are slim unless some special bond, expertise or service makes the American indispensable.

The Chinese will negotiate anyone into the ground, an "old friend" included. They know that if the North Americans do not make the necessary concessions, the Swedes, Japanese, French or some other group of Americans will. Among Latins a long history of obligations will always come first; a North American is rarely going to get closer to any Latin than his family relations or friends cultivated over a lifetime! So why bother working so hard on relationships? The point is that relationships are essential for doing business but they are not guarantees. The traveler cannot count on relationships, but must nevertheless cultivate them and keep reminding the foreigner of them.

Rule 4: Appearances count

The Arabs say: "What is written can be judged from its title." First impressions make a big difference. The international business person should always dress conservatively. Even in unbearable heat, proper suits should be worn, and in developing countries, women should avoid sleeveless blouses or short skirts. In Europe, people seem to notice your shoeshine much more than in the States—a good polish helps.

A would-be industrial real estate broker made a very persuasive presentation to a Saudi developer, complete with market analysis, cash-flow projections, charts and graphs, and pictures of the perfect buildings to buy in Salt Lake City. The Saudi was sold on the idea, but there was absolutely nothing to keep him from sending his own crony to Salt Lake City to make the investment. So he did. They were not friends; he owed this man nothing. The American was left out in the cold. His mistake? He should have sold *himself* (as a local Salt Lake City expert). Instead he only sold the project.

Successful businesspeople must learn how to walk into a room, greet, sit and communicate. The minutiae of social grace are extremely important to the conduct of business: they establish the tone and set the scene for conversation. Awkwardness will not necessarily foil a deal, but absence of awkwardness is an advantage. (See Chapter 8 for details on business and social etiquette.)

Rule 5: Admit to being American—but one interested in the local culture.

Many an American panics when told to "slow down and establish rapport" before doing business. "My God, if not the product, what do I talk about?" asked a young man planning to sell video games in the Middle East. Good question. Many subjects are taboo or unlikely to establish the desired tone. The easiest solution is to good-naturedly admit that you are American, have been that way a long time, and for better or worse, that is the way you are. But don't go overboard. Constant comparisons are irritating to all foreigners. If you belabor the point or repeat "This is how we do it in the States," you run the risk of appearing patronizing or false.

Having apologized in advance for all unwitting gaffes, you should proceed to evidence a deep understanding and appreciation for the culture. The best way to do that is by asking intelligent, informed questions: "I'm sorry I know so little about the art of the Ming Period, but I have admired the Southern style of Shen Chou. His landscapes are honored in a gallery back home in Kansas City." This kind of remark (especially if Shen Chou is pronounced correctly) is bound to make the right impression, particularly if your foreign contact is interested in art. In Canada, asking questions that indicate you know the geography (the provinces and where the cities are) or understand the national politics will be impressive; most Canadians are under the correct impression that

Americans are ignorant of or indifferent to their neighbor to the north.

Dale Carnegie said almost fifty years ago, "If you want to make people like you, talk in terms of the other man's interests." It certainly helps in the United States, but it is absolutely essential abroad. Sometimes it is hard to find out beforehand what an individual's interests are, but it helps at least to know what conversations work best in that culture. Whether it be art, family, history or sports, there *are* patterns and conversational rituals, somewhat subject to change depending on current events or official policy. The best course is to follow the lead of the host. And if there is little to say, the best conversationalist, even in America, is the good listener. The aim is to get across that you are *simpático,* trustworthy and committed, and pleasant as a business partner. You won't do that if you do all the talking.

Rule 6: Talk to people the way they are used to being talked to.

Selling is a matter of style, but the American style makes people suspicious, defensive or embarrassed in different parts of the world. Latins complain we are too boastful; they become irritated and resistant to our sales pitches. The British say we talk too much about nothing, or talk about things we know nothing about, so we lose them, too. Asians feel we are not sufficiently humble and they become skeptical when they feel we are overconfident. The Swiss say we are too absolute in our claims. The Arabs say we are too loud —they prefer a soft-spoken sell. Proclaiming ourselves the best, biggest, newest and fastest may be necessary at home but sounds like wild bragging virtually everywhere else; often we would do better as *"one* of the best." Africans may suspect ulterior motives if we appear too task-oriented. In any culture, the communication style is as important as the message, and care must be taken to find the right emotional and intellectual tone. (See Chapter 5 for more on communication, including a section on presentations.)

Personal selling is not for every salesperson.

An American company preparing to launch its household consumer product in Brazil invested a large amount of money in recruiting and training forty young Brazilians in sales techniques. The training was intensive and the students seemed to lap it up. At the end of a week the trainees were told they were ready for their first sales run; on Monday they would go door to door selling the product. But on Monday fewer than half the workers came to work, and even those who showed up were appalled by the assignment. The Americans learned that it is beneath the dignity of Brazilian men to ring doorbells and talk to women about a product.

ADVERTISING

More than $100 million in U.S. advertising money was spent abroad in 1984, most of it in foreign magazines and newspapers. The figure is overshadowed by the $60 billion spent domestically, but it is growing as American marketers try to stave off foreign competition. Much of foreign advertising is developed and placed in the media by local firms. Nevertheless, it is essential for the American marketer or advertising account manager to understand the realities of the overseas advertising context. Any firm with aspirations to global marketing must become particularly conversant with the world's cultures.

Like habitat models in a natural history museum, commercials display the cultural environment in high relief.

Quite possibly the fastest way to figure out a market is to examine a few successful, locally produced magazine ads and television commercials. More than most media, ads summarize and reflect the most important values of a culture. Advertising is the best indicator of *current* culture because ads are always expressed in the rhetoric of the times, always changing with the moods of a country or population group. Examining successful ads also gives clues to secondary values in the culture, reflecting trends in language, fads, tastes in music and graphics, as well as changing political and social trends.

Rule 1: *You may adopt or ditch entirely the local style, but you'd better know what it is.*

Absorbing core cultural values does not mean pursuing "me too" advertising. You may decide to totally abandon the local style, but you must have good reasons for doing things differently. Your ads must not clash with the cultural context. In markets that are particularly unsophisticated in advertising, some firms have found a good (and economical) balance in introducing fresh creative concepts without the high-tech wizardry so popular in America. Advertising in Canada, for example, is much less developed than in the United States, and an American firm can get great mileage from just a little sophistication; electronic razzle-dazzle would be overkill.

Rule 2: *Appeal to the right need with the right benefits.*

People buy the same products for different reasons. Take toothpaste, for example. Not everyone around the world is interested in cavity prevention, so fluoride has a less than universal appeal. In some places, such as the north of England and French areas of Canada, bad breath is the predominant reason for buying toothpaste. In the United States, bicycles are a sport or leisure item; in India, they are an important form of transportation.

Some products, or course, can succeed with a consistent appeal around the world. Certain cultural sub-groups have much in common—teen-agers, for example. Consumers of industrial products and high technology normally have highly specialized needs that are quite similar. Some market analysts say that the rich around the world have more in common with one another than they do with people in lower socioeconomic levels from their own country, so luxury items such as watches, furs, luxury cars, perfume and imported liquors can succeed with consistent marketing appeals abroad. Very functional items too may have universal appeal: detergents are for cleaning, everywhere. But even if the need for cleaning is universal, the best design for a detergent package may not be. In Italy the large economy size is popular, but in Japan, where space is very tight, the average housewife shops three and a half times a week and prefers a small package. In Mexico much of the laundry is done by servants, and a housewife prefers to have individual packets to give the laundry woman, in order to control pilferage. Moreover, detergent itself must be reformulated to work well with local water conditions.

In introductions, appeal to a need at the beginning of the product life cycle.

Marketers taking a domestically established product overseas make a common mistake: they forget or don't even realize that their product is thrust back to the beginning phases of its life cycle. Advertising in a new market must be introductory, possibly educational, and may not need to address competition.

In Japan, for example, Procter & Gamble has succeeded in creating demand for disposable diapers, but the marketing message is very different from that in the United States. Here the question is *which* convenient disposable diaper to buy—stress is on the competitive extras such as refastenable tape, gathered contours and "more absorbent." In Japan the marketing task was to convince the Japanese mother (and *her* influential mother) that she is not lazy or uncaring if she uses disposables. Kraft had to go back to basics in Hong Kong because most Chinese hate cheese and dairy products. To get the five million Chinese in Hong Kong to learn to love it, Kraft created ads that played on Chinese concern about nutrition, showing kids full of energy from eating lots of cheese.

Advertising may also have to position a product quite differently abroad, going after more appropriate niches and using appeals that make more sense in the foreign culture. Grey Advertising couldn't pitch Tang as a substitute for the morning glass of orange juice in France because the French drink little orange juice, and almost none at breakfast. (The French breakfast is a croissant and coffee.) Instead, Grey positioned Tang as a multiflavored refreshment, good anytime. The 35mm Canon camera is pitched as a high-tech, complex, professional product for the sophisticated

Japanese but is positioned "for people with shutter shudders, meter jeeters, and f-f-fear of f-stopping" in Canada and the United States, where people are technologically naïve and want professional-quality pictures from a product that is simple and easy to use.

Rule 3: Reflect the right values in the context of the ad.

In any culture, ads have more power if they communicate in contemporary imagery and play on prevailing sentiments. If the models in the ads are going to be effective as models for buying behavior they must reflect the right man-woman and parent-child relationships and evidence of an individual's place in society. In Islamic countries, ads showing women in non-traditional roles may be censored, while in developed countries, ads suggesting sexism may be forbidden. France and Germany, for example, are taking issue with sex discrimination in advertising. In some countries, men and women should never be shown close to one another or touching. Even the widely traveled Marlboro man has had to change his stride in different countries. The rugged individual alone in the wilderness had no appeal in Hong Kong, where being part of a group is important. Not only that, he was too old for the Chinese. Philip Morris had to round up several younger cowboys for the ad. In some countries the hot and dusty scene was unappealing and a more lush setting was needed. In Britain, "heroic figures" such as cowboys cannot be used in cigarette advertising because children might be influenced. Getting rid of the cowboy was not enough—authorities complained and the saddle and riding gear had to go too. In the end, ads showed a non-cowboy driving around the country in a jeep.

Props are an important part of the total message, and mistakes can give out unintended signals. In England and America, for example, pets are our "best friends," and the family golden retriever curled on the rug (or romping on the beach) is a commercial cliché. Elsewhere, especially in Islamic areas, dogs are considered filthy and would be as appealing in a commercial as a bat would be in the United States. Greyhound buses there do not carry the famous greyhound logo.

The right tone for an ad, even in cultures similar to ours, may be very different from what would be right at home. American ads are explicit, direct and visual, but British ads are more participative, implicit and non-verbal. The reader is invited into the situation; British ads don't shout, at least not as much. In Japan the tone and manner should be emotional rather than logical, and the ad should rely heavily on innuendo rather than direct communication; images are very important to the Japanese. Instead of claiming to be the most delicate watch in the world, one Japanese watch ad suggests: "Like the moonlight, it lightly touches your arm."

Advertising must adjust to the limitations of the consumers' experience. Can they read? With literacy rates so low in many parts of the ad world, this is a serious consideration. Imagery must be within an audience's ken. The same is true for humor. What is intended as amusing might be taken seriously or offend. It is very hard to know what is funny in another culture, and to get the right balance. If foreigners are in the ads, every effort must be made to treat them with dignity; any sense that they are being made fools of will backfire.

Rule 4: A rose by any other name would not sell so well because it would not have the centuries of poetic propaganda and customer satisfaction behind it.

The importance of the good will embodied in a product name cannot be underestimated domestically or abroad. But brand names that sing in one country may be totally unappealing in another. Some years ago, on our way to a crusader castle in Sahyoun, Syria, we were served an orange soda pop that the Syrians had given what they must have thought was a very distinguished brand name, Mobil Up. The Japanese tried to sell a baby soap called Skinababe in the United States and a hair product called Blow up. We may find all that amusing, but Americans, too, have not paid enough attention to clearing product names for travel abroad. There are hundreds of examples of American products with names that have unintended meanings in foreign markets. When Coca-Cola was first brought into China, the shopkeepers took it upon themselves to make their own signs. Unfortunately, the calligraphy that made the sounds for Coca-Cola translated as "bite the wax tadpole" or "beat the mare with wax." Coke researched 40,000 characters to find a variation that meant "may the mouth rejoice." (Chapter 5 deals with communication and the art of translation.)

The auto industry has had its share of naming problems. American Motors' Matador suggests not only strength, but a "killer," not a positive image where traffic fatalities are high. Ford's Fiera means "ugly old woman" in Spanish, and Pinto in Portuguese is slang for a small male organ. General Motors' Nova, as many know, means "It doesn't go" if pronounced no-va in Spanish-speaking countries. Rolls-Royce had to change the name of the Silver Mist in Germany when it found out that Mist means "manure" and is a mild expletive in German. Esso had difficulties in the Japanese market, possibly because, phonetically, "esso" means "stalled car."

SOURCE: *Big Business Blunders,* David Ricks, Dow Jones-Irwin 1983

Rule 5: Colors and symbols have meaning, often not the ones you think.

The well-known anthropologist Edward T. Hall years ago noticed how casually Americans treat colors. We use color situationally and decoratively. Certain colors and combinations may be pleasing, but the colors themselves have little or no significance. Elsewhere this is not so. Colors are ranked just as we rank gold and silver. Some colors are good, others bad.[3] Americans tend to underestimate the symbolism of color because we use color inconsistently, but in many parts of the world, colors have great significance. Depending on the occasion, the color of clothing, gifts or gift wrapping can cause great embarrassment, not to mention destroy an ad.

Green, America's favorite color for suggesting freshness and good health, is often associated with disease in countries with dense green jungles; it is a favorite color among Arabs but forbidden in portions of Indonesia. In Japan, green is a good high-tech color, but Americans would shy away from green electronic equipment. Black is not universal for mourning: in many Asian countries it is white; in Brazil it is purple, yellow in Mexico, and dark red in the Ivory Coast. Americans think of blue as the most masculine color, but red is more manly in the United Kingdom or France. While pink is the most feminine color in America, yellow is more feminine in most of the world. Red suggests good fortune in China but death in Turkey. In America, a candy wrapped in blue or green is probably a mint; in Africa the same candy should be wrapped in red, our color for cinnamon.

The marketing and packaging implications are obvious: in some countries we should use colors that would be unthinkable in the U.S. and, of course, we must never use our criteria of taste to decide color schemes.

Symbols, too, are potent: in every culture, things, numbers and even smells have meanings. Lemon scent in the United States suggests freshness; in the Philippines lemon scent is associated with illness. In Japan the number 4 is like our 13; and 7 is unlucky in Ghana, Kenya and Singapore. The owl in India is bad luck, like our black cat. In Japan a fox is associated with witches. In China a green hat is like a dunce cap; specifically, it marks a man with an unfaithful wife. The stork symbolizes maternal death in Singapore, not the kind of message you would want to send to a new mother. Combustion Engineering changed its copy in an ad depicting India when it found that "more than 8,500 sunsets ago," had negative tones in Arab countries: sunsets are associated with death and sickness. Symbols are used in advertising because they work on a subtle level; needless to say, inadvertent use of symbols that have negative meanings abroad can destroy a campaign.

Some symbols are part of the national or religious pride and cannot be commercialized without running the risk of causing resentment. Using a picture of Buddha, for example, is risky; printing words across the Buddha would be defacing it. Outraged Saudi Arabian religious authorities recently protested to the Taiwan embassy when a Taiwanese company distributed "blasphemous" shoes. The word "Allah" was inscribed in the sole, and to wear them would be to walk on the sacred name. Landor Associates, when designing the logo for Serfin, the largest banking group in Mexico, created an eagle, which was perceived as American; a topknot was added to make it a Mexican eagle. Designing the package for Sapporo beer, Landor had to change the red star to copper in Hong Kong and Singapore because the red star suggested the People's Republic of China. Be cautious using flags, pictures of royalty, and other symbols..

Just as bad as using wrong symbols is using wrong terminology. Avoid "North Korea" or "North Vietnam" and use instead People's Republic of Korea or Vietnam. In the People's Republic of China it is safest to refer to Taiwan Province when speaking of Taiwan. Never refer to Red China or mainland China, since this suggests there is another China. Most Arab states refer to the Arabian Gulf, not the Persian Gulf. Scots are Scottish and prefer not to be confused with Scotch.

In April 1984, two American businessmen launched a campaign to establish a nationwide MADE IN AMERICA symbol so that manufacturers could "take a new sense of pride in American-made goods." The promoters did not realize that the symbol, based on the okay sign (open hand with thumb and first finger touching to form a circle) had insulting or obscene meanings in other countries. In France and Belgium it means "You're a zero." In Greece, Ghana and Turkey it is a vulgar sexual invitation. In southern Italy it is an insult with anal connotation. In Malta it means male homosexual. Moreover, "Made in America" is about as meaningful abroad as "Made in Asia."

Rule 6: Watch out for restrictions.

Restrictions are an important consideration both for product strategy and creative campaigns. Laws that regulate advertising, product use and conduct of business may vary every few hundred miles for some products such as medical supplies, food additives, pesticides and pharmaceuticals. Syntex, for example, sells Naproxin, a nonsteroidal anti-inflammatory drug, in 140 countries, but what Syntex is permitted to say about the drug, its side effects, contraindications, and so on, varies widely with the regulations of any one market. Marketing to doctors is prohibited in Britain, but in Latin

America, educating the physicians is an important aspect of marketing the product. Some twenty-four countries require prior approval of advertising for ethical, or prescription, drugs. England limits a company's ethical drug advertising expenditures in the trade press to 10 percent of sales.

Use of children in advertisements is prohibited in many places. In Australia, an ad that uses popular children's images is forbidden if it promotes a product that is not suitable for children. A cigarette ad using Robin Hood had to be altered because the Australian authorities felt it was too appealing to children. Product comparisons are dangerous where competitors are able to go to court and ask for proof of any implied or stated superiority, as in Germany. Finland disallows ads for politics, religion, alcohol, immoral or intimate products, and weight reducers. Islamic law prohibits advertising of all alcohol; Saudi Arabia and others do not allow even the slightest hint of alcohol consumption in an ad—no wine glasses on a table. French laws forbid the use of foreign words in advertisements, and recently fines up to $700 have been charged for failure to translate such words as hamburger *(bifteck haché)* or show biz *(industrie du spectacle)*.

Canadian rules for truth in advertising are more stringent than ours, and typical American "puffery" could be construed as illegally misleading. Promises of benefits are prohibited in many places. In Soviet advertising, the essential principle is to provide information that does not "create artificial demands," a qualifier that would eliminate almost all American advertising, leaving only the most objective technical or economic facts. China recently promulgated regulations requiring foreign advertisers to have health and quality-inspection certificates, to keep content of ads "clear and truthful," and to place ads according to state "propaganda policies and economic policies."

In an effort to promote local industry and conserve foreign exchange, some countries require commercials to be made with local talent. The Australian Broadcasting Tribunal, for example, insists that Australian crews must film commercials under certain circumstances.

Government regulations are sometimes obscure, and only officials involved can interpret them for you. In some countries, such as England and Australia, all advertising must be approved; in Canada and Mexico, food and drink commercials must be approved. Whether or not it is required, it is worth the time to talk with the right officials.

Rule 7: Don't overlook practical problems.

Joseph Coogle, president of Ketchum International, stresses how important it is to "set schedules to allow for the increased time it takes to accomplish goals across language and cultural borders."[4]

Poor printing reproduction can spoil an ad that relies on subtle images, fine print or recognition of faces in the pictures. Overseas creative and duplicating services may not be able to provide the quality you need. Before losing time and money, it makes sense to examine local capabilities and alternatives.

Rule 8: There are more media abroad than just the international editions of American publications.

Americans may be the creative leaders in advertising, but we have never been particularly strong in international media research, planning or placement—that business is centered in London. American firms typically underspend in foreign media, and when they do invest in overseas advertising, they make two mistakes: they tend to stick to the publications they know, and they apply the same media-mix formula used in the United States. Very seldom can you successfully implement the same mix from country to country because media habits and the options differ radically. And ignoring the indigenous media means missing the boat; if you want to reach foreigners, you have to reach them in their language in the media to which they are exposed.

Michael Hook of Ogilvy & Mather International Media in London says: "Being at the front line in international advertising means knowing about television in Qatar, radio in Nigeria, posters in France, cinemas in Oman and video magazines in Saudi Arabia, as well as magazines in Germany and newspapers in Singapore."[5] In countries where illiteracy is a problem, or in places such as Kuwait, where a large percentage of the population is foreign, visual media such as billboards (using more images than words) are important, and magazine advertising may be uneconomical. Radios in Africa are important. Most Paris agencies even have a talent pool of diverse African accents, from Abidjan to Cameroon. Norway, Sweden and Denmark have no commercial television, and the time allowed for TV ads is severely restricted in most of Europe. Average advertising available per channel each day in the United States is three hours; in Western Europe the average is thirty-four minutes. Perhaps because of limited availability, TV can be a powerful buy.

Thousands of foreign publications are represented in the United States, either through their own offices (usually in New York) or by independent publishers' representatives who specialize in certain markets. Their job is to sell ads, and to do this they often provide important market and media information, as well as handle currency conversions and speedy access to publications. But many more media are not represented in the United States. One source of information is the six-volume International Media Guide from Directories International, Inc., in New York.

PROMOTIONAL CAMPAIGNS

Promotions that are standard operating procedure in the United States may be disallowed, impractical or disastrous abroad.

One exporter planning to introduce a new product in Indonesia thought it would be a good idea to put a sample on the front doors of people's homes, just like in Darien or Cleveland. Fortunately she learned before it was too late that a package at a door would last just seconds before someone stole it. Another company that had successfully used Christmas pudding in their promotions in England was surprised to find itself saddled with 20,000 unwanted Christmas puddings in Scotland; English taste for this cake has apparently not crossed the border. A promotion involving gifts of coins of any kind is problematic, even illegal in places such as China, where foreign currency, even commemorative tokens, is not allowed.

Premiums are often restricted, notably in Europe. In Austria, consumers cannot be given preferential treatment, thus most premiums are not allowed. In Finland, premiums are permitted but not with the offer of anything "free." In France it is illegal to sell for a price at less than cost, or to offer a customer a gift or premium conditional on the purchase of another product. West German law on promotion, is so stringent and complicated that a lawyer should be involved to help interpret the restrictions.

TRADE FAIRS AND EXHIBITS

"Coming to market" is a centuries-old tradition in the Middle East, Europe and Asia.

Trade fairs continue to be much more important abroad than in the United States. For some international companies or individuals going international, certain events must not be missed. They can be an invaluable way to get experience in a market, exposure among potential suppliers and customers from all over the world, as well as to nurture existing relationships. There are over twenty thousand international trade conventions, and numerous publications that discuss them. It helps to subscribe to the various exhibition publications such as those of the Commerce Department, but reliable colleagues are a better source of information—ask around when considering which trade shows to attend.

Leipzig is not Chicago, and the booth design and dynamics at foreign fairs are not what one expects at American events. Simply because attendance is greater and people coming have higher expectations, the presentation should be taken more seriously than it might at home. More salespeople should be on duty, larger conference areas arranged, and more attention paid to gracious food and beverage service. Salespeople should be prepared to engage visitors in much deeper discussions about products, company history and marketing aims. And a greater time commitment must be made, since most overseas shows go on longer than is common in the United States. The semiannual Guangzhou (Canton) Export Commodities Fair in China runs for three weeks. The Hanover fair lasts nine days.

The major European exhibition cities: Lisbon, Barcelona, Lyon, Paris, Zurich, Basel, Brussels, Amsterdam, Rotterdam, Brighton, London, Birmingham, Harrogate, Cologne, Hamburg, Frankfurt, Hanover, Milan, Leipzig, Vienna, Bucharest, Poznan, Brno and Moscow.
The major exhibition cities outside Europe: Sydney, Melbourne, São Paulo, Guangzhou, Tel Aviv, Tokyo, Osaka and Johannesburg. One caution: China's fairs are only for Chinese sellers and foreign buyers. Only business firms specifically invited by an official PRC organization may attend China's fairs.

SOURCE: Robert F. Roth, *International Marketing Communications*, Chicago, Crain Books, 1982

Attendance information is generally unreliable except in England, Canada and Germany. Figures are likely to be distorted by including all registrants regardless of attendance, or by re-counting the same person at each entry, or they may be simply false. If you plan to participate in next year's show, you should visit *this* year's show while it is still in progress to determine whether the event is right for you, to reconnoiter the site and to learn what you will need to do to manage it. If you decide to participate, you will need to start planning a full year in advance.

The physical design of your booth will be different from what is usual in the United States. Be prepared for different electrical systems; you may want to bring current stabilizers or transformers. And to avoid having to run to a hardware store in a strange town, bring all the materials you might need for setup: hammer, tape, nails, extension cords, and the like. Almost everywhere, instructions must use metric measurements and be in both English and the language of the host country. A local national should help you to make sure your instructions will be understood.

Just as at home, pre-exhibit promotion and advertising is important. You should have calling cards in your own and the foreign language, as well as give-away items of several kinds: inexpensive items for anyone coming to the booth, and gifts more appropriate for important customers and prospects. In some places free give-aways are not advisable. One China hand says: "The Chinese will knock down a booth going after freebies. Don't give things away, except quality gifts to those who spend a long time at the booth."

Managing the work crew during setup and dismantling is important, too. As far as the crew is concerned, you are here today and gone tomorrow. Workers have little incentive to perform when not under your surveillance, so you must be at the exhibit hall early every day to supervise. You can feel free to pitch in and help with setup, but always try to maintain executive dignity. During unpacking, carefully mark and store together all shipping materials to use again after the show. In order to get out quickly, groundwork will be necessary during the exhibition: seek out the management and establish rapport. Invite the key officials to come by for drinks, give special gifts or drop hints that you can leave part of the exhibit behind.

Preparing Goods for Foreign Shipment

A marketer who wants to stay in business in a foreign market will see to it that the product gets through when promised and in good condition.

Many American firms are inclined to process domestic orders first, and foreign shipments tend to be pushed behind—an unfortunate mistake, especially since delivery is further delayed by overseas shipment and customs. This makes it much more expensive for the foreign distributor who has posted money with a bank to issue a letter of credit, which is good for only a limited time.

Engineering or redesign may be necessary to make the product appropriate for another market. Before anything is shipped, you should check to make sure the product meets foreign electrical standards, is metrically correct, and has taken into account local design, grade of material, color preferences, and so on. Shipping and climate conditions affect what kind of packing is necessary. Some foreign customers are much more finicky about the appearance of their packages—Japanese customers often reject products that are chipped or arrive in boxes that are crushed or ripped; the Chinese tend not to be the slightest interested in packaging, preferring the lowest price. Crates should be marked so that instructions can be understood regardless of language; some exporters suggest crates be marked with distinguishing colors or extra large symbols so that they can be easily found on a dock.

Documentation must be complete. Roughly one half of all shipments are delayed by documents that arrive late. American firms repeatedly send incorrect documentation, causing shipments to be stuck in customs. Delayed shipments are very costly: a few bad experiences will drive away customers, and some countries (USSR and East European) exact heavy penalties for late deliveries even if caused by paperwork. Shipping documents include a vast array of licenses and declarations. One study revealed that the average shipment required 46 documents and more than 360 copies, with an average per-shipment documentation cost of $375 for exports. Some countries require certain inspections *before* shipment. Generally, it is wise to hire an international freight forwarder to handle shipment documents, and a bank to handle the payment documents. The Commerce Department should be consulted.

MARKETING SUMMARY

General Principles

RULE 1: The fact is that ancient differences in national tastes or modes of doing business are not disappearing.
RULE 2: Even on a clear day, you can't see Belgium from New York.
RULE 3: Sell to the customer. (Who that is, is not always obvious.)
RULE 4: Identify national goals; promote national pride.
RULE 5: Don't go it alone in unfamiliar territory.

Personal Selling

RULE 1: Make personal contact, and lots of it.
RULE 2: Sell yourself before your products or services.
RULE 3: Make alliances inside and outside the organization.
RULE 4: Appearances count.
RULE 5: Admit to being American—but one interested in the local culture.
RULE 6: Talk to people the way they are used to being talked to.

Advertising

RULE 1: You may adopt or ditch entirely the local style, but you'd better know what it is.
RULE 2: Appeal to the right need with the right benefits.
RULE 3: Reflect the right values in the context of the ad.
RULE 4: A rose by any other name will not sell so well . . .
RULE 5: Colors and symbols have meaning, often not the ones you think.
RULE 6: Watch out for restrictions.
RULE 7: Don't overlook practical problems.
RULE 8: There are more media abroad than just the international editions of American publications.

Promotional Campaigns

Promotions that are standard operating procedures in the United States may be disallowed, impractical or disastrous abroad.

Trade Fairs and Exhibits

"Coming to market" is a centuries-old tradition in the Middle East, Europe and Asia.

Preparing Goods for Foreign Shipment

A marketer who wants to stay in business in a foreign market will see to it that the product gets through when promised and in good condition.

CHAPTER 4

NEGOTIATION

How to win in foreign negotiations

A TRADE REPRESENTATIVE who accompanied American negotiators in South Korea noticed that in meeting after meeting, the Koreans said the same things to each new group of Americans. They seemed to have a rehearsed script and a list of stances. Finally the American was driven to ask one of the Korean negotiators about it. With a little prodding, the Korean admitted that their positions were worked out by personnel at the Korean embassy in Washington who had been studying the American negotiation style for years. The Koreans were thoroughly prepared—every word out of their mouths was uttered according to strategy.

The Americans, on the other hand, went into each negotiation expecting to "play it by ear." With scant preparation or team coordination, they stood little chance against the foreign opposition which knew so much about them and had so carefully planned for the negotiation.

In international business, a lot rides on the success of negotiations.

The ambitions and plans of corporate planners, marketers and contractors are foiled when negotiators fail to win the required permissions, contracts or operational arrangements. And costs can be terrific when no equitable agreement is reached. The stakes in a foreign negotiation are often much higher than they would be in a comparable situation domestically because so many other aspects of the international operation may hinge on the outcome.

One U.S. Department of Commerce source estimates that for every successful American negotiation with the Japanese, there are twenty-five "failures." A consultant in the Arab world says that Americans never really win in negotiations with Arabs. A Chinese broker says Americans do so badly in negotiations in China that by the time it is all over, American negotiators are thankful to get out with the shirts on their backs.

Everyday business involves countless negotiations, for the exporter or the diplomat, the missionary or the multinational manager, the engineer or the lawyer. Negotiating is not confined to big deals. In some countries it seems that virtually every transaction, from settling a taxi fare to buying a loaf of bread at the market, is a negotiation. The traveler who does not appreciate the local rules for give-and-take is at a serious disadvantage. Anyone doing business abroad should know how the local people bargain and when to call in a professional.

Negotiating is often described as a game, and players are seen as opponents or adversaries who accomplish their objectives in a series of moves. Skill is the winning factor. But it is not that simple in most business negotiations. Home or abroad, negotiating is not a game requiring mere skill but an art requiring forethought, imagination and strategy as well as skill. Whether bargaining for a copper pot in an Egyptian *souk* or negotiating an arms deal with a foreign government, it has less to do with overcoming an adversary than with creating a new picture of reality that is acceptable from two different points of view.[1] If negotiating must be likened to a game, it is a game of perspective.

In every negotiation the participants have different points of view and more or less different objectives. If they did not, agreement would be automatic and negotiation unnecessary. But in international talks the negotiators are less likely to have a common frame of reference and value system; their perspectives are further apart. When arguments fail to address what is important to the other side, the resulting suspicion can bring negotiations to a halt.

International negotiations are further complicated by purely physical constraints and bureaucratic nuisances. A *New York Times* bureau chief in Beijing described the frustrations facing Americans in China: "The bloated Chinese bureaucracy has been streamlined from 98 ministries, commissions and agencies to a more manageable 52. But negotiations are still plagued by procrastination, inefficiency, nit-picking, secrecy, and internal rivalries, not to mention a hazy legal system that leaves potential investors confused about their rights."[2]

Negotiators who have worked abroad agree: the international arena is no place for amateurs or slow learners.

BEFORE THE NEGOTIATION

What you do before the negotiation starts is as important as what you do during the negotiation.

Since Americans so often treat negotiations like games, they go into them relying on superior strength and mental or physical agility. But the traveler who counts on being able to think on his or her feet is going to find a negotiation debacle. The real art of successful negotiation is in the preparation.

Rule 1: Make sure that what you are negotiating is negotiable.

A team of U.S. negotiators spent a year and a half flying back and forth to Japan negotiating a coal sale. When discussions were hopelessly stuck, one of the American members asked, "Look, if we gave you the coal *free,* what amount could you use?" Initially confused by the hypothetical question but after some explanation and supportive assurances against loss of face, the Japanese answered, "No amount." No matter what the Americans did in the negotiations, the Japanese were not going to buy their coal. They had already closed a deal with some other country and were going through the paces of negotiating with the Americans only out of politeness. Belatedly, the Americans asked themselves, "What the hell are we doing here?"

Some things are non-negotiable. Some problems cannot be resolved, some differences cannot be reconciled, and some negotiators really have little interest in reaching agreement. In some cases, the parties simply must go their separate ways. In other cases, negotiators should work on reaching a tolerable *modus vivendi,* a means for both sides to live with their differences while leaving the door open for solutions that may come later. Circumstances do change.

When there are facts of life that cannot or will not be changed, find a way to work around them. Dick Burns, director of trading and sourcing for Levi Strauss's Eximco, says one of the mistakes he sees negotiators make in China is to argue about a schedule. The Americans have a preconceived notion of how much time is needed to manufacture a particular product; the Chinese simply will not meet the deadline even if they have agreed to it. You can save a lot of trouble if instead of negotiating a non-negotiable, you ask, "When do I have to commit our final figures for you to meet our fall production?"

Rule 2: Define what "winning" the negotiation means to you.

All too many people go into a foreign negotiation with a view to getting "as much as we can get." Without a target, however, you will be shooting into the trees, and your score on "whatever we can get" will be substantially lower than what you could get when you are aiming at a clear set of objectives.

Be precise about what you want but think through a wide range of possibilities. Research findings suggest that skilled negotiators explore almost twice as many options for action than others.[3] Think through all the variables that will affect the deal—price, quality, quantity, timing, means of delivery, warranties, costs, terms of payment, labor arrangements, inspections, and so on. "Standard business practices" vary around the world. Take nothing for granted.

Be ambitious but set a realistic walk-away.

Many Americans fare badly in international negotiations because they fail to set their sights high enough—they tend to start out from a basis of what they think is fair and reasonable. They may "think big" in planning but are too embarrassed to make what might seem to be preposterous demands. In countries where haggling is the norm, such as China and the Middle East, Americans lose because their proposals start too close to the goal, without enough room for numerous concessions. Even where haggling is not customary, as in Europe and Canada, higher demands bring higher settlements. If one side opens with high demands, the other will probably reconsider its position and is likely to counter with something higher than it was planning to. The reverse happens also; by asking for too little or offering too much, you reduce your chances of a winning outcome.

When you define what "winning" means to you, also define what *not* winning means. Reaching an agreement is not necessarily winning a negotiation. At the point when an agreement no longer benefits you, you must be able to *walk away without a deal,* no matter how disappointed you are. No deal is better than a bad deal, as many companies are finding out around the world.

Rule 3: Get the facts.

If you want to get what is important to you, you are going to have to understand what is important to the other side. Never assume that the foreigner wants what you want or is motivated by the same needs. You have to study the facts of the situation as well as the constraints on and the aspirations of the individual negotiators on the other side.

Before any negotiation, it is normal to have pre-negotiation meetings and information exchanges. In addition, arrange informal get-togethers. During this time, try to get inside the foreign organization. It may operate quite differently from its American counterparts. Who are the decision makers and how are decisions made? Often the decision maker is not at the negotiation table or may keep a low profile during the negotiations. What are the delivery schedules? What are the budget allocations—can you find out how much has been budgeted for *your* project? Where does the company want to go? What are the concerns of the decision makers? Have they had unhappy experiences doing business with Americans? How badly do they want this deal? What other commitments have been made, and on what terms? Particularly, find out what you can about members of the negotiation team—their authority to make a deal, their personal goals and their perspective on this negotiation. Find out how they think. As Tom Klitgaard of Pillsbury, Madison and Sutro says: "How they think will affect their reactions to your proposals."

Just as important as understanding the other side is understanding your own organization, management goals and negotiation parameters. Some negotiators, especially in a foreign situation, get so wrapped up in details that they lose sight of the bigger picture and reach agreements that may seem good for the deal at hand but are bad for the long-term interests of the company. You should know how important the outcome of the negotiation is to the company, and to your career. You also need to know how much rope you have to negotiate elements of a deal, such as price, time and terms. Your credibility will suffer if you have to keep checking with headquarters for each decision. If you feel you will need more time or staff support, negotiate with your superiors to get it.

Rule 4: Have a strategy for each culture and each phase.

A good strategy is like a road map—it doesn't show just one road, but provides a number of routes to the same destination. If you miss the turn you wanted (and it is easy to make a wrong turn in a cross-cultural negotiation), there are a number of alternate ways to go, some more scenic, some faster, some with more roadside facilities. A good strategy allows you to make minor adjustments along your path to get to the same place. The key is flexibility. Dick Burns of Levi Strauss says that one of the biggest mistakes he sees people make abroad is rigid adherence to a "slick" strategy. You must not lose sight of the objective.

Your first strategic decision should be how to position your proposal.

Americans approach a negotiation as a problem-solving exercise, hence they tend to concentrate on the problems, differences or areas of disagreement between the negotiating sides. There is evidence to suggest, however, that successful international negotiators give much more time to common ground and pay a lot of attention to areas of anticipated agreement. Instead of devoting all your energy to developing counters to the arguments you may expect, put more effort into figuring out what the other side will find appealing about your proposal.

In negotiating, as in marketing, it is important to influence how the other side perceives your proposal, particularly relative to all other competing options. You must position your proposal so that it will stand out favorably among all available alternatives. To do this well you must try to see the situation from the foreigner's point of view. Fit the proposal to local economic goals and the ambitions of the negotiating team. What are the deciding factors? What political, social or organizational pressures can be brought to bear? What does the foreigner *want* from you? Richard Pascale, co-author of *The Art of Japanese Management* and negotiation professor at Stanford Business School, says: "People rarely negotiate on the basis of price alone . . . The ability to create deals which benefit both parties is where the action is in international negotiations." Think about "creative packaging" for your proposals, including variations in guarantees, financial arrangements or participation of the players in the deal.

Second, decide whether to be competitive (win-lose) or cooperative (win-win).

Don't always use the same style, even if you think you have developed it to perfection. Instead, determine which approach will work best in the foreign culture, given the circumstances.

There is a lot of evidence that the competitive negotiator wins better deals than the cooperative negotiator, perhaps because in de-emphasizing differences, the cooperative negotiator may give up more, while the win-lose negotiator often sets higher stakes and encourages less compromise. The Soviets, for example, are able to force us to give and give more. Says one executive working in Moscow: "The Russians never lose by putting pressure on the West; there is no win-win with the Russians." Asians, particularly the Japanese, may use cooperative styles when negotiating among themselves but can be ruthlessly competitive with outsiders. Do not assume coincidence of interest in seemingly cooperative negotiations. An appearance of cooperation and harmony should not be allowed to obscure the goals of the foreign partner.

Many Arabs are much more truly collaborative. Despite the haggling, a negotiation is not a true win-lose if you have established a relationship. If you are bargaining over an object in the market with someone you have chatted with several times in the past, you are likely to get a somewhat better price than the total stranger. The Arab often says, "For you, my friend, special deal." (It may not be a *good* deal, just a better deal.) Says Gary Wederspahn of Moran, Stahl & Boyer, cross-cultural consultants: "You'd better protect your flank, but when you are negotiating with the Saudi, you are, in a sense, forming a new tribe to go out against the world."

In international negotiations, a cooperative appearance is recommended; both sides must perceive a win-win. Competitive styles make sense only when power is a major element or when a one-time deal is being negotiated. Even if the competitive style is the one you choose, do not make your negotiation a contest. Never "go in for the kill." Remember, in most cross-cultural negotiations you are not just negotiating a deal but negotiating a relationship. This must color your approach whether you are at the bargaining table with a banker, landlord, supplier, employee or contractor. That does not mean be subservient—your foreign partner will not respect a loser.

Third, set your opening offer.

Opening proposals are an important signal to the other side. At this early stage, foreigners are not likely to take the proposal itself seriously but will use it to size you up. The foreigner is always more interested in *you* than in your product or project, so make your opening bid inspire respect and trust.

The rule of thumb of professional negotiators abroad seems to be to ask for as much as you possibly can without making yourself appear imperialistic, foolish or blatantly bluffing. To make the right opening price demands, you must know two things: the cultural bargaining norms in the country, and the market realities. Not knowing these things makes you vulnerable to exploitation and loss of face, whether you are buying olives at the market or oil in the international exchange. In any country, the market realities provide ceilings and floors on the range of settlements, and it is always assumed that both sides know what the real market values are.

How much to overstate your demands depends on the country. The Chinese, Koreans, Japanese, Arabs, Israelis, Russians and others are likely to start off with an extreme position. Never express irritation—in many countries the opening bid is ritualistically extreme because the negotiator expects to back down. In China the negotiator is likely to be a professional whose only job is to negotiate. If he cannot show that he obtained "discounts," he is not doing his job. The Arab will start with an outlandish position, then retreat and claim, "See how generous I am."

Fourth, plan to control your concessions.

First, make an inventory of all the concessions you might be willing to make, not just the obvious ones from your point of view but any variations that might be appealing to the other side. Think of concessions that may mean nothing to you but a lot to the foreigner—what Stanford's Richard Pascale calls "free ice in winter."

How you present your concessions can make a big difference, depending on the culture of the negotiators. Compromise and concession are not virtues everywhere. In some places an early concession might get the wheels turning, but elsewhere it might hurt your position. To the French, a thoughtful position should not be compromised unless something was wrong with the reasoning. The Mexican will not compromise, as a matter of honor, dignity and integrity.⁴ The Arab fears loss of manliness if he compromises. It's a question not of face but of control—he would rather feel he is giving out of generosity, not necessity. In Russia, "compromise" has a negative connotation; principles are supposed to be inviolable, and compromise is a matter of integrity. A negotiation is treated as a whole, without concessions. However, in the USSR and other countries where compromise is not the cultural mode, issues can be bartered, quid pro quo, without the stigma of concession.

In Persian, the word "compromise" does not have the English meaning of a midway solution which both sides can accept, but only the negative meaning of surrendering one's principles. Also, a "mediator" is a meddler, someone who is barging in uninvited. In 1980, United Nations Secretary-General Kurt Waldheim flew to Iran to deal with the hostage situation. National Iranian radio and television broadcast in Persian a comment he was said to have made upon his arrival in Tehran: "I have come as a mediator to work out a compromise." Less than an hour later, his car was being stoned by angry Iranians.

SOURCE: *Getting to Yes,* Roger Fisher and William Ury of the Harvard Negotiation Project, Penguin Books, 1983, Page 34.

The timing of concessions can be revealing or confusing when people from different cultures negotiate. Americans make trivial concessions right away and continue to make concessions throughout the entire course of the negotiation. We make our concessions in sequence, and the final agreement is little more than a summation of all previous agreements. Not so elsewhere. Some people don't make concessions until the end of deliberations when a total package is agreed upon. In these countries, Americans who make concessions along the way find they have "given away the store" needlessly. During the Cuban missile crisis John Kennedy stood firm against the Russians (who make concessions late), resisting the American inclination to concede early. Japanese negotiators are not normally able to compromise without going through the organization again.

Sincerity and consistency are important practically everywhere, and improving your offer abruptly can undermine the other side's confidence in you. The first to make a unilateral concession frequently is marked as the weaker player in the negotiation, either because the opening bid seems insincere or because the first to back down appears to need agreement more than the other side. Avoid making concessions or agreements along the way when negotiating in cultures where agreement is reached as a total package at the end of deliberations.

Sometimes it's better to negotiate than to make a quick decision.

In his first loan negotiation, a banker new to Japan met with seven top Japanese bankers who were seeking a substantial amount of money. After hearing their presentation, the American agreed on the spot. The seven Japanese then conferred among themselves and told the American they would get back to him in a couple of days as to whether they would accept his offer or not. The American banker learned a lesson he never forgot.

Rule 5: Send a winning team.

Who a company sends may determine the outcome of a negotiation or whether it will be able to enter negotiations at all. In the Middle East, the top man makes the decisions and prefers to deal only with other decision-making executives. In Africa and some European countries such as Germany, authority generally comes with age, so the representative at the bargaining table should be at least middle-aged. In China, team members must have expertise, not just authority. When Chevron Overseas Petroleum negotiated there, the Chinese team was led by a woman who had a degree in chemical engineering and twenty-five years in oil production. Russian negotiators are specialists in their fields, and in addition have several years in the academy of foreign trade. They are trained negotiators.

Everywhere in the world an essential ingredient of a negotiation is the creation of trust and a sense of long-term interest in the country. It does not create confidence to send a representative without much authority. Even where a deal will be hammered out by middle management, a senior manager should make opening contact. The interest of top management gives your project a sense of urgency. But keep in mind that any upper-management meetings should merely set the tone and not deal with substance. In most places the top management will not be directly involved in negotiations and you will only embarrass the other side by sending your highest people to negotiate. The novelty and prestige of doing business in China has attracted many chief executive officers there to initiate talks with the Chinese, and the Chinese have not hesitated to use these executives' general statements to their advantage when subsequently negotiating with middle managers.

Don't go alone.

Foreigners will almost always have more people on a team than Americans are inclined to have. You may not be able to match them (the Japanese and Chinese will always add more people), but do try to reach some balance in authority and power. Being outnumbered is a psychological as well as practical disadvantage. You need the help of a strong team to be able to carry on all the simultaneous activities of a negotiation: giving information, persuading, listening, thinking, preparing arguments, formulating questions and revising strategy as necessary to continue moving toward agreement. It also helps to have a number of nodding (or frowning) faces on your side to give an air of support and unity.

Always have your own interpreter.

Never rely on theirs. Remember, the interpreter on the other side is working for *them*. (See Chapter 5 for rules on briefing and use of interpreters).

Exclude lawyers and accountants from the negotiating team.

Few foreign negotiation teams will have attorneys at the bargaining table, although lawyers are very important behind the scenes. As a general rule, bringing a lawyer along will do great damage, arousing suspicion in some countries and contempt in others. Some foreigners snicker at us for relying on the law when we should rely instead on religion, humanity or common sense.

Foreigners who mistrust attorneys may assume from their presence that you are planning deception or that you are more interested in the fine points of a contract than the relationship. American lawyers tend to negotiate contracts when the foreigners are negotiating a relationship; lawyers concentrate on looking at words rather than the character of the business partners.

The attorney in international business plays a role that is quite different from the domestic attorney's role. The international lawyer must have a conscious appreciation of how differently business is conducted around the world, and a talent for working with these differences to accomplish legal protections and commitments while not impeding the process of business. An attorney who understands the cultural context can be a great asset.

Lawyers must be kept abreast of developments so that they can prevent later embarrassment. The final legal papers are essential, of course. You must have a trail of documents, letters of intent, or agreements to fall back on if and when a deal begins to unravel.

Ford Motor Company, when Lee Iacocca was running it, wanted to buy Ferrari. Some of Iacocca's top people went to see Enzo Ferrari and they came to an understanding: Ford would acquire not the race car but the production side of the company so that the Ferrari name could be used in the United States. The deal was made on handshakes between gentlemen. Soon, though, Ford's attorneys arrived in Italy with contracts, and a crew arrived to take inventory. This was normal business procedure for the Americans, but Ferrari was disgruntled—to his thinking he had an understanding with a gentleman, not with a group of attorneys and accountants—and had second thoughts. The deal fell through. In the end, Fiat stepped in and gave Ferrari the money he needed.

In some cases, use a go-between.

Victor Kiam, president of Remington Products, tells the story of his first efforts to set up an organization to sell Remington shavers in Japan. He flew to Hiroshima and met with the toiletries buyer at Japan's biggest department store. Everything seemed to go well. The Japanese nodded and smiled a lot, and Kiam left after an hour thinking he had a deal. But his interpreter explained to him that actually he did not. In Japan you know you have a deal when you are told the name of the man who is going to pick up the goods that you are selling. Mr. Kiam didn't get a name. Eventually, through the intervention of a banker, the buyer agreed to meet again with Kiam, but Kiam had to go through his entire presentation again, word for word from the first hello, as though he had never met the buyer before. This way everybody could save face and the buyer could place an order.

In many places it is best never to open negotiations with a company yourself. Use someone who is known to the foreign management, such as a banker, a trading agent, a respected professor or a member of a trade association. The go-between must be equal in status to the personnel involved in the negotiations, generally at middle-management level. Often the go-between uses some neutral ground such as a hotel for the meeting. Contact, of course, must be in person.

Don't change negotiators in midstream.

Much of the foreign negotiator's energy is concentrated on getting to know you. Your company goes back to zero when it brings in new faces. Moreover, by changing personnel, you will seem unreliable, confused and insincere.

Rule 6: Allow yourself plenty of time, and more.

Americans go into negotiations with an eye to the end result; our orientation is toward an outcome. Most other cultures are oriented to the process of the negotiation itself, thus they feel no sense of rush and have infinitely more patience. At the beginning of the Vietnam peace talks in Paris, Averell Harriman checked into the Ritz on a day-to-day basis. The North Vietnamese took out a two-year lease on a villa.

Experienced travelers recommend trebling the time you think a negotiation will take. With the exception of a few European cultures, most foreigners will prolong meetings, both to get to know you better and to go over details again and again until total understanding is reached. Many more people will be involved in the foreign decision-making process. Often days will pass while authority from upper management is sought. And throughout the tedium of delays and repetition, you must maintain harmonious relations if you are to keep the negotiations alive. Chevron's Robert Armstrong says that the Chinese repeatedly told him: "Always remain flexible." Don't get mad. Try never to appear rushed. If you had set aside one day for meetings, prepare instead for three days; if it should take a week, plan on three weeks.

Never tell the other side when you are leaving.

Some foreigners, if they know you are in town for ten days, will take you on tours, dinners, and continuous entertainment and meetings to keep you from talking to a competitor. As one executive says: "We've all experienced it—the jet lag, the toasts, the seven A.M. meetings. It's like brainwashing. They wear you down to malleable form." When it is about time for you to leave, they will hand you an agreement, saying, "Please sign here." Mortified to return home empty-handed after an expensive junket abroad, some travelers may sign, especially if making a straight sales deal.

When the foreign negotiators (or their personnel) ask how long you are staying, say you haven't made any plans for your return. Just in case they call your hotel to inquire about the length of your reservation (as they have been known to do), you might make reservations for an indefinite period. Your opponents are likely to proceed into negotiations, and you will be less likely to be pushed into a deal on the way to the airport. Finally, give yourself enough time so that you go into meetings rested. Henry Kissinger has stressed the importance of stamina: you must be able to persist, to hold fast while goals are ever so gradually fulfilled, and you must be able to manage stress. Be sure to schedule plenty of time for sleep and relaxation; don't engage in late-night partying before important sessions.

BEGINNING THE NEGOTIATING

Rule 7: Make the opening scene work for you.

The practice in Hollywood is to throw away a script if it doesn't grab the reader in the first ten pages. Ten pages transforms into ten minutes on the silver screen, and average moviegoers decide whether they like the film in the first ten minutes. So the first scene has a big job to do. In international negotiations, the first scene counts too. The central characters and the thrust of your "story" are introduced. The other side's first impressions will be hard to shake. If your partners are not hooked in the beginning, it will be hard to involve them as the drama of the negotiation unfolds.

As with all international business transactions, do not expect to get straight to the point, unless you are in northern Europe. Your first negotiation meetings may seem more social than businesslike—informal gatherings where the opposite side can check you out. Do not misconstrue the casualness of these meetings. Do not behave informally at informal occasions. Be personable, not personal. And most of all, do not be careless in your remarks. Use this time to check *them* out.

In the United States this first period of "feeling out the players" is usually very brief, often no more than introductions and a few pleasantries. Elsewhere, this first phase can take a long time. Don't rush it, and try to take advantage of it yourself.

Think about the agenda.

Whether you are a visitor on foreign soil or whether you are negotiating with foreigners here in America, don't just accept the agenda proposed by the other side. Read it carefully for what it contains and what it leaves out. Consider what priorities it reveals. What will its effect be on your concession strategy—does it force your concessions too soon? If you are concerned about it, take extra time; ask for a break to study it and propose adjustments.

Watch the physical arrangements.

Most people seem to agree that you have the advantage if you negotiate on your own turf, but you can use being the visitor to your advantage too: you can see their operation and how they operate within it. You can get more time, play on their obligations as hosts, and so on. Wherever the negotiation, avoid arrangements where you face the sun, and avoid noisy rooms. Be prepared for sweltering heat in summer and unheated rooms in winter.

The overture should make music.

Formal negotiations typically begin with what experts call "posturing," the expected generalities and sentiments expressed to set the tone. Use the words "respect" and "mutual benefit" frequently. An air of cooperation will get the negotiations off on the right foot. Avoid any posturing statements that suggest arrogance, superiority or urgency.

Posturing is followed by a period of formal exchange of information. Presentations are made by each side, questions raised, answers sought. Alternatives may be discussed and preferences expressed. Americans are able to dispense with this stage efficiently but may become frustrated in international negotiations. The French enjoy conflict and debate, and will interrupt even the opening presentations with arguments that may or may not be relevant to the topic at hand. The Mexican always seems to be beating around the bush, suspicious and indirect, cushioning opening talks with lengthy conversation but little substance. The Soviets treat business discussions as one form of worldwide political struggle—the unsuspecting traveler can be overwhelmed by the power playing of the Russian negotiation team. Americans in China complain of being "pecked to death by a thousand Peking ducks." The Chinese ask questions that the Americans feel they have thoroughly and clearly answered, repeatedly; yet the Chinese will give only vague and ambiguous answers to the American's questions. In all cases, the only uniform rule is to persist.

The Chinese have been called technological vacuum cleaners. After about a hundred Boeing personnel compiled detailed information and over twenty Boeing people spent six weeks presenting a roomful of literature and making daily technical demonstrations to the Chinese, the Chinese said, "Thank you for your introduction." One who was present in the negotiations explains the Chinese appetite for information: "Remember, their long-term goal is to manufacture airplanes themselves, not to continue to buy from America."

HARD BARGAINING

Eventually, after all the posturing, preliminary information-gathering and presentations of opening demands, negotiators move into a phase of hard bargaining. This is when the deal is hammered out, concessions may be made, and each side tries to persuade or manipulate the other side to give more. This is when your resolve will really be tested.

Rule 8: Control information.

As a rule, keep your cards close to your chest. Throughout, the foreigner will want more and more information, some which may be, at least from your point of view, proprietary and confidential. Give no more information than you think is necessary for the success of your negotiations. Too many of us feel bound to answer a question as though being called upon in school. Don't do it. Field questions diplomatically. Always appear fully cooperative, but remember you can always give partial answers or answer different questions. If the information really is a proprietary secret, say so—most foreigners, even in developing countries, now understand this. Most of all, learn how to handle periods of silence. Many foreigners say that if they are silent long enough, an American will start blurting out information or lowering prices.

Be careful to guard information from the beginning of contacts with a potential negotiation opponent. Information shared casually or formally during preliminary introductions, factory tours, and dinners may come to haunt you in later negotiations. What you said in an effort toward "relationship-building" will be taken into consideration when the other side thinks about its price. Most of us give away entirely too much information even when we ask questions. The typical American will lay out the details of what he or she wants to buy—the product, features, colors, sizes, any special markings or delivery requirements—then ask, "What will that cost if I buy ten dozen?" Worse, we might ask, "Can I have it by Christmas?" Expert negotiators such as Stanford's Richard Pascale suggest breaking down the inquiry to discrete elements so that you will get the information without tipping your hand. For example, start by asking the price of one item. Then explore the discount structure and alternative terms of payment. Discuss scheduling. Consider different features, indifferently. Then inquire about special markings, or delivery, or other variables. The more you understand about the price structure and production schedule, the better you will be able to figure out how much negotiating room you have.

"Americans, especially American men, don't ask enough questions," says a businessman from Guyana. "You always try to show how much you know, but I think we end up knowing more than you." His point: Ask your own questions, or the other side will end up with more information, and you with less. The point is not to catch your opponents off-guard (as you can arouse hostility if they are embarrassed and unprepared), but to learn as much as possible. (The task of getting good information is so complex and challenging that we have devoted Chapter 5 to it.)

> **Don't tell them everything.**
>
> An American trader participating in a trade fair in the United Arab
> Emirates set out looking for helium tanks and regulators to fill balloons
> that would decorate his booth. He found one store open, got a quote on
> the tanks and agreed to rent the regulators. Thankful, he told the Arab
> how relieved he was—the balloons were going to be a big deal at the booth
> and he had been unsuccessful finding anyone else who would rent him the
> regulators. When he arrived to pick up the equipment, the Arab told him
> there had been a misunderstanding—and the American had to pay a
> highly inflated price. This kind of thing happens all the time. The message:
> Never give too much information even *after* the deal has been struck.

Rule 9: Watch your language.

An American negotiator might reassuringly announce, "Well, we seem to
be thinking along parallel lines," meaning "At least we seem to agree in
attitude or point of view." Some foreigners might take this as less than
reassuring; to many people, the same expression describes two unfortunate
parties going down two separate paths that have no hope of ever meeting.

Many negotiations flounder because of communication problems. The
Russians and Americans had a hard time at the SALT talks because of
confusion over words. When the Americans thought they had an agreement
(meaning conclusive commitment), the Russians said it was an understanding (meaning an expression of mutual viewpoint or attitude). And when the
Americans thought they had an understanding, the Russians said it was a
procedural matter, meaning they agreed to a process for conducting the
negotiation. Because words, body language and even concepts mean different things in different countries, negotiators can spend days talking past one
another in meetings, accomplishing little more than large-scale misunderstandings. It is a good idea to agree with the opposite side on the specific
meanings of certain words, including procedural terminology.

Wording is especially problematic between countries that have little
experience in working together. When AMC was negotiating a joint venture
to build Jeeps in China, a dispute erupted over the word "exclusivity" in
the contract. The Americans wanted a guarantee that no other company in
China would be given the technical documents for manufacturing Jeeps. In
Chinese, "exclusivity" has negative overtones; the words "undivided heart"
were substituted in the Chinese version because of their more pleasing
connotations of "complete attention," a more meaningful concept among
the Chinese. A Chevron attorney spent three weeks in Beijing negotiating

the word "profit." It was finally struck and replaced with "remainder." At one point during negotiations one of his colleagues remarked, "To resolve this issue [in the contract] will require the wisdom of Solomon and the patience of Job." Never make that sort of comment—they wasted an hour trying to explain it.

Rule 10: Persuasion is an art. Don't paint your argument with the wrong materials.

Artists know you can't use watercolor on an oil-paint canvas—it just won't sink in, and neither will your arguments if they do not fit into the prevailing thought and logic "fabric" of the culture. Like acrylic on oil, some of your efforts may appear to work, but eventually you will see that the message didn't stick.

Americans tend to be factual—the facts speak for themselves. And we are inductive thinkers: we amass our data and then draw conclusions, but we respond to new evidence. We worry about presenting our data clearly, with evidence documented, and are less concerned with the thought process. It is the specifics of a deal that concern us, not the principles.

What convinces an American will fall on deaf ears in many places. Other cultures are less factual but more intuitive, deductive or normative than we tend to be. In many places "evidence" is interpreted according to already established principles. The Soviets, for example, think from the general idea to the particular. Soviets deduce implications from axioms rather than the other way around. The French are philosophically analytical, believing that cold logic leads to the right conclusions. The Mexicans and Japanese are much more affective than logical in approach; emotion and drama carry more weight. The Japanese are also data collectors, and hypothetical reasoning does not convince them.[3] Arabs are more normative; relationships and value systems are important. The Chinese focus on practicality; they deal in the concrete and particular, but they are artists in using general principles to gain an advantage in negotiation. And they are sticklers for consistency. Many an American feels that if one explanation doesn't work, perhaps another will—an approach that will backfire in Asian countries, where inconsistency may be suspect. Sometimes it is better to repeat the same explanation in different terms or even use the same words.

Thinking on the same plane is important.

Americans like to think big and talk big—we like to deal with big volume, big ads, and so on. This is inappropriate in a culture where people think in smaller, or unit, terms. Joe Garcia of Mattel says: "I've seen Americans in Spain, Germany and Hong Kong trying to negotiate their big deals, when local businessmen were worried about piece counts and profit per piece; they pick on little points. Many Americans get antsy talking about nickels and dimes and cut them off, but you have to listen to where they are coming from. Address their needs. It works."

Don't forget your concession strategy. With new information, you may need to adjust the strategy often, but wherever you are, make your concessions count. Whether you make concessions along the way or at the end of deliberations, think of them as tools in the negotiations, not required giveaways. And don't think you have to make a concession each time the other side makes one, but try to make your concessions only when the other side gives too. Don't worry about being seen as stubborn—you will be respected for your consistency. Generally it is a good idea to let the opposite side volunteer its own concessions rather than suggest them yourself.

Whenever making concessions, keep them small. Every inch should make good mileage. The other side needs to have something to chip at—giving too much too soon doesn't allow the process of negotiation. Old hands recommend accompanying each concession with sweat and tears, emphasizing the importance and generosity of the concession. One might cry, "Mr. Wong, if I gave any more, I would be out of a job! I would lose face and could never come to Taiwan again!" And throughout, keep track. Deidra Deamer, director of trading at Unison Corporation, warns: "When negotiating in China, you'd better keep the total picture in mind, or you will end up with a long tally of concessions that add up to more than you realized."

Whatever the style of your arguments, they must contain the necessary content. Many foreign governments, for example, must be convinced that a deal is consistent with their country's overall economic priorities: an import must be deemed needed for the good of the country, there being no domestic substitute available, or a project must provide for technology transfer and jobs for local laborers. Reliability may be as important as cost savings, considering the state of technology in the country. Price and quality are of concern everywhere, but other factors may be more important. Track record is usually more impressive than plans and promises. Don't waste your breath on the wrong information.

Be wary of the persuasion strategies Americans love.

Many favorite American negotiation gambits can spell disaster abroad. The most outstanding approach to avoid is the "good guy–bad guy" routine. In many places the "bad guy" may generate so much hostility that negotiations will come to an end. Another American stratagem is to decompose a problem down to its smallest parts, to solve each issue separately. Many foreigners don't think this way and become suspicious when we try to force a decision on one piece without considering the whole.

New negotiation stratagems come along all the time, some of them impressive. The rule is: Whenever you learn a new technique, do not use it without questioning how appropriate it will be to the foreign culture.

Rule 11: Get in stride with the locals.

Negotiations abroad are not likely to proceed the way you'd expect them to back home. Americans are uniquely linear, attacking issues sequentially, resolving one issue after another: quantity, then price. We assume we are halfway through when we are halfway down the agenda. But in many cultures, especially in the Far East, a negotiation is holistic: all issues discussed at once and no decisions made until the end. Americans tend to panic when the steps don't seem in order and when expected milestones are gone. As one expert says: "Don't fall off your horse when you lose stride. Learn to vary your pace."

Sometimes it is better for you to be active and involved; at other times you should be passive or removed. At times you will be more effective if you talk or argue your points; at other times you should be quiet or agreeable. You must be sensitive to the flow of the negotiation to know when to be flexible or determined.

Most important: Take time out.

Most businesspeople don't take enough time out from negotiations to think. Whatever the local pacing, you must know when to call a caucus. Stanford's Richard Pascale insists: "Always, always, always give yourself time to think." The Vietnam peace talks were 90 percent caucus and 10 percent talks. It is vital to find ways to buy time. Like the time-out in football, the caucus is an important time for you to reconsider and prepare countermoves. Pascale suggests getting the other side to present its position before breaking for the evening, arranging to get phone calls or going to the bathroom. An interpreter or technical person can also be helpful in slowing down the negotiations. But you don't always need to be coy. It is perfectly reasonable to ask for a recess to study an issue.

Proper pacing also allows for "acceptance time," the time it takes for a new idea to sink in and become acceptable. Given enough time, people often change. Try to provide for plenty of time when you introduce new data, requirements or ideas. Unless you give time and help resolve the other side's concerns, logic will not prevail.

Rule 12: Go behind the scenes—that is where minds are changed.

It is occasionally possible to see that the negotiator on the other side is blocked by some organizational, legal or policy constraint. It is often possible to move the discussion to those issues and help him resolve them, thus gaining favor and freeing up a "win" for both sides.

In some countries, particularly in the Far East, the negotiation session is less a forum for working out issues than it is a formal and public expression of what has already been worked out beforehand. It is always wise to resolve differences before a meeting. Come early to meetings so that you can chat casually, and linger again afterward. It will not be difficult to find ways to meet informally, since *houmani*—the back-door approach—is the customary procedure in so many places.

Rule 13: Give face.

People who lose face can go to extremes to act out their resentment or get even behind your back. Almost every negotiation is a face-saving situation, and the successful international negotiator will carefully avoid making people uncomfortable. Be careful in your choice of words so that the other side is not offended. Grandiose presentations may seem arrogant and make the other side defensive. Always avoid criticism that might be taken personally. Many experienced international negotiators say: "The successful negotiator is the one who treats the person on the other side with respect and fair play. Do that and they will always come back and work with you."

If you must object to certain requirements or constrictions, try to deflect the blame to things outside the control of your opponent, or to "others" in the opposite side's organization. But if you need a scapegoat, be wary of treading on loyalties. In Japan you might offend people if you point blame at the government; indeed, in countries with military governments it is positively dangerous to point blame at the regime and may lead to your arrest.

Rule 14: A deadlock means neither side wins, but both may lose.

No negotiator likes to deadlock, but in international negotiations, deadlock is frequently the outcome of days, weeks or months of meetings. Sometimes there is no solution and the parties must go their separate ways. But before giving up, there are a number of ways to try to get the negotiations "unstuck."

When you are stuck on a certain item, try to expose the root of the problem ("Why are we stuck here?") and make some accommodations such as minor concessions or creative repackaging of the proposal. Now would be a good time to use your go-between. He can ask discreet questions of junior employees in the company to find out what the problem is or who is resisting the deal.

You may be able to get "unstuck" by changing the deal in some way, such as by changing the timing or financial arrangements affecting cash flow or risk. Alternatively, shelve the subject temporarily and work on issues that can be resolved. Some negotiators suggest breaking a deadlock by adding to the tension level: showing anger, walking out, and postponing discussions until there is a readiness to deal with the issues. In international situations, however, these tactics should be used with extreme caution, if at all. In most countries, emotional outbursts or behavior that threatens loss of face may close the door permanently behind you.

Do not hasten to conclude that every impasse is a deadlock. In China, and in many other countries, every negotiation occurs within a complex institutional background. When progress stalls, keep in mind that the negotiators may be waiting for bureaucratic approvals. In Japan a seeming deadlock can last for weeks but is no cause for panic. Even if meetings have ceased, much can be done behind the scenes by meeting in private to rebuild the relationship and sense of interest and understanding. Throughout these trying times, always maintain harmonious relations.

Rule 15: Don't be browbeaten into a bad deal.

The emphasis on harmony and cooperation in some cultures does not mean that the other side will not play tough. Often you will get ultimatums, threats, accusations and occasionally personal slights. When this happens, remember that you do not necessarily need to take abuse to win.

It is not unusual for foreign negotiators to protest loudly, "We have been your loyal allies and now you are picking on us." A U.S. trade representative describes a South Korean negotiation that began with a pathetic comparison of the rich imperialistic nation pitted against their (the Koreans') poor struggling developing economy, and ended with a condemnation of U.S. political and military position in the world. In short, they tried to make the Americans feel guilty before the negotiations even began. Infuriated, one of the Americans stood up and calmly but firmly gave it right back to them. He told them how he had fought in Korea and how many of his buddies died there. The Koreans sheepishly went into reasonable negotiations. The trade representative said, "They do play hard ball, and at the same time, the Korean Blue House controls the media, so you hear only the Korean side. They can come on like a buzz saw."

You must be able to walk away.

Before the negotiation you should have defined your walk-away. When you reach that point, walk! Many international business people are lured into unprofitable agreements in hopes of future business. A bad deal, however, only sets a precedent for future bad business. You can't change your prices next time. You don't need to take a loss to establish a relationship —don't do it. But walk away gracefully, tall and friendly, so that the other side is not too embarrassed to call you back. Never be bitter, or the door will be closed forever.

You must also be able to walk when you find business practices or personal conduct that is illegal or contrary to our standards. Usually there will be warnings that all is not right, and if you pay attention to these warnings there will be time to back out. The project manager of a joint venture between Triad International and a group of American agribusiness companies that were to transfer agriculture technology in the Middle East backed out just before the venture blew up. But, he says, "When the deal is big, Americans can be so dazzled that they miss the danger indicators. Everyone wanted to keep going for the big payoff. They should have paid attention to the red signals."

Don't let your walk-away limit your ability to integrate new information during negotiations and look for new solutions. The picture can change rapidly and there is always more to learn. The point is, you must be able to say no to a bad deal.

Agreements

Rule 16: Get your agreement signed before you leave.

Once you are out of the country, it could take months to get a contract that you thought was agreed upon, either because of the foreigner's reluctance to deal through the mails or because other matters become more pressing when you are not there. Very likely you thought you had nailed down all the points of agreement but find that the written contract produces more unresolved issues. If more people become involved after you are gone, you may be back to zero.

Rule 17: Both sides should agree on the significance of what you are signing.

The American contract formalizes a bargain and protects against either party breaking the bargain—the relationship is legal. Foreigners say Americans are bound by law, not by relationships, tradition, religion or culture. We will honor a contract to the letter, whatever circumstances later arise. But the meaning of an agreement varies around the world, making it very hard for mixed cultural groups to know precisely the significance of the documents they sign or the seriousness of a handshake.

Few Americans, Germans or British will conduct business without some form of written contract. In the Arab world a person's word may be more binding than many written agreements, and insistence on a contract may be insulting. Even so, the Arab (or other nationality) might not fulfill an "agreement" since a Westerner can mistakenly hear words of commitment when only politeness was intended. In many parts of the world, open refusal to do as another requests is rude. In some cultures, it is assumed that any agreement may be superseded or negated by a later conflicting demand, particularly by a superior or a relative. As an outsider, you will always be at a disadvantage because no foreigner will feel he owes you loyalty, and the concept of face only applies to friends, relations and colleagues.

Contracts serve different purposes around the world—often definitely un-American. A Greek sees a contract as a formal statement announcing the intention to build a business for the future; the negotiation is complete only when the work is accomplished. The Japanese treat contracts as statements of general intention, and they assume changes will be made as dictated by developments. Mexicans treat the contract as an artistic exercise of ideals and do not expect contracts to apply consistently in the real world. At the opposite extreme, a German contract cements details that contracts of other countries, even the United States, might leave to standard trade practice. Yet even there, the German Civil Code can supersede a contract, imposing duties or prohibiting items not provided for in a contract.

When the two sides of a negotiation do not define agreements or contracts in the same way, each side is likely to suspect the other of unethical or illegal practices, and future business will be jeopardized. The American who is inflexible in treatment of the contract is going to be accused of shady dealings by many foreigners. Confronted with the various points of view, you have several choices: you may choose to adopt the foreign practice and assume a contract that will be modified with circumstances, or you may try to get the foreigner to understand that you can only make the kind of agreement that is interpreted from the American point of view, i.e., abided by to the letter.

Rule 18: Be willing to give up cherished notions of the proper contract.

A New York lawyer who is given a hundred-page legal brief will nonchalantly look it over on the commuter train home and breezily take issue with a few items the next day. For the U.S. attorney much of the contract is boilerplate, which can be passed over, and any deviations from boilerplate are immediately obvious.

But where contracts are short—in many places a one-page agreement is customary—the American's hundred-page contract will cause problems. Negotiations may be reduced to a continuous assault on the inevitably long and complicated American draft. The foreigner will usually insist that the document be simplified, and may not read it until it has been pared down.

Foreign organizations commonly enter negotiations either with no draft contract or with a simple standard form contract that may have been only a little revised to fit the present negotiation; they will be incomplete compared to what the Americans expect in contracts—the job will be to fatten them. Americans must come to grips with what is not in the contract and negotiate in the points that are important. Typically, you will have to write in statements about quality control and trademark protections, testing procedures, how to deal with rejects, and so on. That will not be easy. In

China, for example, there is a handbook of acceptable contract terms, and if the clause is not in it, it is unlikely that the the Chinese side will accept it. Foreign sellers' contracts are less detailed and stringent than their purchase contracts, so the American seller will have to meet more exacting requirements than the foreign seller. A double standard is often distinct—for example, in delivery and payment requirements. It is important to scrutinize these contracts and determine if you can live with the imbalances. As a rule, shorter is better when negotiating foreign contracts—aim for clarity and leave out all the unnecessary protections and provisions that so clutter American contracts. Use language that fosters trust rather than suspicion, as it is the relationship that will keep the business going, not the written piece of paper.

You must be willing to give up legal jargon that has no meaning, or confusing meanings, outside the United States. For example, acts that constitute force majeure vary, and if they are not defined, you may find certain things that are beyond your control not accommodated in the contract. Definition of an "act of God" may be a problem in some cultures, such as China and Russia. Always search for alternative language. Many companies have found that people who are unwilling to specify acts of God, labor unrest or strikes, will agree to "conditions beyond the control of the parties" as constituting force majeure.

Pay attention to formalities or rituals of signing agreements. Ask a knowledgeable person (even the other side) if there are any sensitivities you should be aware of. In Saudi Arabia, for example, don't send a senior executive in to sign the contract, as the Saudis may take offense when finding that they have not been dealing with senior people all along. In Korea, don't sign a contract in red ink, as it means you expect it will come to a bad end. In many countries you should leave time at the end for the banquet after signing—and you may be the host.

BEYOND THE CONTRACT

Rule 19: Discussions are always preferable to court settlements.

Many people around the world have become used to American insistence on detailed contracts, and many foreigners will sign them. But even then, don't count on your contract being treated as literally binding. Be ready to discuss new events, to "renegotiate" and to reach a new understanding. Handle contract violations tactfully, and you will do much better than insisting on precise adherence to the written deal.

In many countries, going to court would mean a major loss of face for all parties involved, as well as being costly and inconvenient. The foreign justice system opens up a whole new set of cultural unknowns and risks.

Check List for Contract Drafting:

Terms of contracts will vary depending on whether the agreement is a sales contract, technology transfer, joint venture or other transaction. Just a few of the considerations include:

1. State simply the intentions and purposes of both parties.
2. Describe the responsibilities of each party.
3. Specify which codes will apply regarding choice of law and jurisdiction.
4. Define measures of accomplishment (i.e., how you will determine that the job has been done) and methods for evaluation.
5. Agree on what standard principles of accounting will be used.
6. Make provisions (as applicable) for:
   delivery and terms
   discount structures
   payment and credit
   security
   dispute resolution
   taxes (local and foreign)
   force majeure
   controlling language
   notice provisions
   logistics
   expenses of personnel
   work permits for your personnel
   entry visas
   penalties
   exclusivity
   licenses and sublicensing rights
   payment of duties, and other charges
   warrantees and guarantees
   insurance
   installation and start up
   quality control
   disclosure of information and reporting requirements
   safeguarding of trade secrets
7. Translate the contract into the foreign language. Again, be careful with interpretation of meaning: use an interpreter who knows the terminology appropriate for your business.

Often a third party who is familiar with the respective sides can be a bigger help than court or arbitration.

Rule 20: Remember—without a relationship, you have no deal.

Whether you have negotiated an agreement with a distributor for your product, or a supplier for your materials, or a construction contract, your foreign business depends on maintainance of good relationships. You must visit your associates repeatedly—it's a courtesy and a necessity everywhere in the world. Wherever possible, include your foreign colleagues in incentive schemes, training, translated support materials—anything to keep them working for you and with you.

SUMMARY

In international business, a lot rides on the success of negotiations. If negotiation must be likened to a game, it is a game of perspective. What you do before negotiations is as important as what you do during negotiations.

Before the Negotiations

RULE 1: Make sure what you are negotiating is negotiable.
RULE 2: Define what "winning" means to you.
        Be ambitious but set a realistic walk-away.
RULE 3: Get the facts.
RULE 4: Have a strategy for each culture and phase.
        Position your proposal in the best light.
        Decide whether the negotiation is going to be win-lose or win-win.
        Decide on your opening proposal.
        Plan to control your concessions.
RULE 5: Send a winning team.
        Don't go alone.
        Always have your own interpreter.
        Exclude lawyers from the team.
        Use a go-between.
        Don't change negotiators in midstream.
RULE 6: Allow yourself plenty of time, and more.
        Never tell the other side when you are leaving.

Beginning the Negotiations

RULE 7: Make the opening scene work for you.
Think about the agenda.
Watch the physical arrangements.
The overture should make music.

Hard bargaining

RULE 8: Control information.

RULE 9: Watch your language.

RULE 10: Persuasion is an art. Don't paint your argument with the wrong materials.

RULE 11: Get in stride with the locals.

RULE 12: Go behind the scenes—where minds are changed.

RULE 13: Give face.

RULE 14: Deadlock means neither side wins and both may lose.

RULE 15: Don't be browbeaten into a bad deal.

RULE 16: Get your agreements signed before you leave.

Agreements

RULE 17: Both sides should agree on the significance of what you are signing.

RULE 18: Be willing to give up cherished notions of the proper contract.

Beyond the Contract

RULE 19: Discussions are preferable to court settlements.

RULE 20: Remember—without relationships, you have no deal.

COMMUNICATING

❖ ❖

How do I talk with these people?

INTERNATIONAL BUSINESS requires communication between people from different cultures. Whatever the assignment, whether consulting, teaching, selling, buying, supervising, preaching or representing a government, the job will require ability to get across information and ideas to employees, suppliers, customers, students, the media, and government officials. The American way of "telling it like it is" is often the wrong approach abroad.

The job is also likely to require the skillful acquisition of information. In international business, very crucial information is lodged in foreign subsidiaries, joint ventures or customer companies. It can be difficult to extract unless you know how people provide information in those countries. In most places you can't just ask questions to get what you want. You have to have a strategy for how to extricate information, and that strategy must vary from country to country.

Most executives agree that the single biggest problem for the foreign business traveler is language.

Every time language barriers must be crossed, important nuances are lost and potential misunderstandings jeopardize business. International travelers agree that it is always easier and less treacherous to do business when there is no language gap. Even with an interpreter, much is missed.

"They speak English, don't they?" Less than you think.

It is simply not true that most people around the world speak English. Outside the major cities and in most of the new construction projects or field offices, the average worker, engineer or official does not speak English. Gregory Zaretsky, president of The Corporate Word, a Pittsburgh-based translation service, says that American executives often talk with a foreign buyer who speaks perfect English, not realizing that their proposal will be passed along to be reviewed by others in the company who do not speak English. In such instances, the others are likely to pass over the proposal in favor of a rival's proposal in their own language. A Bechtel executive stationed in Hitachi village, outside Tokyo, says the American perception that all Japanese speak English is entirely wrong. In Hitachi, most of the people can read and write English as they were taught in school, but they cannot speak it or understand an American talking to them.

Many foreigners complicate the situation by not admitting when they don't understand you. Or they may speak your language, but have great difficulty understanding what you are saying because you speak too fast, unclearly, in an accent they haven't heard, and use too many idioms. Walter Hayes, vice chairman of Ford-Europe, says: "The American executive makes a big mistake thinking that people who speak English will understand what you are saying. Comprehension can be fairly superficial."

A growing number of foreign nations are now insisting that government contracts and negotiations be conducted solely in the local language. Defense ministries in West Germany, Belgium, Spain and Thailand, among many others, insist that their contracts be written only in the national language. India, Pakistan and Sri Lanka, too, are moving in this direction. Once there was a great incentive for people to learn English; they needed it in order to read most technical and medical journals and to watch TV and American movies. Now more and more media are in the local languages as well as English. If anything, English is becoming less of an international language.

Increasingly, the international business traveler is likely to have to deal with a medley of languages. Assembly-line workers at the Ford plant in Cologne speak Turkish and Spanish as well as German. In Malaysia, Indonesia and Thailand, many of the buyers and traders are Chinese. In Belgium, French and Flemish are spoken, and the visitor should be careful *not* to speak French to the Flemish-speaking crowd or vice versa. French, not Arabic, is the respected commercial language in some Arabic-speaking countries, such as Tunisia and Lebanon, and not all Arabs speak the same Arabic. Algerian, Egyptian, Syrian and Kuwaiti Arabic are all very different. In India there are fourteen official languages and considerably more unofficial ones. Some eight hundred languages are spoken on the African continent.

Language failures can be extremely costly.

When *Shogun* was being filmed in Nagashima, one of the scenes called for Blackthorn (Richard Chamberlain) and Lord Toranaga to blast their way through the evil Lord Ishido's ships at the mouth of a harbor. By prior arrangement, the samurai were to start firing when Chamberlain yelled "Now!" The director was on edge: he was desperate to get the scene before sunrise. Finally everything was set and the ships were moving into position when Chamberlain realized that the director hadn't told him when to start firing. He yelled over, "Jerry, when do you want me to say 'now'?" Of course, the Samurai heard "now" and began firing away, long before the boats were in position or the cameras ready to roll. By sunrise, the ammunition was gone. If the director had taken the time to learn just one Japanese word, a lot of money would have been saved.

Ignorance of a language can be embarrassing too. President Reagan tells a story about a speech he made in Mexico City. After his speech, he says, "I sat down to a rather unenthusiastic and not very impressive applause, and I was a little embarrassed. It was worse when a gentleman followed me and started speaking in Spanish, which I didn't understand, but he was being applauded about every paragraph. So, to hide my embarrassment, I started clapping before everyone else until our ambassador leaned over to me and said, 'I wouldn't do that if I were you. He's interpreting your speech.' "[1]

Mistakes abound even when contact is by mail. A European or Canadian customer expecting shipment or other action by January 6, 1986, written 6.1.86 in Europe and Canada but 1/6/86 in the United States, will be irritated (at least) when action is delayed six months because of the reversal of numbers. Newcomers to the British, Australian or Canadian business scene should talk to others in their line of work to uncover possible communication pitfalls. A Mobil Oil executive says: "In a way, the worst language difficulty we have is in the U.K. or Australia, because you feel like a fool asking people to repeat themselves." When you don't understand something, you should admit your confusion.

The hardest time to get information is when you really need it.

Faced with a problem, an American manager likes to call a crony into the office and say, "Hey, what's going on here?" We get information, then we go out and fix the problem, often by confronting an individual who appears to be at fault. While this may be natural in the United States (even more so in Australia), it would be asking for trouble in most other parts of the world. The manager would find blank stares, deep hostility, or in the extreme, could provoke sabotage.

So how *do* you get information when no one is speaking up? There are a number of ground rules, but the overriding principle is this: Wherever you go, you must watch how the local people who are respected get information from one another and how they try to get it from you. Watch how subordinates, supervisors and colleagues give and get information; the approach may vary with an individual's status or relationship. Wherever you are, you can use the cultural patterns to your advantage if you know what they are. It is easier to sail in the direction the wind blows. Likewise, it is easier to communicate with foreigners by doing it their way.

The English don't speak American.

The British don't have occasion to use the word "billion" very often, because it means a million million (1,000,000,000,000). In the United States and Canada a billion is only a thousand million (1,000,000,000). In England, to "table" a subject means to put it on the table for present discussion. In the United States, "tabling" means postponing discussion of a subject, perhaps indefinitely. Nuances can be confusing too, as when the British say something is "quite good," an indication that something is really less than good or somewhat suprisingly better than expected.

How to Give and Get Good Information

Rule 1: Know where information flows.

In America, information is usually generated outside and flows in to a manager. The system works because responsibility is delegated and initiative is valued. Personnel move toward the managerial hub. In cultures where authority is centralized, such as Europe and South America, the reverse is true. The manager must take the initiative to seek out information, and personnel take less responsibility to keep managers informed. In countries where many people are involved in a decision, there are customary patterns for information flow that might leave out the foreigner who doesn't know the dynamic.

Aside from the formal communication routes, every culture has its informal information channels, variations on the Old Boy network or the executive washroom. The connections described in Chapter 2 are essential links in the chain of communication. In Japan it is standard procedure to go out drinking after work. This is where the problems of the day and personal feelings can be safely aired over a bottle of sake. If you disdain the nightly drinking scene, you isolate yourself from a fundamental fact of life in Japanese business, as important as any staff meeting. In some lines of business this kind of involvement may not be needed, but a newcomer is advised to join in a number of times to be sure.

Rule 2: There is no point in getting straight to the point.

Getting straight to the point is a uniquely Western virtue. In the West we try to get a deal; others try to know us. We like facts, while others like suggestions. We specify, while others imply.

Cross-cultural consultant George Renwick says: "If we want to communicate with people, we have to understand the patterns of their thinking, and we can get glimpses of that by looking at how they talk." When Americans talk, they take the most direct route, one step at a time in a straight line to the finish. Not so the Arabs. They talk about other things before business. Then after they have talked about business for a while, they will loop off to talk about more social things, and eventually loop back to the business at hand. They will continue in this manner forever, and if forced by an impatient American to stay on what the American insists is the subject at hand, will become very frustrated. Renwick says forcing our linear thinking on Arabs only "cuts off their loops," causing resentment and ultimately loss of productivity.

Europeans don't go straight to the point either. An American who wants to talk business with a Frenchman over dinner will find that his French colleague wants to enjoy his meal. He may venture a few business remarks but is unlikely to entertain a business proposition at the dinner table. You need to build up slowly to new proposals, allowing time for the French to digest information and ideas. Indirectly, you can work into any conversation the background or credibility that must be established. French written communication will also be tentative and cumulative. An American will write a detailed letter with all the facts and plans and a sense of completion or finality. The Frenchman will write quite a different letter. It will be the first in a series, full of subtleties that will be elaborated upon in future correspondence. Both will be confused and each will try to second-guess what the other is really trying to say.

Africans, too, are suspicious of American directness. Nigerians complain that Americans have an "espionage mentality," asking for detailed information. Africans also feel that Americans talk too much, especially in public places. Many Africans consider it foolish to talk too much because "people may work against you if they know your plans."[2]

As a general rule, business travelers and expatriates need to learn to slow down and sneak up on information, asking questions indirectly or obliquely, as a courtroom lawyer might. In most places it is best to get information conversationally or "educationally" by asking broader (even hypothetical) nonspecific questions and circling in gently on what is wanted. As anthropologist Tom Rohlen says, you have to learn to "mine for information." In other places, such as China, building a good rapport may be the only way to get people to give you information. Certainly, the direct question will be appropriate in some places, but most often you will need to learn how to beat around the bush.

Rule 3: Speak simple but not simple-minded English to a foreigner.

When speaking English to your foreign counterpart, speak slowly and avoid cumbersome words. Don't be condescending, but say "letter" instead of "communication," "pay" instead of "compensation," and "soon" rather than "momentarily." Avoid slang and jargon such as "blue chip" or "profit maximization." Become familiar with the metric system and convert dollar figures into the local currency. Don't pack too much into one sentence, and pause between sentences. Enunciate clearly and remember *not* to raise your voice.

In their exuberance to be friendly, many garrulous travelers add extra banter to their communications with foreigners. Asking a Chinese waiter, "Hey, hate to trouble you, but would you mind going along to get me some ice? I'd sure appreciate it," will have the poor fellow thoroughly confused. Better to say "Ice, please."

Throughout any conversation with someone who speaks English as a second language, try to ascertain how well you have been understood by asking questions, but avoid "yes" or "no" questions.

Rule 4: Don't mistake a courteous answer for the truth.

Americans think "telling the truth" is especially important—honesty is the best policy. We respect candor, "telling it like it is," straight talk. Other cultures are no less honest or dishonest; they simply draw the line in different places and have their own ways of communicating real meaning.

Naked candor in many places is not as high a priority as other values such as courtesy, sensitivity to feelings, loyalty to family, and "face." Asians, for example, are more concerned with the emotional quality of an interaction than with the meaning of words or sentences. Form is more important than the actual communication, and social harmony is the primary function of speech. Leonard Woodcock, former ambassador to China, recounts the story of a group of Americans on an agricultural tour of China. The Chinese asked the Americans for their criticisms. After the third pig farm on the tour the Americans, who knew about pig farming, gave their honest and no doubt well-intentioned comments. Woodcock says, "They never saw another pig in China."

"Yes" does not always mean "yes."

There is a saying in embassies around the world that "when a diplomat says yes, he means maybe. If he says maybe, he means no. If he says no, he's no diplomat." Probably the worst thing you can ask an Asian is "Give me a simple yes or no." In America the statement is mildly confrontational, but in most of Asia it would be out of step with the whole communication system. Asians rarely say no—there is, for example, no word for it in Thailand. To save face for you and themselves, they will answer in the affirmative. "Yes" can mean "Yes, I have heard you," not "Yes, I agree with you," and not necessarily "Yes, I understand." In Japan there are some sixteen ways to avoid saying no. A banker in Tokyo told us that one of his employees asked him: "What does 'maybe' mean in English? I know what it means in Japanese, it means no, but what does it mean in English?"

"No" does not always mean "no" either.

Just as many Asian peoples use affirmatives in the extreme, Americans are often astonished by the negativism of many Europeans. When San Francisco attorney Lewis Burleigh worked on behalf of the General Counsel of the U.S. Air Force, negotiating NATO contracts in Germany a few years ago, he learned that when the Germans said with finality, "This is false, this is wrong, unacceptable!" they were not the stonewalls that they appeared. Very often minor cosmetic editing of the legal language was all that was needed. The French too often say "no" when they actually mean "maybe" or know they will come around to saying "yes."

Everywhere you go, except in Europe and Australia, people will tell you what they think you want to hear. If you ask a Mexican, Lebanese or Japanese for directions and he doesn't know the way, he will give you directions anyway to make you happy. In any country, from Pakistan to Paraguay, if you ask how far some place is, the answer will be "Not far." Experienced travelers say the only solution is to ask questions in such a way that the foreigner can't figure out what you want to hear. Better yet, don't ask questions but engage the foreigner conversationally in such a way that the information you need will "fall out." When you hear the words "No problem," don't stop worrying.

Koreans take considerable care not to disturb one's *kibun,* the sense of harmony, or "wellness," in a person. They will hold back or delay or "adjust" bad news to avoid upsetting a person's *kibun.* This is not considered dishonest; the *kibun* takes priority over accuracy. It is rare for anyone to give bad news in the morning. No matter how urgent the matter may appear, the news is likely to be given in the afternoon so the recipient can recover his *kibun* at home.

Some people may give us more than we asked for.

At the other extreme from Asian solicitousness, Australians and often the British are so direct that their statements can be quite cutting to an American. An American is flabbergasted and feels attacked when the Briton says "Rubbish" or the Australian says, "You don't know what you're talking about." An Australian executive says the correct response to that is, "I'm sorry, but it's *you* who don't know." You must forge on! In Australia and France, people sometimes find Americans bland because we tend to seek approval and run from a good argument. You are likely to be better respected in those countries if you can be a good sparring partner.

Rule 5: You need to know the context to know the meaning.

Overseas Americans constantly struggle with ambiguity. Even when we get a correct answer, it is not always what we consider a full answer. We get only information that we specifically request, not more, no matter how relevant (to us) the additional information would be.

Some languages are inherently vague, so that even the well-educated have difficulty communicating clearly among themselves. A Tokyo professor specializing in communications estimates that the Japanese are able to fully understand each other only about 85 percent of the time. The language is so vague that in many ordinary conversations people frequently have to stop and trace ideograms in the air or on a surface in order to illustrate their meaning.

Uncompleteness is exacerbated by indirection. "Perhaps," "Maybe" and "We'll consider it" are Chinese stock in trade. When something is "inconvenient" it is most likely downright impossible. "Maybe it is time to go" means "It is time to go." When asked something that seems odd, the Chinese will reply to a question that perhaps should have been asked, giving an answer that may have no relation to the actual question. As a result, the Chinese can be entirely unhelpful even if their intentions are good.

Incomplete information is costly.

During a negotiation some Americans asked the Chinese, "Do you have access to a small computer?" They meant and should have said, "Do you have a computer in your facility so that you can do this software development?" The Chinese answered "yes," but in fact the nearest computer to which they had "access" was over fifty miles away. It was entirely unfeasible for them to develop the software, yet the contract was signed. In the end the American company had to give them $30,000 worth of computer hardware and software for free.

Arabs are equally inexact and confusing to us. With the Arabs, however, we struggle not with lack of information but with overexpression. Arabic is a poetic language conducive to exaggeration, fantastic metaphors, strings of adjectives, and repetitions which enhance the significance of what is said. In the Middle East what one has to say is often outweighed by how one says it. Arab rhetoric makes it hard to interpret precisely what is going on in the Middle East, not only for us but for other Arabs as well. The language allows for people to say things they don't mean, often with terrible results when what they say is taken seriously. During the Arab-Israeli skirmishes just before the Six-Day War, the Arab media threatened Israel with "We are going to burn your homes, rape your women and drive you into the sea." The Arabs were astonished when Israel took this literally as a declaration of war and retaliated accordingly.

In Asia, the Middle East or Africa, Americans need to read between the lines. We need to know the *context* of a communication to understand it, because that's where much of the information is. The anthropologist Edward T. Hall calls these cultures "high context." The opposite are "low context" cultures, such as Switzerland, Germany and Scandinavia, where information is explicit and words have specific meanings.

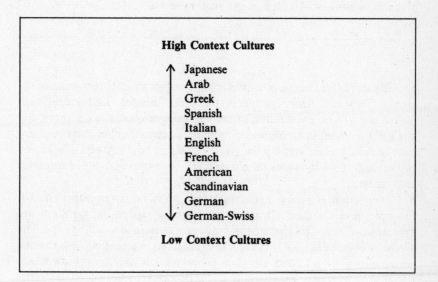

High Context Cultures

↑ Japanese
Arab
Greek
Spanish
Italian
English
French
American
Scandinavian
German
↓ German-Swiss

Low Context Cultures

Rule 6: Make sure your personal style of expression does not communicate things you do not mean to say.

In America, children are taught, "Sticks and stones may break my bones, but words will never hurt me." The Arabs say the opposite: "A sharp tongue cuts deeper than the sword." Thus they attach great importance to compliments, insults or indifference. Jerry Kenefick, an American executive with Whittaker Corporation in Saudi Arabia, found that affectionate mimicking of a favorite Saudi tennis instructor's efforts to say "Smash it," which came out "Smotch it," backfired. The Arab could not be convinced that he was not being ridiculed and was deeply hurt. Americans must be careful with teasing, for the foreigner is not likely to understand ordinary American kidding. Ethnic jokes are almost guaranteed to offend.

A German automobile engineering company contracted with an American supplier to develop a component for a new car. At one point during the project the Americans went to see the company in Germany and tested the component. It wasn't quite right—they would need to work out one small snag. One of the Americans came out with the familiar American quip: "Oh well, back to the old drawing board!" The Germans, assuming more was wrong with the component than was the case, canceled the contract. The message: Watch what you say and don't make light of serious business—people may not understand you.

The words we choose give different impressions in different areas of the world. To some, Americans seem too literal-minded. Latins delight in verbal play. Double entendres, turns of phrase, or quotations, expressed at the right moment in an otherwise ordinary conversation, are an important part of daily speech. In both the Arab world and South America, speaking is like singing—allowances should be made for extravagance of expression and emotion.

Other cultures prefer more restrained use of language. Nigerians, for example, prefer a quiet, clear, simple form of expression. Germans are typically direct and understated, using simple terms and avoiding hype. The German who speaks softly is the one to listen to in a meeting, not the one who makes the most noise. Germans complain that Americans blow things out of proportion and get attention by hyperbole, especially in our advertising.

Many peoples find us obsessed with competition, statistics and measurements of excellence. We abuse superlatives: most, best, biggest. Americans also are self-referenced, using "I" and "my" often. The French seldom put themselves forward in conversations, saying instead, "It is said that" (On *dit que).* When they do say "I," they may add, "I do not want to boast but . . ." A Chinese, too, will avoid the implicit arrogance of the word "I" and refer to "we" even when speaking of himself.

Chinese polite evasiveness can be frustrating, but sometimes charming and effective in assuaging feelings, as in the following rejection slip from a Beijing paper to a British journalist: "We have read your manuscript with boundless delight. If we were to publish your paper, it would be impossible for us to publish any work of a lower standard. And as it is unthinkable that, in the next thousand years, we shall see its equal, we are, to our regret, compelled to return your divine composition, and beg you a thousand times to overlook our short sight and timidity."

The traveler should not be so careful to avoid offense as to become insipid. The French may shun boasting, and the Arabs may resent teasing, but neither are timid about disagreements. Where an American might be embarrassed by a heated discussion or made uncomfortable by conflict, French or Arab men (not women) will find an argument stimulating.

Be careful how you express emotion.

Forms of emotional expression vary around the world. The kiss, for example, is not always associated with romance or love. Some people see kissing as unsanitary and crude, or certainly not something to be done in public. Americans might suspect marital discord if a couple did not kiss or hug at the airport, for example. In Japan you would seem odd if you did embrace when getting off a plane because men and women do not touch in public. While the British and Scandinavians are quite cool in demonstrating affection, the French or Brazilians kiss enthusiastically in public.

Asians describe Americans as hot-blooded, impulsive and emotionally wild. Latin Americans describe us as cold and controlled *hombres de hielo (men of ice),* not in touch with the feelings of the heart. Europeans find us noisy in our enthusiasm and nosy in our questions. We may find the British aloof and the French condescending. The point is that our habits of emotional expression have an impact on how others perceive us and on how effective we are, working with them.

Nor should we come to wrong conclusions when others display emotion differently. In the Arab world, people are encouraged to express their feelings without inhibition. Men are free to weep, shout and gesture wildly.

In discussions among equals, Arab men can attain decibel levels that are obnoxious by American standards. To the Arab, loudness is a sign of strength and sincerity, while soft tones imply weakness or even deviousness. Less expressive cultures are not necessarily unfeeling. Asians are apt to giggle or smile when embarrassed or when told bad news. An expatriate in Hong Kong told us that when her car rolled into a ditch, Chinese bystanders giggled; they also laugh at the sad parts in movies. It is useful to learn to tell the difference between a smile of pleasure and a courtesy smile meant to suppress emotion—often the eyes will tell you.

In most foreign countries, expressions of anger are unacceptable; in some places, public anger is taboo. Even where anger is displayed openly, an American's anger directed at a local will be met with outstanding resentment.

Rule 7: Silence is a form of speech. Don't interrupt it.

Americans rush to fill silences. We talk when we should wait patiently. We tend to crowd our foreign colleagues, preventing them from getting their message across. This hurts our ability to gather information, evaluate a situation and develop the relationships so important in international business.

Many people are put off by our haste to talk. Scandinavians, for example, are flustered by the American tendency to interrupt or finish sentences. Swedes enjoy silence and use it to formulate their next move. Africans are offended by our tendency to talk at them and to interrupt, even when we agree with them. Saying "I know, I know" is taken as a putdown. It is much better to listen quietly and listen a lot.

We need to give the foreigner more air, more time. When the foreigner seems to be struggling with how to say something, be patient, and be careful not to put words into anyone's mouth. If you do, you will surely become more confused because politeness may require the foreigner to agree with your suggestions, no matter how wrong. Klaus Schmidt, director of the Center for World Business at San Francisco State University, says the typical American must learn to treat silences as "communication spaces" and not interrupt them. "Hold on to your chair until you get white knuckles, but don't talk!"

Rule 8: Learn to speak body language.

Westerners assume that most of our meaning can be put into words, so we are more careful about what we say than about our body language. However, about 60 to 70 percent of what we communicate has nothing to do with words; abroad, it may be closer to 90 percent. More important than speaking the language is what you communicate without words.

Many travelers trust that if they don't speak the language, there are a hundred gestures to get across almost any meaning. But gestures have quite different meanings in different parts of the world; body language is not universal. Subtleties are noticed, like the length of time you hold on while shaking hands. On a very unconscious level many of us abroad can turn people off even when we are on good behavior. Thumbs up is considered vulgar in Iran and Ghana, equivalent to raising the middle finger in the United States. Touching a person's head, including children's, should be avoided in Singapore or Thailand. In Yugoslavia, people shake their heads for yes—appearing to us to be saying no.

In general, avoid gesturing with the hand. Many people take offense at being beckoned this way, or pointed at, even if only conversationally. In parts of Asia, gestures and even slight movements can make people nervous. If you jab your finger in the air or on a table to make a point, you might find that your movements have been so distracting that you have not made your point at all. Unintentionally, Americans come across as aggressive and pushy. Yet, in other parts of the world, particularly in Latin America or Italy, gesturing is important for self-expression, and the person who does not move a lot while talking comes across as bland or uninteresting. As always, watch what local people do. Or ask. While in England we once asked, "How *do* you point out someone without pointing?" Our companion dropped a shoulder, raised his eyebrows and jerked his head to the side, as though tossing it in the direction he meant to point. Clear as day, he pointed without pointing.

Body language is more than gestures. You communicate by the way you stand, sit, tense facial muscles, tap fingers, and so on. Unfortunately, these subtler body messages are hard to read across cultures; mannerisms don't translate. We recently saw an American teacher scolding a young Vietnamese boy. Exasperated by his apparent lack of respect, she barked, "Don't stand there sulking; stand up straight and look at me." Standing with arms folded, head down, staring at the ground, the poor boy was showing her the greatest respect, Vietnamese style. An American in the exact same stance would be obviously arrogant, defiant and hostile. To the Asian, it meant only humility.

In many parts of the world, looking someone in the eye is disrespectful.

We are more likely to trust and like someone who looks us straight in the eye than someone who looks away. In Japan a person who looks a subordinate in the eye is felt to be judgmental and punitive, while someone who looks his superior in the eye is assumed to be hostile or slightly insane. The Arabs like eye contact—("The eyes are the windows to the soul") but theirs seem to dart about much more than Americans'. We don't trust "shifty-eyed" people.

An American petrochemical company won a major contract with the Saudi government, but a Japanese firm won the design and construction part of the project. When the American and Saudi managers went to Japan to meet with the Japanese engineers, the cross-cultural problems between the Saudis and Japanese were instant, dramatic and chronic. The Saudis stood too close, made intense eye contact and touched the Japanese. On top of that, the Saudis were enjoying Tokyo's sights. Their leisurely approach clashed with the Japanese work ethic—the Japanese concluded they weren't serious about the project. The tension escalated until Americans became the buffers between the Saudis and Japanese. For once, the Americans were not the bad guys.

SOURCE: Moran, Stahl & Boyer, New York

Subtle differences in eye contact between the British and North Americans can be confusing. According to Edward T. Hall, proper English *listening* behavior includes immobilization of the eyes at a social focal distance, so that either eye gives the appearance of looking straight at the speaker. On the other hand, an American listener will stare at the speaker's eyes, first one, then the other, relieved by frequent glances over the speaker's shoulder. A British anthropologist points out that eye contact during *speaking* differs too. Americans keep your attention by boring into you with eyes and words, while the British keep your attention by looking away while they talk. When their eyes return to yours, it signals they have finished speaking and it is your turn to talk. It seems you can't interrupt people when they are not looking at you. These almost imperceptible differences in eye contact interfere with rapport building and trust.

You can tell a lot about people by the way they walk or sit.

In America we tend to relax in business settings. We often slouch almost to a reclining position, and this has the effect of creating an atmosphere of comfortable rapport. Do this in northern Europe, however, and you reveal that your parents didn't teach you proper posture. In Asia it also means that you haven't achieved the proper physical balance that enhances the spiritual. To make a good impression in Japan or Korea, for example, you must sit with your feet squarely placed on the ground. Your shoulders may be relaxed and your stomach may even hang out a bit. You must talk in a slow, measured pace, showing the body and spirit in balance. All this gives an indication of good breeding, maturity and reliability. After work hours, in a bar or home, you can relax, but never to the degree customary among Americans.

Rule 9: Don't trust people just because they speak English.

A common mistake we make is to affiliate with personnel or business contacts because they speak English. Do not assume that speaking your language is any indication of intelligence, business know-how or local competence. Fluency in our language is only an indication of language skills, nothing more. Needless to say, the reverse is also true. Do not assume that non-English speakers are unintelligent or incompetent. It is hard to estimate people's intelligence when they are struggling with broken English. We habitually gauge intelligence by what is said and tend to discount people who can't communicate. Get some other measure, such as field data of competence or the judgment of an appropriate business colleague.

Rule 10: Learn the language.

If you are going to spend a year or more in a country—definitely, absolutely, do your utmost to learn the language. It will make a tremendous difference to your state of mind. Ability to understand the local language seems to play a major role in adjustment to culture shock and personal success in a foreign world, not to mention enjoyment.

It is not clear why speaking the language makes such a big difference, but it does. Obviously it makes getting around a lot easier. In hundreds of moments of struggling to get something done, from shopping to household repairs to getting directions, just knowing some of the language removes huge portions of aggravation and helps you gain a sense of safety and self-assurance. When people around you are babbling away in a foreign language, you become vaguely insecure and feel isolated. Knowing the language gives you a sense of mastery in situations where you may feel vulnerable.

The mere process of learning the language gets you more in tune with the culture and breaks the ice, putting you in the right frame of mind to adjust. In some places, speaking a second language is important to enhance your image as a well-bred, educated person—you may be somewhat better off even if the language you learn is not the language spoken in the country. One expatriate said he studied the language because he couldn't stand feeling inferior to his colleagues who had learned it.

The frequent traveler should think about learning languages too, of course, depending on the amount of travel and bilingualism of the business community. Speaking a language fluently can permit you to attain levels of relationship and business advantage unattainable by someone who doesn't. In China one might hear, "She's no foreigner, she speaks Chinese." According to the bureau chief of a U.S. news agency: "Foreigners who cannot understand are spoon-fed what their hosts wish to spoon-feed them . . . Many American executives become showroom managers, sitting in well-decorated offices with a staff of secretaries but having little control over operations. Business goes on around them and decisions are made without them."

Fluency in the language will allow the traveler into otherwise exclusive realms of local business. The process of negotiation often depends on behind-the-scenes information flow; the American team left out of these information streams can only operate in the dark. Unison Corporation, in San Francisco, has been tremendously successful in helping American companies get an entrée into China because the company has been accepted by the Chinese in a way that no other American company has. The president, C. B. Sung, is an American, but he is so established in China that he is privy to exclusive information about upcoming projects. During negotiations he gets late-night calls from the other side saying in effect, "Look, here's what's really going on."

Learning the language is no substitute for learning the culture and appropriate behavior. People who are fluent in a language but not sensitive to the culture can make worse mistakes, perhaps because the locals expect more of them. And there are dangers in speaking a language if you are not competent in it. Not knowing the nuances of words or being careless with intonations, you might say things you don't mean. In most languages, some common words have extremely vulgar meanings if pronounced incorrectly. Or you may hear unintended meanings, as when American negotiators become ruffled with the French *nous demandons,* which does not mean "we demand" but, less combatively, "we request." The French call these similar-sounding words *faux amis,* false friends, because they can get you into trouble. You may also be confused by foreign words that have become part of our language; for example, the "entrée" here is the main course, but in France it is the appetizer. Try to find out what common mistakes you should try to avoid.

If you don't speak the language well, it is best to reveal that you have made the effort to learn—but then rely on English or an interpreter. Experts advise that it is generally best to speak the language for socializing and daily activities, but not when transacting business. As a rule of thumb, if you are not fluent and your foreign counterpart does not speak fluent English, always transact business with an interpreter. Traders who meet frequently with foreigners say that while English is the business language around the world, buyers are far more comfortable talking in their native language, and even if they can speak English, it is often better to have an interpreter. They don't have to struggle so hard, and it puts them at ease.

Rule 11: Put your money where your mouth is—get good interpreters and translators.

It is a mistake to assume that anyone who can speak two languages fluently can function as an interpreter. It is even worse to expect that someone on your team who speaks both languages fluently can fulfill that special and demanding function in addition to the job. An employee used as an interpreter may seem to have been demoted in the eyes of some foreigners.

Interpreting involves much more than speaking a language well. It is much easier to speak your own mind in a foreign language than it is to interpret the words of someone else, getting across precise ideas, nuances and connotations. A good interpreter is trained to adjust to the cultural context, turning American idiom into a foreign version with the same message, deleting expletives, correcting for ignorance of terminology (such as Republic of China instead of People's Republic of China), and so on. An interpreter will let you know that a joke has been made, as did Honey, the interpreter in a Doonesbury cartoon, when she told the audience, "The joke has been made. He will be expecting you to laugh at it. Go wild."[3]

You should always make sure your interpreter is thoroughly briefed and understands your requirements. In some countries, interpreters normally play the role of liaison, asserting themselves to assist you or the other party. This may range from answering the foreigner's questions directly rather than telling *you* the question and having you provide the answer, all the way to interfering with the elements of a deal. You may notice that some of your one-word answers become long speeches in translation, or vice versa, your long speeches are summed up in a word. Sometimes this is a function of the two languages, but sometimes it is an indication that the interpreter is overstepping bounds. Keep clarifying the role if you think it is being misused or get a new interpreter.

Good interpreters must be comfortable speaking in front of audiences large and small, and with dignitaries and people of low rank. They must be able to submerge their own egos and take on the personalities of their speakers, like good actors, without overdoing it and becoming too much the ham. When your foreign host provides an interpreter, yours should sit quietly by your side, responsible only for whispering to you modifications on what the other interpreter says.

You must help your interpreter get your message across. You reduce the risk of being misunderstood if you make your interpreter's job easier. A few tips: Before any meeting, explain to your interpreter the gist of the agenda and what you will be saying. If you are in an esoteric field or one filled with its own terminology, give the interpreter a list of words and a chance to prepare. Be as visual as you can be, using charts and graphics more than you normally might. Avoid slang and figures of speech that are difficult to translate and impossible to look up in a reference book. Speak slowly and stop frequently. Don't expect your interpreter to retain long paragraphs of information; if the message is complex, break it down into smaller parts. If you are very concerned about the particular nuance you want to get across, discuss it with the interpreter. During long sessions it may be prudent to have two interpreters so that one is always fresh; interpreting is extremely strenuous.

Don't lose it in the translation.

The perplexing problem of translation can be assuaged by taking a few simple steps each time a translation is necessary. It helps to start with materials that are not highly idiomatic in the first place, and the multinational advertising agency, public relations office, training department and others should keep future translations in mind when writing copy. Colloquialisms will very likely cause translation problems.

Choose a translator with care. If your business is specialized (for instance, medical, legal, scientific or technical), you should get a translator who is particularly well versed in your field. You should also be able to find someone with the right writing style for your needs. Use only a translator who is a native of the country and who lives in that country or travels there frequently, keeping in touch with locals.

Once you have found a translator, make sure your preferences in style and vocabulary are understood. Explain your audience and your message, particularly any ambiguous words. Point out trade names or other words that must remain in the original language. Make notes as to places where you want the actual words translated and where you want simply the idea or mood translated. Also explain the pace of the writing wanted: relaxed or breathless, flowing or staccato. American ads are usually hard-sell; your translator should be asked for more soft-sell language, as appropriate to the culture.

Experienced international business people often involve two writers in the translation process, one for literal and technical accuracy of translation, one for the creative aspects of the writing. There is also security in "back-translation": by having another translator turn the translation back to English, you get a good idea of what mutations might have occurred in the first translation. Finally, allow plenty of time for proofreading, and make sure your proofreader understands your editing remarks. Judy Esterquest of Booz Allen & Hamilton says: "When our U.S. people get into report production in Europe, there are always problems of proofreading symbols not being international." When companies are rushing to meet report-presentation deadlines, it is easy to make mistakes that in a foreign language are not noticed easily.

Rule 12: Your dog-and-pony show may turn into a circus if you don't adjust your presentation to the foreign audience.

By now it should be no surprise that the American style of speechmaking and demonstration may leave the foreigner cold, confused or offended. Time after time an American team comes home complaining its presentation fell on deaf ears, not realizing that the speakers came across as ill-prepared, insincere and rude.

As a general rule, any presentation to a foreign audience should be more formal, orderly and restrained than at home. We may take pride in appearances of spontaneity and "thinking on our feet." We like to sound naturally articulate, not rehearsed. For special effect we mark up our flip charts and transparencies, often with dramatic flair. Many foreign audiences, from Germany to Japan, consider this type of presentation unprofessional. They may feel slighted when they see that the speaker has not made the effort beforehand to rehearse and to complete the visual aids—in their language, of course. Prior preparation and formality are a matter of respect, the more the better.

Presentations must be simple, noncolloquial and presented slowly enough to be translated and absorbed. It helps to stand on the right side of any props in countries where people read from right to left—in the West we stand on the left side so that the eyes come back to the speaker after reading the screen or chart. Visual aids must be simple too. In many places (such as the Arab world), colorful media presentations may come across as entertainment and the message be lost.

Remember that the pacing of business varies around the world, and this will affect the flow of your presentation. Don't launch abruptly into your show in Latin America, Africa, Asia or the Middle East—plan for extended courtesies. Where you must expect many interruptions, notably in Saudi Arabia and the Gulf countries, prepare a presentation which can be delivered in small segments.

In some places you may want to make sure that the people you send are the same age as your audience, or you will face a credibility or protocol problem. People can rise at meteoric rates in American companies, and the young are permitted to do business with their elders; but this is not true everywhere. In some places it would be inappropriate to send a thirty-five-year-old "youngster" to deal with a sixty-year-old executive. Find out if age will be a problem before you go.

SUMMARY

The biggest problem for the traveler is language.
They speak less English than you think.
The English don't speak American.
The hardest time to get information is when you really need it.

How to Give and Get Good Information:

RULE 1: Know where information flows.
RULE 2: There is no point in getting straight to the point.
RULE 3: Speak simple but not simple-minded English to a foreigner.

RULE 4: Don't mistake a courteous answer for the truth—"yes" does not always mean "yes" and "no" may not mean "no."

RULE 5: You need to know the context to know the meaning.

RULE 6: Make sure your personal style of expression does not communicate things you do not mean to say.

RULE 7: Silence is a form of speech. Don't interrupt it.

RULE 8: Learn to speak body language.

RULE 9: Don't trust people just because they speak English.

RULE 10: Learn the language.

RULE 11: Put your money where your mouth is—get good interpreters and translators.

RULE 12: Your dog-and-pony show may turn into a circus if you don't adjust your presentation to the foreign audience.

CHAPTER 6

MANAGING PEOPLE

❈ ❈

*How do I get the
best performance
out of my
foreign employees?*

THERE ARE MANY REASONS for the failure of a foreign operation, from poor marketing to political turmoil. But most often the problems of foreign companies can be traced back to one cause—failure to get performance out of people.

Failure to manage people in the foreign environment hurts the company's profitability *and* can hurt the individual manager's career. Joint-venture presidents as well as employees up and down the line can and should be removed if they don't work well with the local people. It makes no more sense to keep an ineffectual manager abroad than it does to maintain an ineffectual manager at home.

MANAGERS, AUTHORITY AND DECISION MAKING

Each culture has its expectations for the roles of boss and subordinate. What one culture encourages as participatory management, another sees as managerial incompetence. What one values as employee initiative and leadership, others consider selfish and destructive of group harmony.

There's nothing inherently natural or carved in stone about the way bosses or subordinates are supposed to act. Every country has a heritage that has created expectations for people in certain positions. The methods of modern business, *your* business, must not clash with those traditional expectations. You must understand the way things *are* before you can hope to be effective in existing organizational systems or before you can change the status quo.

Leaders get and use power differently.

In many countries, authority in business and government is inherited. Key positions are filled from certain families; hence authority is vested in the person rather than in the position. Elsewhere a manager may command respect by virtue of position, age or influence. In either case, the foreign manager does not have to prove a right to leadership. American managers, on the other hand, often feel respect must be *earned* through achievement or fair handling of subordinates. Thus American managers overseas try to *prove* something that their local employees have already *assumed.* A Mexican manager working for an American firm described one vice president who, he says, "tried to win our respect by showing how hard he worked for the company. Yet he had only a superficial interest in the rest of us. He had it backwards. Of course, we respected him—he was the vice president. But that was about all."[1]

Rule 1: Authority figures must look and act the part.

The respect of subordinates depends on appearance of strength and competence, but what comes across as strong and competent is not the same everywhere. In Mexico, machismo is important. In Germany, polish, decisiveness and breadth of knowledge give a manager stature. This is not to say that you should adopt without restraint any of the more blatant symbols of power in a country; it is foolish to appear arrogant or superior to local subordinates. The point is, you should behave appropriately for your role, or your employees may be confused.

Americans are peculiar in their concentration of interest and effort into a few activities. With few exceptions, industrial leaders in the United States are known only for their corporate identity. Latin American management emphasizes the total person. Leaders are respected as multidimensional social beings who are family leader, business leader, intellectual and patron of the arts. Appreciation for "high culture" is a mark distinguishing the upper classes. French and Italian industry leaders are social leaders. Mr. Dreyfus, who runs Renault, Mr. Michelin, owner of the tire company, the Agnelli family, who own Fiat, and the Olivettis of the typewriter company are industry leaders, but in addition, they have high social prominence and sharp political power. In Germany, power can be financial, political, entrepreneurial, managerial or intellectual; of the five, intellectual power seems to rank highest. Many of the heads of German firms have doctoral degrees and are always addressed as "Herr Doktor."

It helps to know the signals of rank.

In every culture, people are adept at "sniffing out" the power in business relationships. They are also very quick to discover when it is *not* present. Your ability to influence will rest on your agility with the symbols of rank.

In most countries, power is more visible than it is in America, where great pains seem to be taken by the most powerful to appear ordinary. Abroad, people are often shocked when they see American executives pushing a shopping cart or mowing a lawn, or when they see American children working in summer jobs. Local personnel gets confusing signals from our behavior.

To communicate rank or to estimate the power of a foreigner you have to know the local accouterments of success or position. Style of dress, possessions, office setting, even titles do not all mean the same in different countries. Appearance and clothing are extremely important to the Latin Americans. Arab and American businessmen seem to value large offices, expensive automobiles and magnificent homes. British offices of important people may be quite cramped and much more conservatively appointed. Ostentatious displays of power are considered bad form by the Germans.

Authority is also supported by proper decorum and distance.

Managers exude rank by how they behave and interact with employees. Codes of conduct are unwritten but nevertheless firm. In Belgium a newly appointed executive in a major American accounting firm went early to his office one morning to "meet the guys." Leaving his jacket in his office, he sauntered about, stopping to chat with employees of all levels. His good intentions backfired: he upset the routine by arriving earlier than is customary among senior executives (10 A.M.), and violated protocol by talking with employees who were not his "direct-reports." His casual dress and familiar

An American manager at the beginning of his term in France rented a large and beautiful apartment and invited everyone in his office to this place for a big party. The French were horrified—first, most French employees are not invited into the privacy of their boss's home, and second, he had invited employees of all levels in the organization and their spouses, people who normally did not mix socially and who would not know what to say to one another. But they had to go because of his high position in the company. Once at the apartment, of course, they were not blind to the evidence of the American's affluence and personal memorabilia. The party was a disaster, with long-term repercussions.

attitude toward the employees caused great amazement and offense—and it became extremely difficult for him to gain respect in the company.

Rule 2: In relationship-oriented societies, show personal concern for employees.

Generally, outside Europe, Canada and the United States, it is good business to take a strong personal interest in the problems of both customers and employees. You must work at truly understanding their concerns. You must be accessible, available and personal.

American managers are likely to view the organization and its members much more cold-bloodedly than foreigners do. People can be replaced; nobody is indispensable. The American organization is not a family; it is a workplace and profit-making machine. This is not to say that foreign organizations are all big happy families, free of squabbles and petty rivalries. Nevertheless, people in other countries have extremely different commitments and expectations about how they should be treated by an employer.

In the Soviet Union and Eastern Europe, the factory or state farm is the paternalistic provider of many services, such as day care, schools and medical clinics. Many younger workers live in dorms and use the *kollektiv* (group) vacation facilities and Pioneer camps for the children. Employees have a strong sense of being "links in a chain," and collective consciousness is the mode, not individuality. The Japanese also provide seemingly unlimited services to their corporate members: housing, recreation, schools, day care, even marriage-broker assistance. Some firms provide hot meals to be taken home. The Arab expects his boss to help with personal problems— sickness in the family, debt or other misfortune. In Africa a manager might make loans to personnel, to be repaid on payday. Foreigners working for Western companies miss that kind of concern.

Budget hours of talk—and listening—into your week.

In Asia, the Arab world and Latin America, a manager needs a warm personalized approach, demonstrated by appearing at birthday parties and soccer games, walking through the work areas often, recognizing people by name, talking to workers and—even more important—*listening* to them. In Latin America and China, it is important to drop in periodically for social visits with workers, inquiring about their health and morale without mentioning work problems. Without singling out any individual, the group should be complimented liberally to give everyone "face." Evenings out are an integral part of business, most notably in Japan. Plan your schedule so that plenty of time is regularly invested in these personal contacts. Don't depend on memos. Don't be "too busy."

Paradoxically, even where openness is not a local trait, Americans should not try to keep secrets from employees. If you tell one person something, tell them all—they will all hear it anyway and it's better that they get it straight from you without distortion. Explaining your actions will help avoid or allay rumors that can be severely detrimental to your goals.

"Personalized style" does not mean "personal" in the way Americans usually mean it.

There is an art to making warm, supportive personal contact that is not too familiar and that does not bring the executive down to a subordinate's level, causing loss of respect or face or violating privacy. There are signs of respect in tone of voice and manner that denote grades of inferiority and superiority in hierarchical societies. Most Americans are not raised with a strong sense of class distinction. Nevertheless, you should be able to recognize its manifestations.

DECISION MAKING AND DELEGATION

Americans pride themselves on their ability to delegate effectively. Authority and responsibility are dispersed throughout the average U.S. organization. Moreover, delegation allows for flexibility. If an issue does not fall in a specific, prescribed area, some department will eventually take responsibility, even if only after some shuffling.

Actually, Americans seem to be about in the middle on a continuum of decision making/delegation styles, from totally authoritarian and centralized patterns on one extreme to the very participatory style of the Japanese on the other. In the center with us appear to be many Scandinavian and Australian concerns—in both countries, distance between those with authority and their subordinates is small. Nevertheless, American managers in those countries often find unexpected differences. For example, as far as Americans are concerned, Swedes violate the corporate chain of command. When Swedes need information, they'll go directly to the source, even if this means by-passing their immediate bosses. Managers in Sweden are much more conductors, planners or diplomats than their American counterparts. When managing Swedes, you need not feel threatened when an employee goes over your head.

South American, European and European-influenced countries tend to have the most centralized decision making.

American managers all over the world, from Germany to Turkey to India, have been astonished to find multilevel approval needed for authorization of routine items, and poor communication between echelons of management. In so many places, companies are still run very much from above and everything must trickle up to the top executive's office. Even where efforts have been made to delegate decision-making power within an organization, local business people continue to insist on seeing the head person, and employees continue to seek approval of their superiors.

French, Italian and German executives generally believe that a tight rein of authority is needed to obtain adequate job performance, and managers feel there is more prestige in directing than in persuading. Subordinates do not try to influence their supervisors. In India and South America, too, those with authority believe employees want a strong boss who gives orders, and subordinates do not question the actions of their superiors. Cross-cultural consultant Nessa Loewenthal says, "The manager is paid to make decisions. He is respected because he has the ability to make decisions. The employee's role is to carry out instructions, not to question them, not to come up with suggestions that might improve the managerial decision or way of doing something. His role is to please his supervisor, and in his culture, the way to please is to do what he is told."

Where an American group of employees might normally have a give-and-take discussion and present the boss with a recommendation (perhaps reached by vote and majority rule), the German group will expect the boss to give instructions. An American manager who tries to get German workers to make a group decision may be told, "No, let the foreman decide." If the American manager insists it has to be their decision, each member of the group will state a preference and then again expect the boss to decide. Insistence on the part of the manager will be met by more opposition.

England's colonial and civil service heritage left an emphasis on decentralized decision making, but management analysts say that despite considerable lip service to the contrary, decision making in Great Britain generally remains the prerogative of highly placed management. Democratic and decentralized management ideals frequently clash with a leader's class consciousness or basic lack of faith in the decision-making abilities of subordinates.

Rule 3: Involve people in ways they understand.

You can't expect an uninitiated East Indian or Latin American or Italian to understand participatory management. You can train them to participate, but the only way to get them to participate in any meaningful way is by teaching and guiding, slowly and gradually. It will take time to change deeply ingrained customs and in the process you will have to deal with confusion and tension. You also risk losing control. If a supervisor's efforts are taken for ignorance or weakness, foreign workers may disregard the supervisor and pursue their own inclinations.

Arab and African executives have strong traditions of consultation in decision making.

Tribal leaders have practiced council meetings or "palaver" for millennia, and the consultation tradition is supported by the Koran and sayings of Mohammed. Senior members of the ruling families or the community are still consulted on matters of importance; in other matters the family is often asked for input. The consultation method is used almost to the exclusion of joint decision-making or delegation of decision-making responsibility. Arab executives say the practice continues because it works: it is a good human-relations technique, diffusing potential opposition, and it actually produces good input. Arabs prefer consultation on a person-to-person basis; they hate committees and group meetings. Arabs make decisions in an informal and unstructured manner. Some of our professional business approaches seem to them rigid and impersonal. Their heritage is not one of enclosed offices but of open spaces, tents, and generous hospitality. As a result, you may find your meetings interrupted by the constant commotion of people coming and going, telephone calls and servants offering beverages. If you insist on a more formal style, you may be at a disadvantage.

Because Far Eastern cultures and religions tend to emphasize harmony and the perfectability of humans, group decision making predominates.

Despite Japanese emphasis on rank and status, business emphasizes group participation, group harmony and group decision making. The Japanese manager is a facilitator whose role is not to take charge but to improve on the initiatives of others and nurture an environment in which subordinates are motivated to work together for the good of the company. The Japanese executive plays a key role in decision making but not a lonely role. Responsibility for the corporation's success rests with all employees.

The bottom-up style of Japanese decision making can be unnerving for Westerners accustomed to the issuance of orders from above. Americans in Japanese-run companies complain that "our Japanese executives seem to be waiting to rubber-stamp our initiatives, while the American executives are waiting for the Japanese top management to establish objectives."[2] Without objectives from above, the Americans don't know what to initiate.

Managing Japanese employees is by no means a passive function. When a Japanese subordinate brings in a proposal, you must suggest and encourage, and perhaps send that person back for more answers until the proposal is improved enough to warrant being referred higher in the organization, where the same questioning process will be continued.

While employees are involved in the decision-making process, the Japanese system does not require that all participants approve of all actions. Their seals on a document containing a decision indicate satisfaction that their point of view has been fairly heard, not necessarily full approval of a decision. The Japanese consensus-making process may take a long time, but once a decision has been reached, it will be implemented quickly because details have been worked out and support won in advance of the decision.

In Taiwan, Hong Kong, Singapore and South Korea, Confucianism very much affects management practices. Harmony and benevolent paternalism are the guiding principles, and business units are run like families. Each manager is a paternalistic figure to his employee "children," and just as a parent is responsible for the child's behavior, so the superior is responsible for the subordinate's performance. When an employee does not do well, his or her "parent" loses face. There is a strong sense of family pulling together: no employee alone can be responsible for the company. Consensus is important.

In China, too, workers must be involved. The paramount task of a supervisor is to create a cooperative work atmosphere and sense of common purpose. The Chinese ritual of "taking the mass line" is one the visitor to China must learn in order to manage people effectively. The process involves calling meetings of senior and middle-level staff to explain the importance of work goals and methods before a job begins. Employees make suggestions, and having been consulted, are inclined to feel that the job warrants their effort. These managers then convey the "mass line" message down to the workers. The Chinese resist being pushed, and the Westerner who cannot finesse the local management practices may encounter foot-dragging among personnel.

Some reasons why managers fail abroad

Lack of understanding of local culture.
Failure to teach managerial concepts or learn local practices.
Inability to relate to workers effectively.
Insufficient involvement in the business.
Failure to verify information.
Arrogance.
Unwillingness to listen.
Communications misunderstandings.
Decisions made without local input.
Strategies changed frequently.
Too much or too little trust in others.

WORK ETHIC AND MOTIVATION

Americans perceive many foreigners as poor workers. "No work ethic," we say, meaning "lazy." Yet a universal concern of Japanese, Swiss, and others who take over American firms or invest in the United States is that perpetual problem of getting the American labor force to produce. The problem boils down not to laziness but to conflict between culturally different patterns of job behavior, management styles and the role that work plays in the employee's life. To get performance out of people, you have to understand the local meaning of "work ethic."

"We ask them to use not just their arms and hands, but their brains," says the president of a U.S. tire manufacturing company. Yet his workers gripe that they are being overworked and they are unenthusiastic about the 65 percent improvement in productivity since "foreigners" took over the plant. Those complaining are not disgruntled foreign laborers, however, but Americans, and the speaker is Kazuo Ishijure, president of Japan's Bridgestone Tire Manufacturing (USA), which acquired a Firestone Tire and Rubber Company plant in 1983.[3]

Rule 4: Know why people work and how the job fits into their life.

If you want a road built from Oesso to Brazzaville, start at Oesso. Your crew will work harder to get to the big city, a place they want to go to, than they will going through a jungle to nowhere. In other words, recognize the reality of what drives the people you are managing. Chapter 2 touched on cultural differences in people's attitudes toward work. Naturally, these attitudes affect job performance and organizational dynamics. In Japan, for example, employees are wedded to their company. Their attention and energies are concentrated on the company—their personal life is their company life, and its future is their future. Compared to Americans, who are job- rather than company-oriented, the Japanese are generally much better informed about their company's business, and easily step outside their own tasks to help a colleague. American business is more segmented and cellular; parochial attitudes prevail. Americans "mind their own business" and feel little loyalty to a company. When we are displeased with our salary, company policy, or personalities, we resign.

The Latin American, on the other hand, tends to work not for a company or for a job, but for an individual. People strive for personal power.

Relationships and loyalties are much more personalized, and managers can get performance only by effectively using personal influence and working through individual members of a group. Among Turks and Arabs, too, the individual is supreme, although inextricably integrated with family and society. Employees tend to be evaluated on their loyalty to superiors more than on actual job performance. In Islamic societies it is unclear where friendship ends and business begins, when socializing at the workplace stops and work begins, or how one individual's goals translate into national goals.

Your operation can work like clockwork if you set your clocks on local time.

When Dick Burns was the assistant general manager for Sears' overseas buying office in Hong Kong, his superiors complained to him that the employees were coming in too late each morning. They did come late, but they also worked until seven or eight each night. When management at home became irritated with the apparent lack of work discipline, Burns was told to get the people in earlier. He passed the order along: "I get in here at nine, and from now on I want everybody here at nine." The employees did exactly as they were told—all arrived promptly at nine, and left at four forty-five. A lot of work did not get done. Eventually Burns told the employees to go back to their old ways—and they got back to their normal, highly productive rate.

The Australians say they "go to work to get vacation." They have the shortest working hours in the world and they need their frequent "smoke-ohs" (smoking breaks) during the day. To the French the *qualité de la vie* is what matters. Until recently the French government had a minister in charge of quality of life. The French cling to their free time and vacations: they resist working overtime and have the longest vacations in the world, by law a minimum of five weeks a year. German firms, too, are moving in this direction. However, both French and Germans usually work hard during work hours, and have a reputation for being productive and concerned with quality.

Rule 5: *There's no race if nobody wants to run.*

In America, competition is the name of the game: everyone wants to be a winner. Elsewhere, competition in the workplace means everyone loses, either because people go off in their own directions or because they stop dead in their tracks. The international manager must know where to encourage individual effort or group collaboration.

In Greece they say: "Two Greeks will do badly what one will do well." Greek teams work well only when a strong leader is available to set goals and settle conflicts. In South America a team is likely to get stuck in power play among equally strong-willed individuals. Generally speaking, in countries where people are inexperienced in cooperative working relationships, leadership and responsibilities should be clearly delineated. If class, race and other social divisions are strong, it is important to be sensitive to inter-group hostilities and social practices.

In countries where competition is the norm, the objective of the competition must be clear, with measures of what constitutes "winning" firmly understood. If goals and rules are not clear, employees' competitive moves may not be good for the company.

Where cooperation is an art form, as in Japan, Taiwan and other Asian countries, creating competition can bring work to a halt. The goal is to maintain group harmony, but you can effectively stir competition against those outside the group. Needless to say, Japanese concern for harmony does not keep Japanese companies from competing all-out with U.S. firms. In Communist countries such as the USSR, even workers who have no personal ambition can be stirred to compete to prove the excellence of their country, as in the sciences or athletics.

When team members have different points of view, outside expertise may be needed to bring view points together.

A petrochemical equipment manufacturer operating a plant in Vera Cruz had problems getting output up to the level of U.S. plants. The Mexican work force did not seem to be concerned with the productivity. Moran, Stahl & Boyer, a New York–based consulting firm specializing in cross-cultural management concerns, conducted a needs assessment and found not a work-force problem but a teamwork problem. The company's manager in Mexico was American, the plant manager was Mexican, the engineers were American and the workers were Mexican. The personnel organization resembled a Dagwood sandwich—a different culture in each alternating layer. The problems were at the interfaces. The consulting firm worked with the company to build better understanding between the Americans and Mexicans and better teamwork at the interfaces. The Mexicans proved not be be unconcerned with productivity—they spent weekends and overtime to learn—and output increased.

Rule 6: Use the right carrot for the culture.

Carefully consider incentives and rewards—what's appropriate and effective at home may produce surprising results abroad. A financial bonus for a star performer could easily humiliate a Japanese, Chinese or Yugoslav employee. A recent American best seller, *One Minute Manager*, recommends one-minute praisings and reprimands, both of which could immobilize a worker in many countries. To get the best performance out of people, you must understand their desires and goals.

Individual goals are highly personal in any country; people are not the same, nor is an individual necessarily consistent over time. Aspirations may change at different stages of a career. Nevertheless, there are patterns that prevail in different countries, and it is useful to know them.

In America, money is a driving force. Offered money, vacation time, a higher title or a public accolade, the American is likely to take the money. Of course, American managers are motivated by more than just money—they do care about recognition, job security, "interesting" work, job conditions and challenges. Nevertheless, a satisfactory wage is essential, or an American will be extremely discontented. Elsewhere, managers are more likely to emphasize respect, family or job security, good personal life, social acceptance, advancement or power.

In some countries, rewards for workers are limited. In Russia there are few motivational options, and bonuses are the norm, based on a percentage

---

Any incentive scheme that encourages competition is risky where cooperation is paramount.

An American executive in Japan announced that he would send his company's most successful salesman and his family on a holiday abroad.

To the American's surprise, the salesmen were uninterested. He had offered the prize to *one* of them only. Everyone else would be losers. Not only that: Japanese like to travel, but not with their wives.

The American changed the reward to a trip for all if they met the sales target. They did. But then the section chief told him: "Four of the salesmen are first-year people who don't participate in things like this. I would like to return their tickets and distribute the cash evenly among all the office girls and people in other departments who participated in the success."

SOURCE: Condensed from *Doing Business in Japan*, JETRO, 1982

of salary. Asked what would motivate Soviets, the official at the USSR consulate in San Francisco says: "discipline." An American who lived in Moscow says that money is not a motivator because there is practically nothing to buy. Yet there is a tremendous craving for Western goods, and people can be rewarded with *things* instead of cash. If you make Western goods available to a Soviet citizen, however, never accept payment and always make clear it is a gift, because it is illegal for you to sell to Soviets.

Carrots are not green—don't forget nonfinancial rewards.

Many observers say the reward that seems to work best in many places is appreciation. In Taiwan the most highly sought reward is affection and social recognition from the top. Cash bonuses are given out across the board, but departments compete for top management's public praise at the annual celebration.

Japanese companies do offer cash rewards to individuals, but payments are nominal. Matsushita Electric gave a factory worker $13 for suggesting a device to stop solder from dripping down the endplates of television sets and causing short circuits. Another worker received $100 for sixty suggestions accepted in a year. At Mitsubishi Electric, ten members of a quality circle jointly received a cash reward of $200 for suggesting the best cost-reduction idea of the year. Most companies prefer to rely on nonfinancial rewards. At some plants, rectangular cards are hung from the ceiling directly above some of the workers, showing the production count or marking the group for its excellent performance.

There are many alternatives to money: job security, vacations, parties, gifts, sports or health facilities, services, prestigious titles, and public or private praise, to mention a few. The rule is to match the reward with the values of the culture. The wrong reward can be as insulting as extra time off given to the American manager who still hasn't taken last year's vacation.

SUPERVISING PEOPLE

Rule 7: *Avoid blame, avoid shame.*

According to Exxon executive Paul Makosky, a key to success in managing foreign employees is patience and the willingness to permit them to make some mistakes. "You can't operate in an environment where your people fear you will cut their heads off when they make a mistake," he says. If your employees are going to participate in decision making, they need to feel secure in taking a risk that they may make a wrong decision. At first they may need to be right only 51 percent of the time.

Nobody likes to be criticized, especially in front of others. But Americans sometimes fail to take the sting out of "helpful" comments and in the United States one is supposed to accept criticism as valuable feedback. An employee might even thank a manager for being frank. It is a big mistake to behave this way anywhere else in the world, however—with the possible exception of Australia.

To Arabs, Africans, Asians and Latin Americans, the preservation of dignity is an all-important value. Those who lose self-respect, or the respect of others, dishonor both themselves and their families. Public criticism is intolerable. If you use harsh words, or even contradict a person, foreigners will unite in antagonism against you. The result of a confrontation with employees or servants will be such a shock that they may leave the job. In a unionized work situation there might be some kind of employee action. When irreconcilable positions are reached, a third-party mediator is often crucial.

Experienced travelers say that reward systems aside, the only way to enforce a standard of performance is by courteous exhortation, lots of explanation and conversation, humor and an appeal to the foreigner's sense of cooperation. Jim Kelso, after twenty-two years with Occidental Petroleum in Indonesia and Libya, says: "Keep telling them, 'Good try . . . That's great . . . What would happen if you tried it this way?' Never make it personal or emotional." If you fail and cause loss of face, enmity will be undying.

Not long ago, the supervisor on an American oil rig in Indonesia was almost killed simply because he shamed an employee. Exasperated by the poor performance of an Indonesian employee, he finally exploded and barked at his timekeeper, "Tell that man to pack his bags and take the next boat to shore." Even with his limited English, the worker could tell he was being criticized and guessed he was being fired. Within moments, a mob of outraged Indonesians had grabbed the fire axes that lined the rig's scaffolding and went after the American, chasing him around the deck. He escaped and barricaded himself in his quarters. The angry crew was chopping down the door and virtually upon him when help arrived.

This incident is a dramatic example of cultural collision. The American manager had violated certain principles of behavior that are profoundly important to Indonesians. First, he lost his temper in a culture where peace, harmony and emotional restraint are all-important. Second, he disregarded the Indonesian's distinct concept of fairness. Superiors in Indonesia are expected to deal with their subordinates as fathers deal with children, sternly but sympathetically. Third, he shamed the man in front of others. One simply never berates an Indonesian in public.

Rule 8: Supervising is a job that is never done.

A magnificent new hotel in China equipped with the most modern accouterments and grandly decorated soon looks shabby: tiles become loose, potted plants die, and the paint peels. In Mexico a stunning necklace, obviously made with much skill and time, is precariously held together by the flimsiest of tin clasps. In Cairo an ambitious development project is proudly announced but then fails to materialize.

International travelers find a pattern of incompleteness that is most frustrating. The American manager wants to assume that once something is planned and under way, the hard part is over. Not so. In many places, just as much attention must be given to the final stages and to continuing maintenance. The expectation around the world is that managers must follow up on a job once it is assigned.

Supervisors also encounter a lack of support, both in newly opened and well-established offices and plants. Skills that they consider fundamental are unavailable, and on-the-job training becomes a perpetual task just to keep an operation going. Americans are especially irked that secretaries do not take responsibility, as we define it. They may speak English, but they are not educated in clerical skills, can't whip out memos and set up a filing system. They are not trained that way. In Japan they only serve tea and handle personal things. Many of the demands made by an American boss can be very disturbing to them. One Bechtel manager says it made his Japanese secretary physically ill when he tried to make her take responsibility.

When Unison Corporation built the Great Wall Hotel in China, waitresses had to be taught how to set tables—employees didn't know the first thing about Western-style cutlery. Particularly in developing countries, managers must remember that certain things we consider common knowledge may be outside the ken of the employees.

HIRING AND FIRING

Recruitment, hiring, promotion, transfer, discipline and firing are all affected by cultural differences. Western concepts of equal opportunity, appraisal systems, merit promotions and career ladder are not universally accepted or understood.

Western work discipline, such as regular office hours, quality standards, honesty and avoidance of conflict of interest are not part of the value system everywhere. Pilfering, neglect of machinery and equipment, absenteeism and bribery are problems worldwide. Employees and managers may feel no compunction about using company assets and company time for their own personal benefit, even to the extent of starting small businesses using company supplies.

Rule 9: Think creatively about where to find employees.

Sources of personnel vary widely from country to country, and you will have to find people in unaccustomed places. In Thailand, men tend toward the civil service and the legal profession, so businesswomen are a valuable resource in all segments of business. In developing countries, such as Ethiopia, managerial candidates may be found among an educated elite, or among former military officers, who are more likely to have some technical training and refined work values. British managers come from the population at large, but French managers are drawn from the elite educational institutions. Only 6 percent of Italian personnel managers come from blue-collar families, compared with 38 percent in the United States. In developing countries it may be necessary to bring in "third-country nationals" or search for nationals within U.S. graduate schools.

Regardless of the work assigned to them, individuals with certain family or education status often expect the same respect at work that they receive in their local communities. Thus young university graduates in Latin America, the Middle East and parts of the Far East may refuse "degrading" dirty work or manual training. Often, when a young man gets a degree, he expects immediately to have a plush office, staff and an exorbitant salary, even though he has had no managerial experience or business training. The hiring process should take these sentiments into consideration. In some jobs it may be best to hire totally inexperienced workers who have not learned work habits that clash with your needs. Often trainability is more important than prior training or experience.

Rule 10: There is more to a job applicant than work qualifications.

What Western society condemns as nepotism, another values as family loyalty. When a foreign company is acquired, numerous relatives, family members and friends may be found employed in key positions.

When one American multinational corporation set up a model operation in Pakistan, the American managers had to deal with job-seeking relatives of customs officials and government officials. The first year was difficult—often approval to import needed materials depended on the hiring of someone's nephew. The company worked hard to be firm without being arrogant and adopted a policy of hiring relatives who had the skills but not those who didn't. Once management established a reputation for being fair, a singular level of trust was attained. The plant became Pakistani-run in only five years—an outstanding success. The lesson is that you need not adopt the local hiring norms, but if you don't, you must be sensitive in your handling of the situation. The company was able to make clear that in return for providing top-notch training, opportunity and good pay, management expected an unusual degree of responsibility.

Applicants abroad are evaluated according to different values.

The American boss tends to look at employees in many separate but not equally important categories. "Bill is the best salesman in the business," we hear, "and he also plays a great game of tennis." To the American, it is the work performance that is of primary importance. The employer considering hiring an individual in America will weigh evidence of the applicant's potential strengths and weaknesses in performing the job.

In Islamic countries the employee's personality and social behavior in the workplace is more notable than his specific knowledge or skills. A Moslem manager might easily say, "Hussein is a nice man. I am most pleased to have such a fine person with my company who is also such a good engineer." A manager considering two job applicants will be less concerned about previous experience or education if the individual seems well-intentioned and able to learn. He is more likely to ask: Is the employee a good person? Do I like him? Does he need the job financially? Will he be loyal? And, finally, Would it please God to provide him this job?[4]

If a first-rate Chinese carpenter went to a furniture company to find work, the interview would probably be something like this:

Employer: Have you done carpentry work before?

Carpenter: I don't dare say I have. I have just been in a very modest way involved in the carpenter trade.

Employer: What are you skilled in, then?

Carpenter: I won't say "skilled." I have only a little experience in making tables. [He may have been making all kinds of tables for the past twenty-five years].

Employer: Can you make something now and show us how good you are?

Carpenter: How dare I be so indiscreet as to demonstrate my crude skills in front of a master of the trade like you?

By this time the employer might just be fed up and say, "I'm sorry but we don't take novices" and show him the door. But if the employer is more subtle and persistent, the carpenter would probably respond: "If you really insist, I'll try to make a table. Please don't laugh at my crude work." With that he commences to work on a table, saying a few more times, "Please don't laugh at my crude work . . ." and gives the final touches to a perhaps beautiful piece of art in the shape of a table.

SOURCE: "The Importance of Being KEQI," in *Communicating with China*, Robert Kapp, ed. (Yarmouth, Maine: Intercultural Press, 1983).

The job interview may be unlike anything you have seen at home.

An American executive recruiting a Lebanese office manager was surprised when the young man brought his uncle to the interview and the uncle did all the talking. In Lebanon it would be immodest for a job applicant to speak highly of himself, hence the need for a spokesman who can expound on the applicant's merits. In India and Pakistan an interviewee presents school records, diplomas and awards, all of which are closely scrutinized by the interviewer.

In China, workers will very modestly present their talents. For the American, an interview is a lesson in humility beyond most Westerner's experience. Even the most highly skilled job applicants will minimize their skills, and the employer will have to know their history or see evidence of their work to get the true picture.

Rule 11: Don't assume any foreign appearance will do.

An American advertiser recently thought he was being culturally sensitive by hiring a Chinese-American woman to produce his commercial in Japan. Fortunately, she told him how wrong he was. There is still tremendous animosity between the Chinese and Japanese. Moreover, a second-generation Chinese- or Japanese-American is far from the real thing. Along the same lines, a South American complains, "It's a real insult when they send down a Latin exile to manage us."

Another common management mistake is to send a U.S. manager to the company's operations in one single country and then bring the manager back to the home office as the expert for the entire area. A year in Egypt does not make anyone an Arab expert, nor does a year in Venezuela make anyone a South American expert. Any such "expert" should have a least a second-country assignment to provide exposure to differences as well as to fundamental similarities. As one expert suggests, the aim is to *beware* of generalizing from one country to another, but also *be aware* of what they do have in common.

Rule 12: Easy to employ, difficult to discharge.

International managers struggle with the problem of finding good personnel, but a tougher problem is getting rid of employees who don't work out. From Switzerland to Mexico to Indonesia, the unsentimental American "hire and fire" habit seems unnaturally brutal to foreign employees. Foreign personnel are usually more firmly attached to their company, and they are used to being protected during their working lives. Firing is never abrupt or taken lightly.

Foreign workers are protected by strong labor laws and union rules, and the employer who is unaware of them will risk costly lawsuits and penalties.

Ignorance of the law is no excuse. A Mexican labor law, for example, gives workers complete protection. After a thirty-day trial period they are regarded as virtually permanent employees. British law protects a manager against "loss of office." Belgian labor laws are among the toughest in the world, and Belgian social benefits the most liberal in Europe.

In Indonesia you can't fire people without a long process of government red tape. An employer must give three written warnings over a year, specifying the bad work, with written copies distributed to certain officials. A manager must meet with the employee to suggest changes in performance, and do it diplomatically. One old hand advises, "Offer him a transfer somewhere else in the company, and over three years you can move him from job to job until he can be eased down to the kitchen and out the back door."

In the USSR, workers are guaranteed jobs—the government boasts there is no unemployment—and only serious infractions justify dismissal. Visitors to Russia must hire Soviets through the UPDK (Agency to Provide Assistance to the Diplomatic Corps), the agency that supplies all personnel. You can fire an employee, but the UPDK is not likely to make a replacement for a long time.

Even where laws do not tie employee to employer, firing is not without consequences. In Taiwan and other paternalistic cultures, dismissal is considered the failure of the superior, who has failed to get adequate performance from his "child." It is better to shift unsatisfactory workers to "uncles" in other departments.

Personnel problems are not easier in a joint venture.

You can't always rely on your foreign partners to play fair when it comes to choosing local staff, and you must beware of becoming a dumping ground for all the people your partner doesn't want. It is common company practice to divert people who are no longer needed in one company into ventures considered less important. But if you accept these rejects it is virtually impossible to get rid of them, and you have little choice but to try to get the best you can out of them.

A great deal, of course, depends on the motivations of your foreign partner in entering a business relationship. The more the foreigners have invested in the joint venture and the more concerned they are for its success, the less likely they are to give you poor personnel. Executives with experience in foreign joint ventures and partnerships say that quality of staffing must be clearly defined during negotiations; it is too late after a deal is made.

SUMMARY

Managers, Authority and Decision Making

RULE 1: Authority figures must look and act the part.
Know the signals of rank.
Maintain decorum and distance.

RULE 2: In relationship-oriented countries, show personal concern for employees.
Budget hours of talk—and listening—into your week.
"Personalized style" does not mean "personal."

Decision Making and Delegation

RULE 3: Involve people in ways they understand.
Arab and Far Eastern cultures emphasize harmony and group decision making. African executives have strong traditions of consultation.

Work Ethic and Motivation

RULE 4: Know why people work and how the job fits into their lives.
Job satisfaction is relative.

RULE 5: There is no race if nobody wants to run.
Competition is not for everyone.

RULE 6: Use the right carrot for the culture.
Carrots are not green—don't ignore nonfinancial rewards.

Supervising People

RULE 7: Avoid blame; avoid shame.
RULE 8: Supervising is a job that is never done.

Hiring and Firing

RULE 9: Think creatively about where to find employees.

RULE 10: There is more to a job applicant than work qualifications.
Applicants abroad are evaluated differently.

RULE 11: Don't assume any foreign appearance will do.

RULE 12: Easy to employ, difficult to discharge.
Personnel problems are not easier in a joint venture.

CHAPTER 7

SKILLS TRANSFER AND TRAINING

❀ ❀

*How to teach
in a foreign culture*

NATIONALISTIC LABOR LAWS and management exigencies are requiring multinational organizations to employ more local supervisors, professionals and labor. In the developing countries this has meant tremendous pressure to train local people in even the simplest of technologies and management methods. From the oil wells of Gabon to the mining operations of Papua, New Guinea, modern industry could not be imported without importing construction and operations know-how *and* some system for passing that know-how along to the local population. It used to be called manpower training; now it comes under the general heading of technology transfer.

Technology transfer is occurring not only in the developing nations but in thoroughly industrialized and sophisticated countries as well. In Japan, for example, Bechtel's engineers are an essential part of the construction of a nuclear power plant, passing on their knowledge to their Japanese counterparts.

In business literature and seminars across the country, technology transfer has become the hottest subject since the personal computer. Unfortunately, it is handled in much the same way as hardware and software, as though technology transfer were a tangible product for import or export. This outlook reduces the subject to issues of capital investment, potential profits, marketing, protection of licenses, and socioeconomic implications for the developing country. But transfer of technology is more than the sale of a license; in most cases, it involves more than engineers, financiers, marketers and lawyers. For technology to be transferred successfully, a major commitment must be made to giving the local labor force thorough instruction in the technology to be transferred, assistance in installation, and ongoing training and assistance in utilization. Obviously, once a plant is constructed, a number of people who know how to run it are needed.

Multinationals differ in the degree to which they are attempting to train local people. Some are willing to run the risk of developing local talent, while others choose to face the political risks of importing skilled labor from outside. The training route is inevitable, extremely difficult and rarely satisfying *in the short term*. Even the best of the newly trained personnel will be severely constrained by inexperience, particularly inexperience working with fellow workers. A group of athletes does not become a team overnight, nor does a new group of workers, foremen and engineers immediately fall together to run a plant smoothly. Being taught and supervised by people of another culture does not make it easier.

OBSTACLES TO SKILLS AND TECHNOLOGY TRANSFER

Technical experts and trainers in the United States will be confronted with six major obstacles to technology transfer.

Obstacle 1: The small pool of potential managers and skilled employees.

Inadequate education and intellectual deprivation in developing countries result in a pool of workers that is ill equipped to learn the technical or administrative skills necessary to implement new methods or technology. In many Third World countries the adult literacy rate is estimated to be from 10 to 20 percent. Local people are so extremely disadvantaged by deprived home life, poor quality of village schools, and lack of intellectual exposure that they offer little to the developing industries in their own countries. The problem is exacerbated by lack of vigor—hunger is a problem for the majority of the world's population. Many potential trainees are simply too undernourished or ill to participate in training.

In most countries there are pockets of potential talent; you simply need to know where to begin looking. In developing countries the educated elite and gentry may produce candidates for management. Their station in life may call for ownership, however, rather than purely professional management. Since few in this group will have ever worked in any meaningful way, they will not have any real know-how.

University graduates in many developing countries are too few and inadequately trained, and worse, they can be hostile to business and Western interests. In many parts of the world a degree is an end in itself, not preparation for a career. Educational systems stress memorization, not the problem-solving skills that are needed in business. Nationals educated in the West and who have returned home are more likely to support Western interests.

Obstacle 2: More than a technology gap.

It is easy to think that if the knowledge or skills to be transferred can be reduced to their simplest elements and clearly presented, anybody should be able to learn them. Americans like to say breezily, "Don't worry; we'll teach you." It is not that simple, however, because the difference between the technology-owner and the technology-receiver is much more complex than a matter of what they know or don't know about the technology.

One consultant who has spent years working with developing countries makes the point dramatically: "If all the Swiss were to move to Ghana and all the Ghanaians were to move to Switzerland, within only a year Ghana would be a rich, booming economy and smoothly running country, while Switzerland would be unrecognizable, a shambles from the point of view of a Swiss." The problem that is perplexing the high-tech world is that the people needing technology training belong to a totally different civilization; they have different cultural values, inadequate knowledge and are innocent about the game of business and the rules by which we play.

Silvere Seurat, president of the French industrial consulting firm Eurequip, says: "The know-how gap spreads into relations with other people, their attitudes to problems, and even their professional and social values." He gives an example of a shepherd seeking a construction job. "He lacks not only technical know-how, but also an understanding of the abstract, of how to interpret even the simplest technical drawings. His background is also at odds with an industrial society. He does not understand the importance of time, an essential consideration in all production systems. He does not realize why a work team should all be present at the same time for a meeting. The need to make machines work properly, and alertness to breakdowns, are foreign to him."[1] He will completely miss indications of equipment failure such as noise or overheating. Finally, he is likely to feel absolute loyalty to his manager, not to the company or the job. Thus long-term interests of the company are not his concern.

Some academics have complained that it is unfair and ethnocentric to apply American tests and standards to foreigners. In reply, James Lee, dean of the College of Business Administration at Haile Selassie I University, argues: "If foreign nationals are to perform a 'Western' job, e.g., supervise the maintenance of a Boeing 707, oversee the production of pharmaceuticals, or manage the distribution of 4 million gallons of gasoline per month, a Western test is a better prediction instrument than any other tool available. There is no known way to Nigerianize or Indianize a Boeing 707, or the manufacture of antibiotics."[2] Nevertheless, when Lee was employed by an African airline to help with the selection of pilot trainees, an African manager complained to him that it was unfair to make applicants perform within the time limits of the American aptitude tests. Lee said he would agree to double the time limit if the African manager would go around the world and double the length of the runways in the world's airports. In the end, only 16 African pilot trainees were selected out of 700 applicants. They required five times the hours of dual instruction to solo, had six accidents, demolished one airplane, and produced 6 pilots.

Religion, tourism and social class systems in some places retard the local people's capacity to learn, change and adapt to new methods. The native language in some countries adds to the educational problem. Sometimes many languages are spoken, making communications difficult and translation a greater task. Moreover, languages in the developing nations lack the vocabulary for translating modern technology. Forty-five percent of our 700,000 English words are technical and scientific terms. Words such as "manager," "responsibility," "cooperation," "probability," "capital" and "torque" have no equivalents in many languages. Other words take on emotional meanings that affect their interpretations. The word "plan," for example, can evoke ideas of state planning, antiliberalism, or the opposite. Even where English is the official government and business language, it is a second language for the majority of the trainee population.

Don't assume your common sense is their common sense.

"At one point during the long months of building a nuclear facility in Brazil, the control boards in the computer room started to light up like Christmas trees. Horns sounded; the computer printers went wild; everything was going crazy. Water was leaking somewhere. We weren't worried because the system was not yet loaded with the reactor source, but the Brazilians were horrified: it was their first reactor. Somewhere at the bottom of the plant a main valve was open. When we got down there, we found four Brazilian cement workers taking a fresh-water shower. They had just opened a valve and were draining the reactor's primary feed water. But this kind of thing happens every day."

Obstacle 3: Hostile attitudes.

In most of the developed nations, the primary purpose of a business is to make profits and return capital to its investors; even government is supposed to return services for taxes. These ideas are in radical contrast to what most people in the rest of the world believe are the appropriate objectives of an enterprise. In developing nations the prevailing belief is that an enterprise's first purpose is to provide jobs and welfare. Even the most educated managers, government officials, and opinion leaders do not really comprehend the principles of risk analysis in capital investment, nor do they appreciate the role of profits or savings in economic growth and creation of jobs. Rates for return on investment no longer seem fair once the exploration or development risks are over, and often the repatriation of profits seems more striking than the benefits to the local economy.

Hostile attitudes can be severely destructive to the multinational operation, since the foreign manager who believes his employer is a ruthless profiteer is unlikely to be motivated to help the company achieve its primary objective of providing a return on investment to the United States parent. In a very revealing survey, Ethiopian and Pakistani managers and graduate students, when asked about their opinion on a number of business-related questions, showed strong socialistic attitudes. They were against private enterprise and overestimated profits, and belittled the role of capital.[3]

Obstacle 4: A dearth of trainers and training materials.

Any large multinational corporation is likely to need training capabilities throughout the world. Trainers may have to work with students whose first languages are Urdu, Tagalog, Chinese or Arabic. Their second language may be any of the widely spoken languages: German, French or Spanish, for example. English may be their third language. On the whole, American training and human resources development have been U.S.-oriented; films, audio tapes and seminars on stress, time management, sexual harassment, sales calls and a hundred other programs are in English, for Americans. Inevitably, trainers shifting their attention to local personnel will not know enough of foreign languages or cultures to be effective. Multinational organizations must design specialized training adapted to the foreign cultures.

A lot of technology transfer is accomplished not by professional trainers but by company managers. An oil-company executive warns that people in these positions sometimes resist releasing technology to the local people, in an effort to perpetuate their own position. In such instances, local management may never become ready to take over responsibility.

Obstacle 5: Resistance to American techniques and style.

American teaching styles and Western approaches in general clash with the expectations and needs of people in many countries. Typically, American training includes a combination of coaching and appraisal, or "feedback." But what is comfortable for us may be extremely upsetting to foreigners, who may react to direct feedback as if it were punishment.

Most other cultures of the world are more sensitive to perceived personal criticism than we tend to be, and our frank appraisals do little more than trigger an assortment of counterproductive defense mechanisms. In cultures that have little experience with criticism, an employee might discount a manager's or trainer's remarks as American idiosyncrasy rather than something to listen to or learn from. In other cultures, where criticism causes loss of face, a worker or trainee might avoid more humiliation by shunning the learning situation that caused the humiliation, or by leaving the program altogether.

Because of the different cultural attitudes and habits of the worker in developing countries, an American manager, trainer or technology-transfer consultant cannot effectively discipline or motivate as he or she might at home. Our favorite techniques—"the good talking to," the appeal to good will, or joking but meaningful remarks—don't work the way we expect.

American teaching methods also call for participation, risk taking, questioning, trial and error, and practice. Foreign trainees are often terrorized by the American way of learning because in their educational experience, they were encouraged to avoid risks and never to question superiors or to speak up in class. The Western training program that fails to address these habitual learning resistances cannot succeed.

Obstacle 6: Americans overlook what the foreigners do know.

An American and a German company experienced tremendous difficulty in South America trying to build a nuclear power plant. The Indian laborers shook their heads over the seaside construction site, a place whose Indian name means "weak rock." The engineers paid no attention to them until too late, when it became apparent to all that the rock really *was* weak and that the ground actually shifted with the tides. Because the turbine building was on unstable ground, the reactor turbine shaft would trip at high rpm's. Altogether, around $3 million in cost overruns was spent over the next few years trying to shore up the buildings, to little avail. In retrospect, those involved wished they had heeded, instead of evicted, the old woman squatter on the land who had cursed them and sworn that the reactors would never work.

Considering the educational deprivation in developing countries, and the severe lack of sophistication of the local work force, it is easy for the outsider to discount "information" from the local people. But many an American has found that what appears to be superstition may well be founded in reality. It pays to listen to the people who live in the country. They may be wrong about many things, but right about many things you don't understand.

THE MAJOR COMPONENTS OF SKILLS TRAINING

Experience shows that canned American training programs do not normally work abroad as well as they have in the United States. When the training is not culture-specific, trainees may be very dissatisfied with it, fail examinations and develop dangerously little technical competence. The real damage will emerge in operational failures.

A successful technology, knowledge and skills transfer requires a training plan that specifies responsibilities and schedules for trainee recruitment, selection, training, start-up supervision, and evaluations.

Step 1: Analyze "receiver" country, company and conditions.

The first "givens" for any training program are the requirements of the local job, i.e., what is the new technology in the foreign country supposed to accomplish, and how? What jobs are there, what skills must go into those jobs, and how will the jobs interface?

Any technology transfer must take into consideration the local work force. Are there enough workers in the vicinity of the project and is transportation adequate? Are potential workers the right age and in good health? What is their level of education, experience and general aptitude for the jobs? What languages do they speak? Will they work together? Cultural idiosyncrasies should be examined for impact on work. Tribal or religious conflicts, for example, might make it impossible for certain employees to cooperate. Some countries permit importing of labor from neighboring countries, and these populations should be considered too, along with the questions of how they will be fed, housed and received by the local population. These are big questions and must not be taken lightly.

The training task is defined by the distances between the worker's capabilities, the requirements of the job, and the resources needed for training. Cultural variables will obviously affect the cost efficiency of training certain groups: local attitudes about training, work, American employers or particular jobs can make a big difference in the trainees' motivation.

Step 2: Analyze the "sender" company.

Any company that is selling or moving its technology or management overseas must look at its own resources. First, who in the company has both the technical or professional know-how *and* the cross-cultural training know-how, or which team of individuals would together provide this combined expertise? Are the technical experts willing to be trained in the cross-cultural communications necessary for skills transfer, or can trainers be adequately brought up to speed on the technology that is being transferred? Are the trainers themselves adequately skilled in the culture of the destination country? Who will train the trainers?

Analysis of resources should also include a look at what similar operations the "sender" company has elsewhere. Trainees might be given some hands-on experience in a similar operation under conditions that resemble those in their own country. In that case, personnel there should be prepared for the foreign trainees and alerted to cultural differences.

Step 3: Prepare teachers.

Transfer of knowledge depends on the ability of the teacher to establish rapport and communicate effectively with the trainee. If the cultural gap between them is too wide, intermediaries will be needed, but then the valuable interpersonal rapport between trainer and trainee will be missing, a factor that many experts believe to have great impact on the learning process. The best trainer is often someone of the same culture, a role model for trainees to emulate. Preparing for the next generation of trainees, local teachers must be readied to take over the training function.

Trainers must understand the technical, cultural and organizational situation of the people being trained. They must also have a high level of cultural self-awareness and be able to recognize and interpret the cultural background that they themselves bring to the training situation.

Step 4: Recruit.

The search for qualified local personnel typically requires extensive use of personal contacts cultivated over time. Job advertising will be relatively futile in most places. To the greatest extent possible, personnel already working for the organization need to be given the opportunity to train and advance, so as to avoid political repercussions and to bolster employee morale.

Job history analysis, testing and other recruitment methods must be accommodated to the cultural norms of the country, such as company loyalty to employees, and manager's obligations to relatives. Recruitment must take into consideration the effect the new technology will have on present jobs.

Step 5: Train.

This is where cross-cultural skills really come into play. Training always must be customized to the capabilities and needs of the trainees and to linguistic and cultural barriers.

Rules for Customizing Training to the Local Situation

Rule 1: Make training meaningful from the perspective of the trainee.

The essence of education is not teaching, but learning. You will be more effective if you worry less about what materials to teach and more about how to enable the student or trainee to learn. First, you must empathize with the trainee, looking at the educational task from the trainee's current point of view and making training relevant to the individual. A peasant, for example, might be quite fascinated by systems for measuring land but will be lost when it is explained in mathematical deductive logic. Accommodate your materials to the trainee's own experience and knowledge. Second, gear the training to a desired outcome, presumably the development of an individual who has the particular knowledge or professional behavior necessary to perform the new job. Training is not an event, but a process; you must concentrate on helping the trainee get from where he *is* to where he wants to *go*.

One "truth" in education that seems to cross borders is that newly acquired skills must be quickly put into practice to make them part of one's repertoire. New ideas or skills will be learned more easily if applied to an actual task or event. Any technology transfer should permit timely practice and application of the transferred know-how.

Rule 2: Training groups should consist of people with similar backgrounds, destined for similar jobs.

Skills transfer works best when it is carried out with trainees of the same educational level and destined for identical or similar jobs. This is true in the U.S. too. However, most foreign countries are less equality-minded than we are. If you mix people of different status in your training, you may cause great discomfort, loss of face, or insult, jeopardizing the program.

Give the trainees realistic problems to solve together. Since team relationships will be a new experience for many foreign trainees, you should be prepared to help with group dynamics. (See Rule 9.)

Rule 3: Conscientiously try to gain respect and trust.

Cross-cultural expert George Renwick states in our *Going International* films: "You can have years of technical training and experience and valuable expertise, but you will not be able to transfer your knowledge if you don't establish rapport, a relationship with the person you are trying to teach." When information is passed from one person's head to another person's, the style of the transmitter and the receptivity of the receiver make a big difference. As a result, it is important for the teacher to establish the right personal image.

The American trainer has a distinct style, which is informal compared to most foreign educators' styles, and, unfortunately, many foreigners underestimate or lose respect for the American who violates the local norms. An American may get the class going by asking people to introduce themselves, one after the other. "State very briefly your name, organization, position and country," we say. Some trainees will be surprised by this type of meaningless presentation—too rushed and inappropriate data. In more hierarchical cultures, this type of introduction may seem the opposite—too personal and time-wasting.

After introductions, the American trainer will explain the direction and aims of the course. In the United States a course is always described as "intensive" or "extensive" and students are warned that there will be lots of material to get through in the limited time. They are told that by the end of the course they will be able to analyze the problems in their organizations and make the changes that are necessary.

McGill Professor Nancy Adler says that this kind of presentation will shock the foreign student: "Do they have problems in their organizations or do the students only perceive situations that must be accepted and lived with? How can they be fully responsible for change? Is God willing? Are others willing? People do not fully control their world. Further, if there is so much material to cover in the course, why not allow more time? What is the hurry? And when do we get to know each other? Isn't that the real reason for getting together?"[4]

Whether a trainer, technology-transfer consultant or manager, you must establish your credibility at the beginning of a program. In the Arab world, students are supposed to fear the teacher like a god. Among Latin Americans, the teacher is like a surrogate parent. In most countries, students stand when the teacher comes into the room, and bow when they see him on the street. A trainer who demands less than the utmost respect is generally not taken seriously by the students, be they Iranian, Indian or Italian. If the teacher is casual and familiar with students, authority will be jeopardized. The teacher should be cautious with frank admissions of personal limitations. American students may be charmed by the "real humanness" of their professor who admits to mistakes or gaps in knowledge, but such modesty is risky abroad. Students generally will respect a teacher who has demonstrated competence in the discipline.

You must also be respectful toward apparatus used in teaching, such as the desks. When the famous historian Henry Steele Commager lectured at a university in Japan, he decided to make his talk informal. He walked around the room, casually leaning and sitting on vacant desks. The students murmured—in appreciation of his wit, he thought. Eventually, though, one student dared ask, "Excuse me, sir, but why does the bottom of honorable professor sit on honorable desk?" The whole time, the students had been so disconcerted by his disrespectful treatment of the desks that they missed much of the lecture, and Commager had lost face in their eyes. Asians, Latins and others are shocked by U.S. students' apparent disrespect and flippant interchange with teachers and casual posture in the classroom.

Rule 4: Accommodate training to second- or third-language discomfort.

Learning in a second language is usually much more difficult than learning in one's native tongue. If you are teaching in a radically different culture, the language problem is exacerbated by the impossibility of precisely translating certain concepts which may not exist in the other culture. You will have to search for alternatives to such words as "achievement," which doesn't exist in some Asian and African languages, or "management," which doesn't have a direct translation in French.

Some trainees who are uncomfortable in the second language tend not to participate, and typically do not admit what they do not understand. Others may swallow embarrassment and struggle to understand or be understood, but the stress can inhibit learning. If you are sensitive to language difficulties and trainees' feelings, you can ameliorate or avoid exacerbating the situation.

Tips for teaching where English is a second language

Speak slowly and enunciate clearly.
Do not use idioms, jargon or slang.
Repeat important ideas expressed in different ways.
Use short, simple sentences; stop between sentences.
Use active, not passive verbs.
Use visual reinforcement: charts, gestures, demonstrations.
Have materials duplicated in the local language.
Pause frequently and give breaks.
Summarize periodically.
Check comprehension by having students reiterate material.
Encourage and reward, as appropriate to the culture.
Never criticize or tease.

Rule 5: Adjust to learning habits.

American teachers abroad commonly complain about the passivity of students, and sometimes erroneously conclude that their foreign pupils are duller. Students are passive because that is the role they have learned in school. Teachers teach and students are supposed to sit quietly and learn, never challenging a professor with questions that might cause loss of face, or competing with other students, which could disrupt harmony. In many countries, such as Vietnam, student participation has been discouraged by corporal punishment, and the lesson is not soon forgotten. As a result, speaking out in class is hard for the Vietnamese and for other students with similar backgrounds. Do not, however, mistake shyness for apathy.

People reared in different cultures learn to learn differently. Some are taught to learn by rote, without reference to what we consider logic. Others are conditioned to learn better by demonstration and passive observation. Latin Americans, for example, much prefer demonstration and oral explanation over any written instructions. Americans tend to learn by doing. The Chinese are in some respects even more pragmatic than Americans. They believe the purpose of all study is to learn something useful so that one can make a contribution. Hence they are often amused by American tourists in China who profess to be there to learn *about* China rather than *from* China. Practicality is the priority in learning, and the primary way to learn is through the successful experience of others. In China, demonstration models are used for practically everything: there are model factories, communes, schools. "Learn from" campaigns are used to an extreme. An American student at a large Chinese university discovered that he had been selected as the "model foreigner" and that the Foreign Affairs Office had instructed everyone in his department to observe him, to emulate his diligence and to learn from example how a foreigner ought to behave in Chinese society.

The ways we learn are basic, and emotion-laden. Once people have

Nancy Adler of McGill University was once conducting a training program for American technical instructors being sent abroad. One American instructor complained that his foreign students hadn't paid any attention to his presentation. Yet, upon questioning, it was obvious that the students had listened very carefully. The confusion resulted from the American's observation that none of them took notes, an activity which in the U.S. indicates interest and attentiveness. In much of the world, students expect lectures to be verbatim from the text, hence they do not take notes.

learned to learn one way, it is very difficult for them to learn any other way. We encounter terrific opposition when we try to impose our learning habit upon someone with another style. We tend to be very smug about our educational methods, but apparently without justification considering the increasing illiteracy of our high school graduates and the fact that so many of our children hate school. To succeed as a teacher you must appreciate different learning habits and adjust your class plans accordingly.

Rule 6: Yield to differences in thinking patterns.

Not only do people learn in different ways; they also think and problem-solve in different ways. Successful skills transfer depends on the adaptation of teaching methods to these different ways people think, i.e., the different ways they intellectually process the information they receive.

Typically, Americans are fact-oriented, scientific in process and practical in application. We find meaning in results. Trial and error, not deductive logic, is the path to truth. We pay little attention to philosophy, compared to other peoples who, to us, may seem pointlessly obsessed with it. From experiments and specifics we leap to generalities, we think from small to large. We think outwardly from ourselves at the center to our local situation, to the state, to the nation, and then to the world, not the other way around. Many other peoples start from the philosophical or the universal idea and the world at large, narrowing down to the close-at-hand, particular facts.

How we think affects how we give answers. Alison Lanier, publisher of the *International American* newsletter, says: "If an Indian, Japanese or Mexican asks an American about an overall goal, a basic theory, or a principle, he often feels buried under detail in the answer he gets. He is confused with a flood of statistics or a long description of method before he hears any overall purpose or plan. People say, 'Ask an American the time and he tells you how to build a clock.' Americans, on the other hand, feel equally frustrated when they ask for a specific fact or detail but then are subjected to twenty minutes of theory, philosophy, or universality without a single concrete fact!"[5]

It is also a mistake to assume that we see eye to eye with other Westerners, particularly Europeans. There is, for example, a chasm between the ways Americans and French think. The French are more principle-minded, placing cold logic and *a priori* arguments over reality. While the American thinks in a straight line, the Frenchman thinks circuitously. The American distrusts complexity and aims to simplify; the Frenchman distrusts simplicity and tends to overcomplicate. Americans feel they can never get a straightforward question from a Frenchman, and the Frenchman feels he can never get a full, sophisticated answer from an American. A Frenchman tries to define a question, the American tries to answer it.

Indians, Mexicans and many other peoples allow more room for contemplation and intuition in their thinking than we do. Japanese trainees are unimpressed by hypothetical reasonings or principles, relying heavily on data. Clifford Clarke, a consultant who spends much of his time training Americans to work in Japan or training Japanese to work in the United States, says the Japanese are horrified when Americans in joint ventures or subsidiaries try to force the Japanese to think in American ways. "Creative problem-solving methods such as brainstorming or conceptualization are totally alien to the Japanese, who see these methods as flippant, irresponsible and a waste of time. If these methods are to be used, trainees must first be helped to see that they can be effective as problem-solving techniques."

Rule 7: Modify instructional materials for the culture.

Most training materials are written on the assumption that reality can be broken down into an orderly series of steps that follow a plan. We assume that the instructions provided will be carefully followed, since surely everyone knows that equipment works only if used properly and if regularly serviced. In many countries these basic principles do not apply. In so many parts of the world, "reality" is disorderly and heavily dependent on chance or the will of God. The Saudi, for example, is not very likely to follow a handbook or a design; he is more likely to deal with each situation as it arises. It will take time and patience for you to help your foreign trainees to understand the practical use of a manual.

Even where trainees are inclined to use learning materials, instruction manuals and seminars on machinery are rarely useful to foreigners who have no experience with the technology. It is not a matter of intelligence but of experience with the concepts presented in the written medium. As anyone who has had to interpret computer software manuals can appreciate, many instruction manuals can only be understood by those who already thoroughly understand the subject.

One obvious solution is to custom-produce meaningful instructional materials geared to the learning styles and vocabularies (both word and pictorial vocabularies) of the trainees. Naturally, explanations and examples should be relevant to the economic and educational experience of the trainee, as well as relevant to the specific job at the end of training. Problems that will occur if instructions are not followed must be demonstrated, and procedures will have to be repeated many times with the help of a variety of teaching methods.

Generally, avoid training materials that are obviously made for Americans and that seem to be preaching American ways. Materials should appear to be made for the local scene, and the examples and data should be home-grown—European cases should be used in Europe, and so on. Avoid examples which will provoke sensitivities. We became acutely aware of this requirement when we produced a five-minute short on the *Going*

International training films for the airlines—we had to edit out all Arab scenes for a carrier which flew to Israel. Even in our new *Going International* films, subtitled *Working in the USA* and *Living in the USA*, we were careful to avoid the implicit arrogance of Americans talking about America. Instead, people of diverse nationalities describe what it takes to succeed here, and all scenes show foreigners interacting with Americans in the workplace or community. The films' pacing, structure and style were accommodated to the foreign viewers.

Rule 8: Reconcile training schedules to the cultural norms.

Often overlooked is the context of a training program. Cultural norms affect the daily conduct of business and education. For example, it might be hard for a class to adjust to a one-hour lunch break in a country where the pattern is to take a three- or four-hour lunch during the midday heat.

Rule 9: Inculcate teamwork and a sense of responsibility to the company if these are important to the transfer of technology.

Some peoples, such as Saudis and South Americans, tend not to be experienced or comfortable with the requirements of teamwork, nor do they necessarily appreciate joint credit. Arabs and Latins are extremely individualistic, and their characters will have to be recognized when organizational structure and group dynamics are considered. If teamwork is vital to the training, you must give considerable attention to changing work habits and providing models for group behavior.

Team building may be impossible in places where different hostile tribes or long-term national rivals cannot work together, or where groups of different status cannot be forced into the same training or work situations. We ran into this problem when we were shooting the India scene for the *Going International* film series: Indians of different castes were very uncomfortable being rehearsed together, even though the caste system is officially banned.

On the other hand, in countries where teamwork is traditional, most American managers and trainers will need to allow more time for the team process—in Korea and Japan, for example. A Coopers and Lybrand executive observed: "If you have to debug a program, an American will go off alone to solve the problem, but the Chinese will do it in a group, all at the top of their voices."

Rule 10: Make rewards appropriate to the motivational systems.

There are enormous differences in what constitute incentives and rewards in different cultures. What makes one student learn in one country may inhibit another elsewhere. (Refer to Chapter 6 for more on incentives.)

Rule 11: Be venturesome.

Notwithstanding all the above advice, don't be limited by local tradition or go overboard in adopting the local learning patterns. Remember, one of the central problems in skills transfer has been the inadequacies of the foreign educational systems. If you accept "This is the way it is done in this country" too rigorously and fail to bring other teaching methods into your training, it is likely you are short-changing your students by not fully using your strengths. Some experts have had great success taking the most unlikely programs into foreign countries. "Assertiveness training" was extremely popular in Hong Kong, for instance, and est in India.

Rule 12: Show an interest in learning your trainees' culture.

While foreigners expect you to be an expert in your field, they don't expect you to be an expert on their country or culture. But they will be pleased to help *you* learn. They will appreciate your interest in *their* methods and country. You can get away with many mistakes as long as you are not arrogant, insensitive and overbearingly ethnocentric. As Paul Makosky of Exxon says: "They'll be willing to listen to you if you show you actually listen to them."

SUMMARY

Obstacles

1. The small pool of potential managers and skilled employees.
2. More than a technology gap.
3. Hostile attitudes.
4. A dearth of trainers and training materials.
5. Resistance to American techniques and style.
6. Americans overlook what the foreigners do know.

The Major Components of Skills Training

STEP 1: Analyze the "receiver" country, company and candidates.
STEP 2: Analyze the "sender" company.
STEP 3: Prepare teachers.
STEP 4: Recruit.
STEP 5: Train.

Rules for Customizing Training to the Local Situation

1. Make training meaningful from the perspective of the trainee.
2. Training groups should consist of people with similar backgrounds, destined for similar jobs.
3. Conscientiously try to earn respect and trust.
4. Accommodate training to second- and third-language discomfort.
5. Adjust to learning habits.
6. Yield to differences in thinking patterns.
7. Modify instructional materials for the culture.
8. Reconcile training schedules to the cultural norms.
9. Inculcate teamwork and a sense of responsibility to the company.
10. Make rewards appropriate to the motivational systems.
11. Be venturesome.
12. Show an interest in learning your trainees' culture.

CHAPTER 8

BUSINESS AND SOCIAL ETIQUETTE

❂ ❂

ASKED IF MANNERS REALLY MATTER, a Saudi sheik told us about an American who stopped over in Egypt on his way to Saudi Arabia. He spent his first evening, as many travelers in Cairo do, visiting Egyptian night clubs. In one place, he insisted on sitting at a table that a Saudi prince usually sat at. Soon the Saudi prince and entourage arrived, and upon hearing the waiter's explanation, the sheik politely nodded to the American as a gesture of offering his table. The American must have misinterpreted the nod, and made an obscene gesture. The incident passed without further ado, until the American arrived in Riyadh, where he was immediately thrown into jail.

This American was particularly rude, and the prince perhaps particularly vengeful. Nevertheless, this type of scene is all too common.

Travelers tend to become increasingly rude in direct proportion to their distance from home.

Asians categorize people into three classes: (1) people within one's own group, (2) those whose background is fairly well known, and (3) those who are unknown—strangers and most foreigners. Very rigid codes of conduct define all behavior among people in the first two categories, but people in the third category are considered non-persons. Asians see no particular need to apply rules of etiquette to non-persons. Saying "Excuse me" when bumping into a stranger is like apologizing to a chair. Since a foreigner is usually in the category of the stranger, we may be treated quite rudely by people known for their politeness.

Most Americans don't realize it, but we also tend to vary our conduct according to those same three general categories of people. We just don't care as much about what total strangers think of us—we may hardly notice their presence. Foreigners are so "non-person" that we may behave as though we were traveling incognito. We tend to become careless in our behavior even in business and work settings.

Business and social etiquette are vitally important. Even the well-intentioned traveler can come across as a boor if unaware of how rules of etiquette differ around the world. What is polite in the U.S. may be seriously rude elsewhere, and vice versa.

You can be dressed for success, and staying in a prestigious hotel, but you will still be mistaken for an ignorant tourist if you don't project savoir-faire.

Experts do not take international etiquette as a frivolous concern. Anyone who has real experience abroad knows that the correct gesture at the right moment can boost your image and effectiveness tremendously. And *your* personal image is tightly linked with the image of your company, as is your spouse's image if traveling with you. The American manager, consultant or company engineer, in the eyes of the locals, is Mr. or Mrs. IBM, Coca-Cola or Bank of America, not Smith. Many Americans find this irksome. They are always on company business. The company affiliation can be a problem in two directions: the ill-mannered traveler can create a bad image for the company, making it hard for other employees in the future; and the stigma of an ill-reputed company can hurt an individual's effectiveness.

This chapter will describe the proper manners and protocol for a variety of situations. But whatever you are doing and wherever you are, the following three principles should guide you:

People tend to like and prefer to interact with people they perceive as similar to themselves.

The more similar two people are, the closer will be the relationship they form. Good cross-cultural manners are a vital part of bridging dissimilarities and hence increasing the possibilities for forming a good business relationship.

Respect for etiquette is deep-seated, deeper than we imagine.

Don't forget that form, in many places, is more important than substance. In general, be more formal and conscientiously polite than you might normally be at home.

Show respect.

Banquet toasts, international treaties and academic exchange agreements around the world often include a vow that the parties will "respect" each other. The call for respect is not a rhetorical one, but deadly serious.

An American woman standing on a train in Tokyo overheard two men talking in Japanese—they naturally had no idea a *gaijin* would be able to understand. The conversation went as follows:

"I think I should get up and give this foreign woman my seat."

"I don't think you should. It's not our custom."

"But she doesn't know it's not our custom. If I don't get up, she will think I am rude."

"But she's in our country. She should know *our* customs."

"That's true, but I don't think she does."

The concerned Japanese finally got up and offered the American woman his seat.

INTRODUCTIONS

It is safe to assume that introductions everywhere will be much more formal and significant than they usually are in the States.

Try to get the names and titles right.

Dale Carnegie long ago said that a "man's name is to him the sweetest and most important sound in any language." While that is not absolutely true in all cultures, it is true enough in enough places so that it is worth paying close attention to both pronunciation and proper use of names.

In Brazil and Portugal, people are addressed by their Christian name, along with the proper title or simply "Mr." so that Manuel Santos is Senhor Manuel. But in Spain and Spanish-heritage South America, the last name is the main one, so that Señor García Alvarez is Señor Alvarez. Some Spanish-speaking people use a double surname, from both the maternal and paternal family names. In China, the first name is the surname, hence Premier Zhao Xiyang is Mr. Zhao, not Mr. Xiyang. The Egyptian President Nasser's real name was Gamal abdelNasser Hussein, the abdelNasser meaning literally "son of Nasser." Some Indonesians have only one name, such as Mr. Gondomono.

Don't use first names until specifically invited.

First, or given, names are used for children, family and intimate friends. This rule applies almost everywhere whether speaking to peers, subordinates or service people. All foreigners agree: Americans are much too hasty in using first names.

We also overlook the importance of respectful titles. Whether you are in Germany or Brazil, it is customary to address a medical doctor and any Ph.D. as doctor (Herr Doktor Braun or Doutor Blanco). In Mexico, professionals may be addressed by profession and name, such as Architecto, Ingeniero or Licenciado (Lawyer) Perez. The same is true in Italy. Even if lacking credentials someone of substance in Italy will be called Dottore. Sheik is a term applied in the Arab world to anyone deserving respect: a teacher, elder, religious leader or member of the royal family. It is to be used discreetly, and some Arabs may politely decline the title.

Although we may feel silly doing it, it is a good practice to use more formal forms of address, such as Senhor and Senhora in Brazil and Herr and Frau in Germany, otherwise disrespect will be assumed. In France, Monsieur or Madame along with a person's name is sprinkled throughout a conversation, as a repeated courtesy and acknowledgment of the other person in the conversation. Not doing this seems aloof.

As anyone who has studied foreign languages knows, many cultures have formal and intimate variations on common pronouns. The word for "you" depends on whether you are family, close friends or mere acquaintances. In Germany, white-collar workers, professionals, civil servants and the older generation in general use the formal form, *Sie,* and reserve the informal *du* for children, family and intimate friends. Two people who see each other daily at work and play bridge together will still call each other Herr or Frau after twenty years. In some places it is proper to use other words of deference, such as Babak (father) or Ibu (mother) when speaking to men and women of rank in Indonesia. In China, once you know people, such as your staff, you can respectfully switch to titles such as Lao (old or venerable) or Xiao (little). You should be cautious with these forms, and probably should stick to English titles until invited to do otherwise or clued in by someone who knows.

Be prepared to shake hands endlessly, and know when to bow.

You are safer sticking to your habitual handshake, unless met with bows. And when bowing, remember that the appropriate bow depends on your relative age and status as well as the situation—do not necessarily bow the same way as the Japanese who are bowing to you. For most business situations, the informal 15-degree angle, hands-at-the-side bow will suffice; the more formal bow is about 30 degrees with hands together, palms down on the knees. Do not confuse the Chinese with the Japanese—the Chinese affect only a slight bow when shaking hands.

You may notice Japanese greeting each other in a ritual of bowing, which you are not advised to try to imitate. It is a highly cultivated art form during which two Japanese ascertain the status of each other so that they will know how to act. For example, if a teacher meets a former student, they both bow in the traditional manner, the student making sure to bob up and down longer than the teacher. The teacher uses condescending forms of speech and the student uses honorifics and polite word endings. If strangers meet, both bow while keeping an eye on each other, watching the depth and frequency of bows while asking polite questions to determine the relative status. When one emerges as having greater status, he switches to condescending language and the lower status individual continues as before, being sure to bow longer and lower than the other.[1]

Watch the exit bows, too. In Korea, for example, if a meeting goes well, the bow at the end will be longer than the bow on entry, showing pleasure or indebtedness. If your colleague or customer gives only a short departing bow, he is likely to be displeased with the meeting.

In Europe and South America, shake hands with all persons present every time you encounter them, even if you have already shaken their hands that day, and even with close acquaintances. In Kenya a man and wife who ate breakfast together and then see each other at 10 A.M. will shake hands. If you are reticent to shake hands, people may think you are untrustworthy or have an attitude of superiority.

Some people say the Belgians are the busiest handshakers among the Europeans, and the French the most reticent. In France a firm, pumping handshake is considered uncultured—the handshake should be quick and crisp. In China the pumping handshake shows pleasure in the greeting. The Arab handshake makes many people nervous, being a little limp and entirely too lingering for the average Westerner. Americans often want to wriggle their hands free, a gesture not missed or taken without offense by many Arabs. (Our firm grip is equally offensive to many foreigners.)

In most countries, etiquette calls for a woman to extend her hand first. In some places, such as Saudi Arabia or Thailand, touching a woman even in a handshake is bad form. It is always best to wait for an extended hand. When hands are not shaken, a nod of the head or even a slight bend from the waist would be appropriate. One also sees the "social kiss" in many countries, on one cheek or two, depending on the country. But unless you are sure you know what the form is, never initiate a kiss.

Play your cards right.

Business cards may be commonplace in the United States, but they are vital abroad. Wherever you are, you will do better with a formal style of card, without advertising, and with clear information in English on one side and the local language on the other side. (See Chapter 2 about printing business cards.)

In East Asia the presentation of business cards can take on special ceremony. Mimi Murphy, an exporter trading with Indonesia and Taiwan, says her foreign contacts are visibly impressed and pleased when she honors the proper forms of handling business cards. Wherever she is, and whatever she holds in her hands, she puts everything down, stands straight and presents the card, using both hands, being careful to have the foreign language facing up in the right direction for the foreigner to read. Never casually flip a card across a table.

Business card etiquette is no mere ritual. In places such as Japan a business card is both a mini-résumé and a ticket to the game of business; a certain amount of gamesmanship is necessary to make the best use of the ticket. The first rule is never to be without cards, any more than a samurai would be without his sword. Never being without cards in Japan means taking fifty or more cards to every meeting. The second rule is to respect the cards, keeping them in a distinctive holder. Keeping your cards in your pocket or in a cheap plastic envelope is like making a business call with a shopping bag instead of a briefcase. The third rule is to handle the card with formality. The card is presented, not merely handed. Japanese books of etiquette even point out a variety of ways to hold the card. Get someone to show you how to do it. Fourth, try to hand cards out in descending order of rank. The fifth rule is to receive another's card gracefully, using both hands and never stuffing the card recklessly into your pocket.

GREETINGS

"Hi" is never enough.

Many foreigners find Americans and Westerners in general to be aloof, rushed and unfriendly because of the brisk manner in which we dispense greetings. When we see someone we know we toss off a "Hi" and keep going. In most other countries an exchange of pleasantries when meeting someone is customary, and greetings are much more elaborate. As always when abroad, the rule is to slow down and invest in relationships. That is how business, in the long run, will get done.

In China the traveler is likely to be met with a unique and potentially baffling welcome. When you are being shown a factory or a school, as you inevitably will, workers or students will clap their hands in applause to welcome you, and again in farewell. The proper response is to clap back with a big smile. If a toast is made, there will be more clapping and again, you should clap back and smile.

DRESS

When on business, look the part.

Dress customs are hard to fathom in any country; Americans wear T-shirts and jeans to business school classes; the British might wear a coat and tie to a picnic. In China, scruffy, scanty or flamboyant clothing will cause ridicule or anger. When in doubt, dress conservatively and more formally than you might at home, and try not to be ostentatious. Whenever making a business call, wear business clothes, even in very hot climates. Always look around and ask about the proper attire.

CONVERSATION

Watch out for pitfalls in conversation.

Everywhere except a few northern European countries, conversations and business meetings begin with the innocuous. A mood of friendliness must precede any business. In Sweden, the opposite is true. Small talk is rare—the Swedes are quiet if they have nothing to say, and their answers are short. In France, business may not be discussed immediately, but the preliminary talk is not idle chatter either. Small talk is associated with the American sales pitch, which the average Frenchman detests. Always avoid familiarity or intrusion.

A normal conversational gambit for fast-moving Americans is to go through a check list of personal questions that will immediately identify what we think we need to know about someone before we can really converse: profession and employer, college, spouse's job, number of children and in what part of town he or she lives. From this data we can surmise a person's income bracket, intelligence and social status, and whether or not we have anything in common. This kind of interrogation seems so persistently rude to so many people abroad, however, that it is best not to do it, anywhere. Keep the conversation general and impersonal, following the lead of the host national. In Moslem countries, do not ask a man about the women in his family—wife or daughters—it shows unseemly interest and is a violation of the man's privacy. In business meetings, do not discuss family or home matters unless asked—many people feel that what happens at home is private. In Africa some people may be offended if you ask to which tribe they belong, especially if they take pride in being "modern."

Don't always talk business.

While business is increasingly an international subject, it is still considered inappropriate conversation in social settings abroad, including the business lunch. With some disdain, a foreigner can always point out the Americans in a restaurant—they are the only ones writing notes on the napkins or passing literature across the table.

Conversations to avoid in any setting, perhaps obviously enough, are politics, religion and sex, and even when the foreigner brings up these subjects, tread warily if you want the relationship to continue comfortably. There are many double standards, so what a foreigner talks about is not necessarily something you may talk about.

Disagree agreeably.

It is generally offensive to flatly contradict foreigners in their own country. The French and Australians enjoy a good argument, but be careful to fight on an intellectual, impersonal plane. Never criticize or correct someone in front of others—including servants, service people, shop assistants or people at work. Be careful too with phrases that might be relatively harmless at home, such as "Don't be silly." Much of what a Westerner barely notices can cause great indignation among foreigners who may take your English literally.

A group of Iranian students came to a New England university for an orientation tour. After an American student showed them the campus, a solicitous dean asked them what they had seen. Meaning to be helpful, the dean turned to the student and told him where he *should* have taken the Iranians. The entire group canceled their registration—they were appalled by the dean's apparent disrespect and discourtesy in criticizing the student in public.

Learn how to say "Thanks."

Also problematic are the compliment and even the standard "Thank you." While most cultures are taught very young to give thanks on hundreds of occasions, Indians use "Thank you" to signify the end of a transaction and relationship, like giving money in the market. Many foreigners think we overuse "Thank you" in the same way the Japanese seem to overuse "Sorry." Displaying gratitude after receiving a gift or favor in many Asian and some African countries is considered improper, and compliments directly to one's face are distrusted as insincere. Appreciation must be relayed indirectly via a third person.

Many Africans and Asians are made uncomfortable by Western compliments after a meal. From their perspective, one who praises the cooking may have come only for the food and did not appreciate the gathering. Asking for a recipe may seem to be insincere flattery, making the friendship suspect. On the other hand, don't get up from Swedish or Norwegian meals without a small bow and a few words thanking the hosts for the meal, or they will be quite hurt.

The rule of thumb for all conversational situations is to let the foreigner lead, unless you are the senior ranking person, in which case respect demands that others follow your lead. And don't shrug off their deference, or you will seem to be rebuffing their courteous intent.

Foreign Hospitality

In business and social settings, accept hospitality graciously.

In the United States you may or may not be offered a cup of coffee at the beginning of a meeting, and chances are that it will come in a Styrofoam cup or odd mug. Furthermore, nobody cares whether you drink coffee or not. In Asia and the Middle East, however, a host will be offended if you refuse food or drink offered to you, rejecting their hospitality. If you are making many visits in a day, you can consume enormous amounts of soft drinks, tea or coffee. Old hands say it is best to "take a sip of this and a sip of that," but don't overdo it, or you will be sorry by evening. In Saudi Arabia or other Arab countries, try to drink at least two cups of tea or coffee, and when you've had enough, decline more by tilting your cup back and forth twice, as you will see others doing. In the Gulf you will be served tea throughout a meeting, and when it is time to go you will be served coffee in a handleless cup. Drink at least one or two swallows before leaving.

In some places—Bulgaria, for example—you might be offered an aperitif like plum brandy or vodka during a business meeting, and it should be accepted. If you don't drink, your host can't drink either, and he may prefer to do business with someone more congenial. If you really don't want to drink alcohol, you can ask for something else and beg your host to proceed drinking what he wishes.

In Far Eastern cultures the host typically serves the guest, repeatedly, even in a restaurant. In fact, the Chinese are sometimes thrown off balance by Western restaurants where the food is presented entirely on individual plates, disrupting the protocol of serving each other. When being offered more food, you have to learn how to say no politely; the best way is to pre-empt the hospitality, saying, "Oh no, *you* must have some more." Or you can just nibble slowly what's on your plate and say "Thank you" with each additional serving.

Generally, do not take food or drink until it is specifically offered to you. The fact that it is set before you on a table is not necessarily an indication that it is polite to help yourself. In Indonesia, for example, you must be invited to taste the food that has been sitting in front of you during the conversation, and then you should, without haste, savor the food and prepare to leave. The invitation to eat is a sign that the meeting or visit is drawing to a close. In Finland you will be offered a drink upon your arrival, but you must hold it and wait until all the guests have assembled. Don't drink until your host has officially welcomed you to his home and proposed a toast to your health. Thereafter, each time you wish to take a sip, you must first toast another person by simply raising your glass and nodding. This will continue throughout the evening, including at the dinner table. In the Netherlands, Switzerland or Belgium, don't help yourself to hors d'oeuvres, and don't drink until the toast is made. In the Dutch toasting ritual, the host makes a toast, you raise your glass, say "Cheers" or *"Prost,"* exchange glances, raise glasses again, and then finally take a sip. It's done a little differently everywhere, and if you do it right, you will fit in a little better.

Business after hours is part of the job.

Japan is notorious for the obligatory night life. It is after hours in the sake bar or night club that male employers, employees and colleagues work out interpersonal problems. Through drinking, men (men only because women should not get drunk) can develop the rapport that the Japanese call *sukinshippu* ("skinship"), a term that describes the familylike rapport you feel when rubbing elbows with a drinking companion. Unlike Westerners who consider it malicious to be plied with drink, the Japanese take it as a friendly gesture—be sure to keep your drinking partner's glass full.

French and Italian business travelers in the United States complain about the "economical" entertainment they receive from Americans. In their countries they honor guests at the best restaurants, with three- to six-course meals and fine wines. They have large expense accounts and spend lots of money. Says one Italian businessman: "It is very disillusioning when we come here and our American partner takes us out for steak and salad."

Whether dancing the night away in Greece or drinking yourself stiff in Iceland, expatriates and international travelers must partake in these evenings of entertainment. It is a sign of respect and recognition. Moreover, being together with your associates on an informal level gives them a chance to say what they need to you with the understanding that they will be safe from loss of face and repercussions the following day. However, keep in mind that the evening is for enjoyment, not shop talk. And watch out for the local liquor—Russian vodka, for example, will not be diluted with tonic or ice, and you may be surprised at the quantities offered.

Don't make yourself at home in a foreigner's home.

It is uncommon for expatriates or visitors to be invited to the homes of host nationals in Arab countries, Asia and many parts of Europe. Home entertaining is not as spontaneous as it is in the United States, and it is usually a long time before you are invited to a home in communities where friendships are formed over the long term. Even close friends are rarely invited to the home. Instead, friends are more likely to meet at a café or pub. In Germany, for example, most people live in a fairly narrow, close network of social relationships that are determined by tradition as well as by an individual's education and job status. The home is a shelter from the outside world and the privacy of one's home is seldom shared. To be invited to the home of a German, or a Dutch, or Belgian is a special gesture of friendship.

Spouses are not always included in invitations—do not assume that they will be welcome. Nor will foreigners always bring their own spouses.

Around the world the guest who brings or sends gifts is always appreciated, and in many places a gift is expected. The main differences concern when the gift should be given and what kinds of things make for appropriate tokens of appreciation. In Europe, flowers are standard, but again, form of presentation differs. In Arab countries it is not proper to bring food to a meal. It is best to find out the local custom to prevent any awkwardness.

"Thank you" notes are much appreciated everywhere. Swedes thank their hosts for the food right after dinner, and for the party the next time they see them, and they call or write a few days later. You will seem ungrateful if you don't repeatedly remember such events. In Holland, if you have been invited to a birthday party, try to remember the event yearly thereafter with a card or gift.

YOUR ENTERTAINING

Your entertaining may be American style, but be ready to guide your guests, and watch out you don't insult them.

In some European countries, the visitor is expected to make the first social move, whereas in the United States the old-timers usually invite over the newcomer to a neighborhood or business. Customs vary, but the traveler should not pine in loneliness for fear of making the first move; you must often take the initiative to begin the acquaintance.

Invitations are seldom informal. Both business and social invitations should be written—a simple telephone call or verbal invitation may easily be forgotten, ignored or rejected. A formal invitation will get a written reply in Europe, but Moslems do not accept an invitation until the last minute. Even then, they may not arrive. In places such as Indonesia, commitments are not made because it is impossible to plan for the future; who knows what imperatives each day may bring?

You can entertain your guests in your own habitual ways, but this should not imply that the local entertaining customs are inferior. Your guests might be much more comfortable being entertained in the ways to which they are accustomed, but you run the risk of being out of your element and making *faux pas.* The best bet is a combination, essentially entertaining in the ways you know, with some accommodation to local traditions, cuisine and tastes.

The schedule of events for the evening is the first consideration. In Europe and South America, dinner is eaten much later than is customary in the United States—you may invite people for nine or nine-thirty and serve dinner at ten-thirty or later. In Africa you may invite people for supper between three and six in the afternoon. In many foreign countries, events occur in the reverse order from what is expected in the U.S. In Saudi Arabia, for example, coffee, tea or fruit drink is served as soon as guests arrive and conversation will continue for a long time. Dinner will be served at the end of the evening (as late as midnight) and guests are expected to leave right after the meal, after the postprandial coffee.

What to serve is also important. Don't serve beef to Hindus, or pork to Moslems. Alcohol is prohibited by Islamic law. Many Moslems now do drink, but with religious fundamentalism on the rise and punishments severe to gruesome, you must be discreet. When entertaining Chinese, either at home or in a restaurant in the United States, forget your inclination to avoid Chinese food. Many people will feel silly offering Chinese food to the Chinese, but actually this is the best choice; most Chinese don't like Western food and much prefer even bad imitation Chinese cooking to anything else.

Don't expect people to be on time. Arabs and South Americans will think nothing of coming to dinner an hour later than the appointed time. Brace yourself and be calm in your approach to preparing and serving the meal. Moreover, be prepared for unexpected additions to the dinner table, since your guests may bring relatives or friends without warning. They will expect the same warm welcome they would extend to any friends or family of yours. Many people come from a tradition of open hospitality for all.

MASTERY OF PROTOCOL

International business as well as diplomacy is marked periodically by major banquets and other affairs of state that demand an ability to finesse the requirements of protocol. Americans often want to skip the banquets, tours and other formalities to get on with business. Don't. It is through these activities that you establish the necessary relationships. However, before participating, check with the protocol officer at the American embassy to make sure you understand the local protocol. For those who will have occasion to meet royalty, find out the proper forms.

Among the most important rituals to master are the ceremonials of banquet toasting, which vary considerably around the world. Whether guest or host at a banquet, always keep in mind that formalities are not superfluous but may be part of the substance to your local business associates or government officials.

TOURING

While on business, know how to be a proper tourist.

Your hosts in many places will want to show you the sights. Touring is part of the business-social package, and you had better make the most of it. If you handle sightseeing with finesse, you can win many points. In exotic places travelers often make one outstanding mistake—they appreciate what is "quaint," when what is "quaint" is *not* what your host wants you to appreciate. Few Americans in developing countries are able to refrain from taking pictures of water buffalo and peasants in the fields. But that is not what developing countries are about. Water buffalo, while scenic, are less common and less a part of these cultures than new textile mills and new tractors. The business person on tour should take pictures of the things that make the people proud—the factories and other modern developments—not the human-interest shots. The wise traveler in China will observe with fascination that the Yangtze Dam, which is boring to the average tourist, will change China immeasurably. Find out what the local sources of pride are before you start taking pictures, and take care not to take illegal or sensitive shots: military establishment, bridges in Eastern Europe or women in the Middle East. Don't take pictures of any people without their permission.

When visiting national or religious monuments, be careful to respect local icons. At the Emerald Palace in Thailand there is a guard whose job is to rush over to you and move your feet if you point them at the Green Buddha. In England, refrain from trying to break the stony gaze of the Palace guards. In any monarchy, speak only respectfully of royalty. Take off shoes in mosques and certain Oriental structures. Never walk in front of someone praying or step on a prayer rug.

Another standard when touring is to honor the guide's restrictions on your itinerary. Sometimes it is a matter of national security, and sometimes a matter of your own protection.

In overseas operations anyone can make mistakes.

President Reagan made headlines on his 1984 trip to China when he overpaid for a souvenir. "Keep the change," he said as he walked away. Humiliated, the shopkeeper ran after him to return the money. Tipping is officially not allowed in China.

GIFT GIVING

Gift giving is a normal part of business almost everywhere, but always handle it with care.

Most businesspeople are somewhat uncomfortable with the process of gift giving, and many delegate that function to secretaries or other assistants. But gifts provide an opportunity to reinforce relationships. At the same time they may be a risky business, especially if given to government officials.

Anybody can make a mistake with a gift. Letitia Baldridge, who was social secretary to President Kennedy and assistant to ambassadors in Paris and Rome, once delivered six dozen signed photographs of the Kennedys to the U.S. embassy in New Delhi, all beautifully framed in dark blue cowhide and stamped with the presidential seal. They were to be presented to officials all over India during the Kennedys' official visit to Prime Minister Nehru in 1962. But the gifts were totally unacceptable. Hindu officials would have been aghast to receive anything made with the hides of cows (which are sacred in India). Within forty hours, silver frames were substituted.

The type of present, its value and the way it is given are very important. If the gift is thoughtless, it may be remembered as a token of the visitor's disregard. A few rules that apply virtually everywhere will make gift giving easier: First, know the local laws—all countries have regulations. Second, do not buy expensive gifts. Go instead for quality, conversational interest or something you know will be meaningful to the recipient. Avoid junk, including logo gifts, unless they are particularly attractive or interesting. Third, let the foreigner initiate the gift giving, except when the foreigner is extending hospitality. Parker Pen Company commissioned a study of gift giving around the world, and found that the safest gifts are fancy chocolates, toys for the children, something intellectual, such as a book, or, not surprisingly, high-quality pens. Something special from your home, such as Vermont maple syrup or Hawaiian macadamia nuts may be appreciated.

Wrapping should be simple and elegant, but find out local form for color of ribbons and wrapping paper. Generally avoid white or black paper. In Japan, avoid bows and ribbons. Do not make a ceremony over gifts unless they are part of a banquet, and do not press the receiver to open the gift in front of you. In many places, gifts are opened later, in private.

Different countries have different ways of dealing with gift giving so that there will be no appearance of bribery. In the Arab world, give your gift in front of others so it won't seem sneaky, but in China, unless your gift is official and presented at a banquet, give it in private. In many parts of the world, such as Japan, it is improper to give a gift to anyone when there are others around, unless you are giving them all gifts.

A mistake that Americans often make is to overly admire something that they see on display in a shop or store or in their host's home. Dr. Phillip Grub of George Washington University tells of a visitor to Korea taken on a tour of several shops and a department store. She commented on the beauty of a number of items of local origin. Later all of the items she had noted on her tour arrived at her room with the compliments of the host. Americans make the assumption that the foreign host is very generous. On the other hand, the foreign host assumes that the American has hinted that the host should obtain the gift.

Check list for hosting foreigners in the United States

Appoint a liaison.
Send advance information to your guests.
Research the delegation members and their industry.
Make hotel and travel arrangements.
Plan menus, seating pattern, and protocol.
Prepare toasts.
Brief your own company executives.
Translate all relevant materials.
Select gifts.
Arrange for photographs.
Print an itinerary, including maps and other logistics.
Arrange security and plan for any emergencies (including medical).
Convert all numbers to the metric system.

SUMMARY

You may be dressed for success, and you may be staying in a prestigious hotel, but you will be mistaken for an ignorant tourist if you don't project savoir-faire. So remember:

People tend to like and prefer to interact with people they perceive as similar to themselves.

Respect for etiquette is deep-seated.

Show respect.

Introductions

Try to get names and titles right.

Don't use first names until specifically invited.

Be prepared to shake hands endlessly, and know when to bow.

Play your cards right.

Greetings

"Hi" is never enough.

Dress

When on business, look the part.

Conversation

Watch out for pitfalls in conversation.

Avoid familiarity and intrusion.

Don't always talk business.

Disagree agreeably.

Learn how to say thanks, their way.

Foreign Hospitality

Accept hospitality graciously.

Business after hours is part of the job.

Don't make yourself at home in a foreigner's home.

Your Entertaining

You can do it American style, but be ready to guide your guests.

Mastery of Protocol
Learn the protocol; learn the rituals.

Touring
While on business, know how to be a proper tourist.

Gift Giving
Gift giving is a normal part of business, but always handle it with care.

CHAPTER 9

GETTING THINGS DONE

✳ ✳

Making the
machinery work

T HE MOST FREQUENT COMPLAINT we hear from international business travelers is that what should be the simplest, most routine tasks are monumentally complex abroad. "You just can't get things done the way you would in the States," they say. People who are high achievers at home can flounder miserably overseas, foiled by incomprehensible systems and officials who seem to create obstacles at every turn. Things we take for granted at home just don't exist in some countries.

Developing countries prove to be especially stressful for even the most rugged of individuals. Conditions are, some travelers say with grim understatement, "difficult." Telephones, for those lucky enough to have access to them, work intermittently. Brownouts and total power failures are frequent. Airplane reservations fall through with regularity. A good secretary is almost impossible to find, a word processor unheard of. The most essential, elementary business data are unavailable, and people must make decisions with insufficient information.

Getting things done in any country, developed or underdeveloped, Eastern or Western, is hard for the traveler who doesn't know the ropes. People who do business in England are often just as frustrated as those in Saudi Arabia, although for entirely different reasons. You can overcome the obstacles preventing you from getting on with your job if you know how to cut through red tape and use the lubricants that make machinery work.

Rule 1: Take advantage of cultural idiosyncrasies.

One Japan expert, frustrated by being ignored and kept waiting in government and business offices in Japan, devised a way to get the attention of people who refused to acknowledge his presence. He would concentrate on catching the eye of anyone in the office who glanced up at him, and then bow instantly, before the person could turn away. He found the short, jerky bow the most effective, as it seemed to force the Japanese to bow back and thereby recognize his presence. The Japanese would then be obligated to come over or send someone to find out what this American wanted.[1]

Whether you call it manipulation or diplomacy, it is fair and sensible to use what you know about a culture to your advantage. People react in predictable ways to certain stimuli, and you will get better results if you push the right buttons or pull the right strings for the culture.

Everything you have learned in preceding chapters will apply to your efforts to get things done. The principles of international negotiation, managing people, communicating, selling, even etiquette and teaching will come in handy whether you are trying to have a telephone installed or to obtain a driver's license. The importance of speaking the language and showing interest and respect can't be stressed enough. Asking the right question (so you don't get a plain "Yes" or "No" or "I don't know") and being a good listener will be indispensable whatever it is you are trying to do.

Rule 2: Rules, like the price of souvenirs, are negotiable.

The international traveler quickly learns the foreign words for "difficult," "impossible," "illegal" and "It's never been done." The traveler who uncritically accepts an explanation and gives up is like the shopper who pays the asking price in an Egyptian souk or Mexican market. You are supposed to bargain, and if you don't play the game, you lose.

In many countries, getting what you want really is a game, and the core skill required to play the game has a name. In Brazil it is called *jeito,* which the dictionary defines as "aptitude, aptness, dexterity, adroitness, skill, knack, propensity, manner, and appearance." *Jeito* is a way of manipulating the system, using imaginative ways to get around constraints and get what one wants. To give or make *jeito* is to manipulate circumstances to your benefit. When your dentist can't see you, you ask his secretary to make a little *jeito* to squeeze you in. Modern street thieves in the cities show *jeito* when they carry bottles of liquid soap to get the rings off their victims. When you are in Latin America you may as well accept the prevailing attitude, which is that "life is spelled out, but you can try to beat it." In America we like to believe hard work will get results; in many countries it is a sense of humor and imagination that can conquer fate.

In China the word for circumnavigating the bureaucracy, rules and regulations is *banfa*. *Banfa* means a way out of a problem, or resourcefulness in finding ways through the myriad of petty, conflicting, bizarre and obscure regulations that choke the Chinese system. Westerners who come up against apparent Catch-22's can use *banfa* to save the day. One British diplomat who needed a Chinese driver's license had to promise never to drive with his glasses on because his passport showed him without his glasses, and his license had to match the passport. In another incident, Chinese firemen lined up outside one of the foreigner's residential compounds in Beijing. They could not put out a fire because permission was needed for Chinese to enter the foreign area. Asked what could have been done, a Chinese official suggested the *banfa* solution: the foreigners could have gone to the gate and invited the firemen into the compound as guests.

Each country has its version of *banfa* or *jeito*. In America we call it creative problem solving. The point is that wherever you are, you must not feel blocked simply because your habitual methods do not work. If you are imaginative and resourceful, and pay attention to how others in the culture seem to work through obstacles, you should be able to accomplish many things, including things that would be impossible in the United States. In many ways foreign bureaucracies, while extraordinarily complex and sluggish, can be much more flexible than our own rigid institutions.

One last point here: for *banfa* and *jeito* to work you must believe, as most foreigners fundamentally believe, that the individual case is special— that *your* case is special. In many countries outside Europe, rules are interpreted variously, depending on the people involved and the situation. In South America and the Arab world an individual and his unique and special circumstance is always more important than an abstract principle or organization. A border official can give you ten reasons why you can't cross over into the next country, but then may say, "But who will see you walking over there?" Given a real person, meaning someone who has emerged as an individual rather than an impersonal foreigner, a law can be bent.

Rule 3: Who you know is the key to getting things done.

You will never get anywhere without connections, and if you can't stand the thought of "using people," you had better stay home. In many parts of the world, patronage, sponsorship or "influence" is a fact of life. The Western version, networking, is the same idea, but nowhere nearly as powerful and pervasive, possibly because we believe that it is always better to get ahead on our own merits. Interpersonal dependency in other cultures is normal and healthy, and certainly would not be a reason to be less proud of one's accomplishments.

In many places, such as Greece and especially South America, one needs a patron to get a job, a loan, a place in a university or even a passport. In the Middle East, family or friendship connections are the key to getting work permits, by-passing government formalities, learning about and winning upcoming contracts. In Mexico, Italy, Spain and many other places one gets ahead by clever use of one's network of influence and the gratuities from being well-connected. In China the word is *guanxi,* meaning literally an intricate, pervasive network of personal relations. *Guanxi* is the relationship of mutual obligations, a way of getting things done through the back door. One with wide and effective *guanxi* will be a success; without it you are lost. *Guanxi* is more than back-scratching; it is not an **adjunct** to business, but its **essence.**

In many places things get done only through unofficial channels. Says one executive: "The informal structure is there for a reason: the official system does not work. The unofficial system is a legitimate solution that creates jobs and allows business to function. You have no right to insist on using the official bureaucracy."

It is virtually impossible for outsiders to ever develop substantial *guanxi* or *compadre* relations, but they can certainly get close. In order to play the connections game, international business travelers must pay their dues, initiating from the start the long and arduous process of building those relationships. It will do no good to try to make connections when you need something. A U.S. project manager once described to us the problems he had when one of his crew died in Saudi Arabia: it took him four long days to get the necessary releases to have the body sent home, and he was successful only because he could call on long-cultivated personal relationships to muster the necessary doctor's slips and proof that the man had not been murdered. He warns: "As bizarre as that incident may sound, anyone working abroad will have to handle the strangest situations, and you had better have lined up your friends long before you need them."

In some countries you will need friends in all relevant departments in a company, and you shouldn't be overly concerned with getting the company's president involved. In Japan, for example, you can ask the head of Research & Development to introduce you to the section head (*kacho*) who will be responsible for your proposal, and once you have appropriately established a relationship, you can ask him to introduce you to his counterparts in other departments, such as Production, Quality Control, and Sales. Eventually, once all the relationships are in place, you should proceed to meet with the president, only to discuss policies and the mutual value of the venture with his company.

Even with conscientious relationship building, don't expect to be able to do everything. Locals will often be much better at getting things done than you could ever hope to be. Use them. Cutting through red tape is an art, and there are professionals who specialize in dealing with the court system, real estate or government officials. In Brazil they are called *despa-*

chantes, and they can be indispensable in accomplishing a multitude of errands that would be routine at home but can be nightmares abroad—such as a simple delivery or pickup. Some say in Brazil there are two languages, Portuguese and a secret code for getting things done. The *despachante* speaks both. In France you will want a *debrouiallard* on your staff, literally a "defogger," an operator who can cut through the fog of conventional barriers when everyone else says "It can't be done." In the Arab world you need to hire someone with *mukh,* street sense. In China you are crazy not to employ an "office manager," one with *guanxi,* of course. A low-level office manager handles administrative matters. High-level managers play an important part behind the scenes in business: they get across messages "off the record," which on the record or made directly might result in loss of face. Hence they are invaluable in helping move negotiations when neither side can officially disclose information or their *real* positions.

In Japan, everybody has rights, responsibilities and restrictions which come with their *bun*, their station in the social order. *(Bun* is pronounced "boon.") Managers, workers, teachers, and students—the behavior of all is controlled by the individual's *bun*, even when they are not at work or in school. Thus it is always important to know the *bun* of people you ask to do things or who represent your company. If their *bun* is limited, you will be wasting your time. Japan expert Boye De Mente says, "The aims of foreign businessmen are often thwarted because they attempt to get things done by Japanese whose *bun* does not allow them to do whatever is necessary to accomplish the required result. Instead of telling the businessmen they can't do it or passing the matter on to someone who can, there is a tendency for the individual to wait . . . until they are again approached by the businessmen, then announce that it is impossible."[2]

Just how to go about cultivating the right connections can be a sticky question. Experts suggest the following steps. First, begin socially, with the proper introductions. Any foreigner will be more favorably disposed toward you if you are introduced by one of their own trusted friends or connections. Second, you must make friends, in every case. Making friends, of course, requires establishment of mutual interests and respect. Third, extend a favor, in a casual way. Your gestures must be done in the spirit of friendship, although the obligation will be understood by all.

Rule 4: If you must grease palms, do it right.

Bribe, mordida, dash, commission, tip or backsheesh—greasing of palms is a daily part of international business. Whether or not to do it is a question that inevitably confronts anyone who continues to work abroad. There is no single rule that will apply to all situations, because no two situations and countries are the same. However, there are laws. Some forms of payment are illegal, and you must know the laws and local practices. It helps to work out for yourself a framework for action so that you will be prepared to decide what to do in any situation.

Cross-cultural consultant George Renwick says: "We all face ethical dilemmas overseas, sometimes very serious ones. My basic suggestion is that if you're asked to do something that would violate your individual sense of right and wrong, or the company's code of ethics, or the government's legislation, don't do it. There is an advantage in becoming known overseas as an individual who will not compromise, even if their standards are different from ours. There is an advantage to becoming known as a company that will do A, B and C, but not D under any circumstances."

Others complain: "We were doing well abroad before the Foreign Corrupt Practices Act. Our share of the business in Saudi Arabia has gone from 34 percent to 4 percent since then. Now we are losing to the Germans, Koreans, French, and anyone else who can let money flow in the customary ways. If a payment is acceptable in a foreign culture, it cannot be considered wrong, and your job is to help your overly moralistic company reconsider its ethnocentric values as they are applied to the foreign situation." The West Germans, for example, deduct bribes as legitimate business expenses. In many countries, government officials are not paid very well and "tips" are a way of compensating them. If you need government approvals or permits in those places, you had better seriously think about legal ways of putting something into the right pockets.

Wherever they stand on the ethical question, whether to make payments or not, people experienced in international business suggest that before you make a move, examine U.S. law and your company's policies, and talk with someone who has successfully done business in that country for a long time. Bribing is always a risky business, and penalties are severe, both for the individual briber, the company, and those accepting bribes. Even where bribery is local practice, laws may be invoked whimsically.

Often the bribery situation will not involve a monumental ethical or legal question, just a monumental nuisance. A typical scene: An American hands his passport over to the Jakarta customs official, who puts it up on a shelf. The American is asked to wait, and he does, until his patience gives out and he asks for his passport back. "I don't know what you are talking about," says the official. The American says, "It's right up there, I saw you put it there," but the official, who has all the time in the world, shrugs and maintains, "I don't know." Even the most naïve traveler will finally catch on and pass over some cash—if it is enough he gets his passport back. If he is unlucky, he is arrested by an unobserved policeman.

Although it is hard to make rules about *when* to make payments, there are rules for *how* to do it. In fact, these things are handled in such traditional ways that you never really have to improvise. The first rule is: Arrange your rewards so that in fact they are not bribes. Instead, "hire a consultant," for example. Add someone's relative to your staff, arrange for an expense account or use of a hotel room, or offer some other acceptable form of business gift or entertainment. Some wealthy international dealers and corporations have found it effective to invest in community projects, such as building schools for the children of customs officials, building hospitals, and so on.

Second, avoid doing it yourself. You must select a local go-between carefully—someone who knows the informal structure and dynamics, and who has finesse and the right contacts. Beware, however, that you may be liable for any actions the go-between might take on your behalf. Third, don't go overboard. Typically the American either fails to make payments at all or goes too far, paying a fortune when significantly much less would do. "You make a mockery of the system when you pay so much," complained one Arab.

Keeping out of foreign jails

Almost 10,000 Americans have been arrested abroad in the past three years. Most of these people didn't know they were breaking the law, or underestimated the seriousness of their offense. The typical American prisoner is the construction worker caught drinking alcohol in Saudi Arabia; or the tourist who tried to take archaeological artifacts out of Greece or Mexico; or the exporter who let his Indonesian importer "adjust the numbers" on the exporter's letterhead invoice, not understanding that the adjustment was more than a currency conversion. In Saudi Arabia a foreigner involved in an accident will always be found at fault, even if you are stopped at a red light and hit from behind.

The best way to keep out of foreign jails is to:

1. Know the local laws and customs.
2. Never buy on the black market.
3. Make sure you have the required permits.
4. Make sure someone who cares about you knows where you are at all times.
5. Don't drive yourself unless you live in the country, are licensed and well prepared. Take taxis or hire a chauffeur.
6. Call your embassy or consulate, but don't count on the ambassador or consul being able to help, and don't expect anyone to honor your American constitutional guarantees.
7. Contact the International Legal Defense Counsel, a Philadelphia-based organization that does legal and humanitarian work for Americans arrested abroad. The ILDC has published a handbook called "The Hassle of Your Life: A Handbook for Families of Americans Jailed Abroad."

Rule 5: Keep things simple, sometimes.

Foreigners remark that Americans are obsessed with the newest and most elaborate of modern equipment; they are concerned with getting the job done through the most efficient means, never mind the cost, because time is more valuable than money. But often old-fashioned techniques that take a little longer and employ a few more local people will work better, in the long run, than imported complex heavy machinery that may be stockpiled, useless, once the project is complete. In many developing countries, expensive equipment is inappropriate for the climate or culture, and doing things on a smaller scale makes more sense.

"In a perverse way," an American executive in the Middle East complains, "the last thing an Arab or African wants is a simple, straightforward solution. You have to make it complex or they will not trust it. They will turn to someone who can give them a more impressive and complicated proposal." The trick to getting things done in some areas is to make them simple enough to be 'do-able' yet appear complex enough to have importance."

Rule 6: Don't be dependent on business services. Bring your own.

An old China hand says all Americans seem to be distraught in China, half of them sweating out difficult negotiations, and the other half running around trying hopelessly to get the business support services they need so that they can get back to sweating out the negotiations with a retyped, revised proposal or copies of documents. "You can't just send papers down to the hotel secretarial service or to the copy place down the street," she says. "In China there are no copiers, no secretaries, no typewriters."

In many countries the only way you will have the business support you want or documents prepared the way you like them prepared, is to bring your own secretary and typewriter (and the proper electrical converters, of course) as well as paper and supplies. Expatriates have a valuable resource in their spouses, who, in most places, aren't allowed to have work permits. Spouses can save themselves from desperation and be tremendously helpful in filling the business services gap.

The telephone presents some of the greatest frustrations in international enterprise. In South Africa, South America, and other places, it can take over a year to get a phone, after an arduous application procedure. But even once you have a phone, or if you are working out of a hotel or office already set up with telephones, the going is not easy. Usually the only telephone directory is in the local language, so you have to speak and read the language before you can track down even the American embassy. In Iran, phones are listed by the owner of the building—you have to know the landlord's name to find someone in the phone book. Whatever government office you call, there is a 50 percent probability that the line will be busy.

In any country that is not technically developed, it may take hours of dialing to get through. The norm is one phone (if any) per office, very few private lines and whole apartment buildings with one or two communal phones. You dial endlessly and the line is busy or nobody answers. Once someone does answer, the *real* frustrations begin. You ask for someone, and whoever answers blurts "not here" and hangs up. You call back, dialing for yet another hour. When you get through, you ask, "When will he be in?" The voice says "Don't know," and hangs up again. You persist. This time you don't mince words: "Take this message." This is probably all you can do, but don't count on your message getting through. It is best for you to pay a personal visit to the office and leave a note. One solution for situations such as this is to get to know someone with a phone who works or lives next to the office you need to call. Better yet, hire an intermediary who is in the network.

If you are making long-distance calls from a hotel in China, a bellboy will arrive at your room after each phone call and present a bill to be paid at once, in Chinese foreign-exchange certificates. And always assume that your telephone is tapped and that Telex messages are read by an official.

Business supports are a problem not only in developing countries. Even in England you can run into difficulties if you have a task that cuts across different union lines. And the telephones can be baffling: when you call long distance, the area code is different depending on where you are calling *from* as well as where you are calling.

Rule 7: Travel with money and lots of small change.

All the big tourist hotels and airlines seem to take credit cards, but they are not commonly used everywhere. You do get charged extra for many things you are unlikely to think about: there are oddities everywhere. For example, it may be much cheaper to call collect than to use a credit card. In some countries, particularly in the Middle East, taxi fares are negotiated when you get in the cab; if you fail to settle on a price in advance, the sky can be the limit when you get to your destination. Asked for restaurant recommendations, a local is likely to send you to a place he thinks a rich American (all Americans are rich) would like. Dinners in the finer restaurants can easily cost $100 to $150 a person.

It is easy to overspend when traveling, simply because you don't know your way around. It pays to ask experienced travelers what pitfalls you should avoid.

Rule 8: Get advice before you travel outside the major cities.

In some countries, travel outside the modernized or "Westernized" cities can be quite a shock even to rugged individuals. Even well-traveled executives find some developing countries impossible. A group that included oil executives, a Peace Corps director, and others who claimed to have been "everywhere in the world," found the China hinterland too much for them, and many of the group cut their trip short. The food made them sick, toilet facilities made them even sicker, the heat was unbearable, they were thoroughly shaken by the suspensionless buses hiccuping relentlessly over miles of bumpy roads, and the Chinese tour guides insisted on a schedule of sights that was in conflict with what they wanted to see. This country may have been particularly tough, but the point is that these people thought they had been around and knew how to cope.

Be Prepared For Terrorist Activity

Most corporate executives probably don't have the faintest idea how they would handle a kidnaping, armed attack or other terrorist activity. And most companies treat the subject with so much secrecy that people in the field don't know if the company has any plans for handling such emergencies. This is most unfortunate because interviews with former victims make it clear that they would have been better able to handle the situation if they had some knowledge and advice beforehand. In crime prevention at home or abroad, a little awareness is important: the subject should be aired even if security dictates that not all plans be known.

It helps to know something of the terrorist's motives. Abroad the objective is usually to gain money and/or publicity for a political cause. Publicity is primary, so hostages may be held for long periods of time and targets are likely to be newsworthy. In kidnapings, men are usually the target—not always the top executive. A company cannot guard everyone: even if the president is protected, the vice president is vulnerable, and so on down the line. Almost anyone from a big wealthy corporation will do. However, high-profile individuals or companies are favored targets.

Most terrorists do a lot of surveillance. Be alert to the signs of being watched; somebody must come and take a good look at you if you are a target, and your routine is likely to be carefully recorded. Always be aware of your surroundings, and the people coming to your home and office. Insist on seeing credentials and checking references of people who work for you. Be unpredictable: vary your routine, don't park in marked parking spaces, go to work at different times and by different routes and if possible in different vehicles. Keep a low profile—don't label your belongings or drive with vanity plates. Think through and make arrangements for contingency plans—prearranged signals, and so on.

Even though "Libya is safer than New York," as one executive put it, terrorist activities are a real threat, and many of the major multinationals do have contingency plans. In an emergency, the first call should be to corporate offices, where there is a greater commitment to protecting employee victims. Then call the police and the U.S. embassy.

It is important to be prepared *before* an attack.

How is this relevant to "getting things done"? If you are researching your market, developing new areas, or simply improving your mind, you will need to get things done outside the cities. You won't do very well if you are incapacitated by the prevailing conditions. Circumstances vary so greatly that you must research the area in which you intend to travel.

Rule 9: Adjust your expectations.

Nothing is going to happen as quickly and easily as it does at home. But more than that, many things are going to be accomplished in a different way from what you may think is the right way. Give it a chance; you will often find that the different way will produce adequate or better than expected results.

Rule 10: We've said it before, but we'll say it one last time: be patient and keep cool.

SUMMARY

RULE 1: Take advantage of cultural idiosyncrasies.
RULE 2: Rules, like the price of souvenirs, are negotiable.
RULE 3: Who you know is the key to getting things done.
RULE 4: If you must grease palms, do it right.
RULE 5: Keep things simple.
RULE 6: Don't be dependent on business services. Bring your own.
RULE 7: Travel with money and lots of small change.
RULE 8: Get advice before you travel outside the major cities.
RULE 9: Adjust your expectations.
RULE 10: Be patient and keep cool.

CHAPTER 10

DEALING WITH HEADQUARTERS

❋ ❋

*What will they think
back home?*

ONE OF THE MOST COMMON REASONS for failure abroad has nothing
to do with poor performance in the foreign country itself but with an
inability to maintain the support and trust of superiors at headquarters.
"You won't last long in international business if you don't have good
communications with the head office," says Jim Peterson, head of international personnel at 3M. "Once communications break down, your superiors
become suspicious. You lose credibility and they think you're goofing off."
You take a career risk in going abroad because it is much harder to show
results and you can lose credit at headquarters if you don't get your message
across.

Almost without exception, expatriates and home-based international
travelers complain that management does not understand their problems or
why they do the things they do in the field. According to Hewlett-Packard's
John Toppel, who set up HP's first sales operation in Hong Kong: "Most
likely, you are dealing with people who don't understand the local situation,
who haven't been overseas, or who think you are going native if you are not
responding the way they think you should." Another annoyed traveler says:
"You just have to remember that they are not small-minded jerks, but their
jobs do require them to be petty sticklers."

The inevitable tension between personnel at home and abroad is an
unfortunate fact of life. Management and administrative staff seem generally suspicious of the qualifications and actions of the people who travel. On
the other hand, personnel abroad seem universally disgruntled, complaining
that headquarters exerts too much control yet lacks sufficient information
upon which to make decisions and persistently demonstrates gross ignorance of local realities.

The simple fact of physical and psychological distance creates communication problems. Time-zone differences limit the number of working hours you can communicate around the world. For many international travelers or expatriates, there simply are no telephones. Bechtel project manager Eric Brown says that when the phone system was installed in their Venezuela project, it still took hours of dialing just to get a long-distance operator. Telegrams were no viable substitute, since they weren't delivered with any sense of urgency. "A telegram would come from the States to Caracas in a day and a half, but then they would put it in the mail, and we would get it ten days later." Now much business is conducted via Telex. But messages bridge only the physical distance, not the psychological.

RULES FOR THE TRAVELER AND EXPATRIATE

How to keep your job and how to get the cooperation and backup you need from your home office are central tasks while you are traveling or living abroad. You simply must make peace and keep peace with the administrative staff, or life may be very miserable. And you must make the right impression with superiors, or your international efforts will be in vain.

Rule 1: Keep in mind two realities.

Anyone working internationally has two realities to keep in perspective, the reality of the local situation and the reality from headquarters' point of view. Experts stress the importance of keeping in touch with both, not hiding out in the local scene, nor staying only within the American community and communicating only with home. Always listen to two points of view, because your job is to seek the best combination that will achieve the results your company wants in the local scene.

Diplomats are familiar with a principle that should be helpful to anyone doing business abroad, which is that any President has two foreign policies, a foreign-foreign policy and a domestic-foreign policy. Very simply, it means you have to make your actions understandable to two audiences that have entirely different points of view about what is important or right. Foreign-foreign policy is what goes on between international leaders themselves and in statements made for foreign media; domestic-foreign policy is what electorates at home are *told* about what is going on. In international business, a similar principle operates; you must put information through a filter, in both directions. Of course the analogy should not be stretched; you should not be out in the field making policy, or lying to the people who pay your bills.

Rule 2: Bring your superiors over.

Tim Dorman, who spent several years in Japan with Bank of America, says: "The main way to get them to understand is simply to invite them over. Chief executives of companies who come to Japan for the first time generally leave with a remarkably different insight and perspective on how things work in Japan. They had to see it first hand because it is very hard to communicate the subtleties of how Japanese do business." Eric Brown, a Bechtel manager, agrees: "It's very important for the management back in the States to get into the country frequently, to be able to get the feel for what's happening to the staff there."

Some people who are given international assignments come to see the overseas operation as their turf and are reluctant to have visitors from the home office. They have a sense of being special, of having special knowledge and power. But in the long run it will hurt not to have people in headquarters who understand and can support you in the ways you need. This applies both to expatriates and to those who travel frequently.

A word of caution: Do not expose your superiors only to the good side of your business. There is a tendency to cocoon business executives, to protect them and to impress them. Joe Garcia of Mattel says: "Don't give them a business review in the hotel. Get them out to your retail business; take them to problem accounts, not just your successes. If they go on a bad call, they are more likely to understand that your problems are not all your fault." An Exxon executive adds: "Don't just pop them in the situation. With someone new to the area it is extremely important to give them a good background. Explain the culture; use maps and visual aids; show how local customs affect business results. If they come yearly, give them updates and keep presentations on file so that you can refer to what you told them last time."

Even those in international business who never or rarely travel benefit from a better-informed organization. The more others in the company understand the international scene and your international functions, the easier your job should be.

Rule 3: Don't treat those at home like numbskulls.

Decision makers at headquarters need information from the field to make good decisions, and providing that information is part of your job. It is not enough to maintain that "This is how things are done here," without explanation. You will greatly enhance your effectiveness if you can improve home office staff's understanding of how the local culture affects your decisions and operations. If people from headquarters don't visit the overseas locations, you should visit them, and make presentations there to colleagues as well as superiors. One consultant recommends another solution: send home quarterly reports on videotape. A "show and tell" will help provide information in a way that will make an impression. Eventually people at home may develop greater trust in your judgment.

Administrative support personnel also need to be educated about the realities of the situation. In many cases, loopholes in company-procedures manuals can be found once an administrator understands your predicament. One traveling executive says: "It doesn't hurt to make friends with all the staff who can make your life easier, from the one who books your flights to the one who will approve shipping your piano." He always brings back a little something for his "home team"—perfume, liquor, small art objects and some good funny stories.

Don't overlook the fact that your superiors at home may well understand your situation, and yet still insist on actions that you consider wrong. Management must make its decisions based on a multitude of objectives and considerations, some of which may not be apparent to you. The best you can do is try to keep yourself informed about the bigger picture, and make sure management is kept up to date.

Rule 4: Don't get confused about whose "side" you are on.

Loel Labberton, who spent several years with Chevron in England, says: "It is so easy to get caught up in a 'their side/our side' confrontation with the people in the home office. You never have enough information and they never understand your situation, so it is easy to get confused about whose side you are on."

Just remember who sends your paycheck and what your employer's objectives are, and balance that with the demands of your own personnel and the local situation.

Rule 5: Like a balloon under water, keep bouncing up.

Those who have succeeded abroad say, "Have fortitude. Hang in there, and if what you are doing is right, it will be understood in due course." Almost everyone, at one time or another, feels like giving up an overseas assignment. Without a doubt, international work is more difficult, problematic and personally stressful than work at home. The irony is, of course, that colleagues at home think just the opposite, seeing the overseas assignment as a long vacation. The task for you is to keep reassessing the situation and keep communications open.

Rule 6: Make sure your overseas employees and contacts know you have the support of headquarters.

Ted Mascott, who was with Merck in the Netherlands for many years, says that he didn't realize that one major obstacle was in the way of his becoming truly effective in implementing certain changes in that office. The fact was that all his personnel knew he would be leaving in a few years. They had, therefore, little incentive to change other than superficially, and little commitment to this American manager who would not be around long enough to affect their careers. International managers must have a mandate from home. If your overseas personnel, agents or other business colleagues do not think you are acting with authority and with the implicit backup of your bosses, your position will be weak. If they think the next manager to come along is going to change everything you have established, they will not be deeply committed to programs you are trying to install.

It is important for you to ask for and get from headquarters whatever manifestations of support you need—visits from home-office officials, placards for the walls, publicity, manuals—whatever makes sense in your particular situation. The blessing of higher-level people who will be around for the long term will very much affect your ability to manage and motivate personnel.

MEANWHILE, BACK AT THE RANCH...

U.S. companies tend to go through at least three stages in going international. In phase one, the foreign market is considered inconsequential, so only a few truly interested and experienced managers take it on, become its champions and build the international business. In phase two, the foreign market becomes profitable but is still small enough to be used as a "dumping ground" for mediocre company executives who have little interest or experience in doing international work. Thus it becomes an unprofitable group and many of the good people leave. In phase three, sometime later, the market and the company mature to a point where management is ready to take it seriously and becomes willing to recruit people with international skills and experience, and ultimately, foreigners.

Rule 1: Senior management must make a long-term commitment.

If senior management is aware of these predictable phases and makes the decision to go international, the trap of phase two can be avoided. If headquarters is serious about developing international business, management and staff must think long term. Staffing for phase three means, for example, recruiting personnel people who know how to recruit for overseas, and controllers who know the budget requirements for overseas. In marketing it may mean extending the life cycle of a product that is winding down or being replaced in the U.S. market but may be in the introduction phase abroad. When management decides to invest in the international arena, executives must no longer think of the phase one ground-breakers as being too small a part of their business to warrant their time. To succeed in international business, you have to be serious about long-term relationships in the foreign country. That means you also have to be serious about long-term relationships with your own skilled and experienced international personnel.

Rule 2: Headquarters personnel must accept that they do not know everything.

A major problem for people in the field is that home-based personnel, both superiors and administrative staff, seem to think they know what is going on overseas—especially if they have done a little traveling. But it is impossible for anyone to know it all because "it" constantly changes. Each visit brings some new, unexpected turn of events. An environment can rapidly change.

Lut D'hondt of Raychem says: "If anyone understands the local situation, it should be the person in the field." Management must either trust the expertise of those people or replace them, because when home management persists in second-guessing the management in the field, only demoralization, errors in judgment and mounting problems for local management will result.

Gary Wederspahn of Moran, Stahl & Boyer says that international personnel "use up lots of chips trying to do what headquarters wants, meeting unrealistic deadlines, targets, prices and general company policy." One of MS&B's clients needed to raise its prices in Japan to cover increased production and distribution costs. Telexes went to the manager in Japan giving instructions for immediate price increases. When nothing happened, a second cable insisted and queried, "What's going on here?" Finally a corporate manager hopped on a plane and flew to Tokyo to give the sales manager and sales team a "talk." The Japanese listened and "agreed" to have prices in line by a certain date. Prices were increased, but the result was that customers didn't pay their bills or paid only the old price. Eventually headquarters got the message: prices are not increased abruptly in Japan. The sales force needs a long lead time to explain and prepare people for increases.

Rule 3: Get out there.

"The biggest contribution headquarters executives can make" says Joe Garcia of Mattel, "is to get out there." But when you do go, be sure that your actions enhance the image of the field personnel. By throwing your weight around (showing who's *really* boss), you can do great damage to field personnel's abilities to do their jobs.

All the advice in Rule 2 for field personnel applies in reverse for the home team: ask not to be favorably impressed but to be realistically informed. Try to understand why things are done the way they are and judge by results, not methods.

Rule 4: Try to relieve, not add to the expatriate's or traveler's stress.

International travelers may expect problems communicating with foreigners but often aren't prepared for the communication problem with headquarters. Field personnel can become extremely discouraged by an unsupportive bureaucratic machinery, especially when they are already thoroughly fatigued by the countless difficulties encountered in the international experience.

One essential element in relieving the stress experienced by international staff is flexibility. Rules need to bend. Solutions often must be unorthodox. Look for justifications to allow field requests, rather than looking for reasons to turn them down. Administrators at home must have the same "can do" attitude that allows the field people to tackle otherwise insurmountable obstacles.

"Visiting firemen" sometimes add to stress by demanding constant entertainment. One Hewlett-Packard expatriate, John Toppel, says: "If you're in a desirable place, having to deal with the tremendous numbers of business visitors can be a very hard thing. They require a great deal of social activity, much more than at home. Sometimes you wish they would take themselves out so you could stay home and read or spend time with your family."

Rule 5: Watch for the right time to bring people home.

After a certain period abroad, many expatriates "go native." This does not mean "doing things their way," but rather, shifting loyalties from the company to people and institutions on the local scene. The ideal is to be culturally assimilated enough to get the job done in the foreign context while still maintaining company standards. Certain things cannot be compromised—safety standards and fiscal integrity, for example. Yet immersion in a foreign culture may change one's own value system and business habits, for better or worse. Some people go native right away, some after five or ten years.

Management must help international personnel maintain the right balance between company and local requirements. One executive says: "After two years a person is just starting to be functional; after five years you have to watch out." And in the next assignment, going native may happen sooner. The only solution to this loss by attrition is to invest tremendous time and effort in preventing isolation: keep communicating and keep international personnel involved in the company process.

Rule 6: If you must send in new players, give them the same script.

One feature of American operations overseas has been the lack of a long-term perspective. Whenever bad news reaches headquarters, the standard solution is to send in a new general. Predictably, new management brings changes. Projects are shelved. New methods are instituted. New directions are taken. When projects are ended, local personnel have to withdraw from commitments, causing loss of trust and "face," which makes it difficult for staff to maintain working relationships in the local community. New management may be totally unaware of these repercussions, while employee morale may be devastated.

When there is constant turnover at the top, the local management and workers become skeptical about the solidity of new policies. Commitment will be low and participation half-hearted. When the top players are changed, the cast must have a sense that the show must go on. Without a script they will begin to make up their own lines. Consistency in direction is vital, and to ensure it, management at home must hire people who are sure to be around a long time, then take good care of them.

Consistency is important not only in management, but also in any function dependent on personal relationships—virtually all international positions. Foreign buyers, suppliers, agents and distributors, government officials and almost any other foreign business associates simply do not want to do business with someone who will be gone tomorrow. When you do have to move personnel, don't take all your people out at once. Stagger the changes so that you always have continuity in foreign country expertise as well as continuity of relationships.

SUMMARY

Rules for the Traveler and Expatriate

RULE 1: Keep in mind the two realities.
RULE 2: Bring your supervisors over.
RULE 3: Don't treat those at home like numbskulls.
RULE 4: Don't get confused about whose "side" you are on.
RULE 5: Like a balloon under water, keep bouncing up.
RULE 6: Make sure your overseas employees and contacts know you have the support of headquarters.

Meanwhile, Back at the Ranch . . .

RULE 1: Senior management must make a long-term commitment.

RULE 2: Headquarters personnel must accept that they do not know everything.

RULE 3: Get out there.

RULE 4: Try to relieve, not add to the expatriate's or traveler's stress.

RULE 5: Watch for the right time to bring people home.

RULE 6: If you must change the players, give them the same script.

CHAPTER II

MANAGING YOUR PERSONAL AND FAMILY LIFE

W E DEBATED about whether to include a chapter dealing with personal life in a book which is strictly business, and we were persuaded when every expatriate, international manager and traveler we asked said this could be the most important chapter of all. In their experience, supported by countless studies and confirmed by international personnel directors, the most frequent cause of an employee's failure to complete an international assignment is personal and family stress. This is of course particularly true for expatriates (employees and families moved abroad for extended periods), but disrupted home life was also a primary reason for frequent travelers to curtail their trips abroad, among both married and single employees.

It is hard enough for nontravelers to manage their jobs when personal and family problems arise. Overseas it is much more difficult to do your job under these circumstances, simply because you and your family members have few places to turn for moral support and emotional relief.

THE FREQUENT TRAVELER

Frequent travelers, both married and single, experience tremendous difficulties sustaining a life outside of work. It is hard to nurture relationships at home and it is often impossible when traveling to get psychic replenishment from family, friends and "outside interests" at home. Travelers say they frequently end up staying in their hotel rooms drinking alone and feeling depressed. One traveler, sent out for months at a time to various Persian Gulf locations, noticed that his Japanese competitors always seemed to travel in teams, and that their morale was consequently much higher.

Frequent travelers who have grappled with this problem say there are a few simple things you can do to reduce the stress of constant travel. First, they say, try to make a home away from home whenever possible. One consultant who flies to Tokyo and Paris says: "Look tirelessly for the right hotel, a homey place where people will remember you, where you feel comfortable, and always stay there, in the same room if possible." And if you are planning to be going back and forth from one location to another, consider keeping your hotel room so that you will not have to check out and reregister each time you return. It may cost a hundred dollars to keep your room in London while you hop over to Brussels, Dublin or Oslo for a day, but it is worth it not to have to pack up all your things. Another consultant advises: "Create a routine for yourself. Whatever you like to do, whether it's exercising or jogging or reading a good book, travel prepared to treat yourself regularly to the pastime of your choice."

The only way to maintain continuity with family and friends at home is to keep in touch, through regular letters and telephone calls. The expense of the communication must be weighed against the personal cost of severed or weakened relationships. Sending gifts to family, friends and even people at the home office helps keep your memory warm when you are on the road.

The single person who travels frequently faces great barriers to the establishment of a normal social life and sense of home. They are so often out of sight that they are also out of mind when friends plan parties or other social events. They may be as lonely at home as they are when traveling.

There is no cure that does not require a lot of effort. If you are single and travel frequently, it is up to you to call your friends when you come back to town (they are unlikely to keep track of your calendar) and to try to get into the swing of things. But more and more travelers are finding that sooner or later they must make a life choice, and frequently that choice is to quit their job and find something that requires less travel. Some have successfully renegotiated their responsibilities with upper management to the effect that they either travel less, have a more fixed schedule of travel, have longer vacations, or get other benefits such as the privilege of taking a "friend" along occasionally.

Because of the very real threat of losing good people who are simply tired of travel, more companies are trying to address the special needs of their single people who must move abroad or travel frequently. If you are experiencing distress, it is worth it to broach the subject with your employer and work toward constructive solutions.

THE EXPATRIATE

Culture shock is part of the overseas passage.

Almost everybody living overseas for any extended period experiences culture shock. It is an occupational hazard for expatriates and for people who travel so much that they spend most of their time in a foreign country.

People who have not spent much time abroad are often skeptical about culture shock. Most people, it seems, have a fairly romantic vision of what life must be overseas, and they assume people who suffer culture shock are like the kid at summer camp who was homesick or just didn't fit in, even when everyone else was having fun. Among those who don't know any better, there is a stigma of weakness attached to the person who has "adjustment problems" in a foreign country.

So let's set the record straight from the start. Culture shock is not poor adjustment. It has little to do with strength of character. The person who suffers the symptoms of culture shock is not weak or incapable.

Culture shock is the result of stress overload, stress caused by the barrage of hundreds of jarring and disorienting incidents, many so subtle we hardly notice and many so disturbing that we may feel seriously threatened. In order to understand culture shock, you have to remember that our ability to function in the world depends on our ability to read hundreds of signs, respond to subtle cues, and to behave according to countless explicit and implicit rules. At home we know how to read street signs, we know how to use the telephone, or how much to tip. We pick up signals when it is time to end a meeting or leave a party, or change a subject. Usually we get the joke. Much of what we do is automatic, requiring little thought or effort.

Overseas the reverse is true. Simple tasks become difficult because our accustomed resources are unavailable; we miss routine things like the telephone directory or shopping bags. Things are done differently, or we can't communicate what we want. Moment by moment we suffer the tiniest anxieties because we don't know how to behave, our actions and words don't get the expected responses, and we don't understand the messages we are getting. The signs we are accustomed to are gone. We are confronted with new ways of doing, thinking and valuing. Our own common sense or logic no longer seems to apply. Anxiety becomes a permanent state of being. As one expatriate put it: "It's like being in an exam twenty-four hours a day." This is culture shock—the disorientation that causes perpetual stress.

Generally, culture shock is experienced by people who settle overseas for extended periods. Tourists do not experience it because they are protected from the culture, not having to worry about repairing shoes, dealing with servants, or the hundreds of other mundane tasks that people living abroad must face. Business travelers, too, are protected because their experience is usually limited to hotels and restaurants where people are trained to serve foreigners.

No one is immune to culture shock, even after many international experiences. And the impact of culture shock does not depend on an individual's intelligence, education, race or job. The ambassador, corporate vice president, platform worker or secretary must all face the stresses of adjusting to a new environment. Expatriates who have lived in several countries say that you experience culture shock in each new country, regardless of where you go. For some, subsequent adjustments are easier; for others, each move becomes more difficult.

The phases of culture shock are predictable.

Experts reject the concept of culture shock as a malady that one catches and then gets over. It is not something that strikes suddenly or results from a single event. Instead, it builds up over time, an accumulation of minor or major cultural confrontations that may be difficult to pinpoint. Experts now prefer to describe culture shock as a "cycle of readjustment," marked by four phases. It helps to know them. So many returned travelers say, "If only I had known that what I was going through was normal! I thought I was going crazy and had to keep it a big ugly secret. I was afraid to seek help."

Phase 1: In the beginning, you go through a euphoric period, the "tourist phase" when you take a lot of pictures and are excited about the move. You may notice how surprisingly similar things are to home, and things that are dissimilar seem merely quaint.

Phase 2: Soon elements of the new culture begin to intrude, and they are no longer always enchanting. Your curiosity is overtaken by irritation, impatience, frustration, anger and depression. Minor nuisances become catastrophic upsets. You feel helpless and drained, emotionally and physically. Family members bicker more than normally or begin to complain about the country and local people. Differences become blown out of proportion, and harsh judgments will be made: "These people just don't value human life." People at this stage show all the symptoms of being under pressure. Some people withdraw, develop obsessions (about cleanliness, fear of foreigners, overeating or sleeping), or become overtly hostile and aggressive.

Phase 2 may last for months, and it is a terrible time. It affects the employee's performance at work, children's adjustment at school, and the spouse's ability to provide family support at home. It does not affect only the individuals involved, but the whole family dynamic. Fortunately, reactions usually hit different family members at different times, so that individuals are better able to help each other. And they must—adjustment is a process to be worked on by family members together.

Phase 3: If they don't pack up and go home during Phase 2, an individual or family eventually begins to learn, to change and to adapt. This is a "pulling-up" period, in which you begin to accept local ways, or accept negative feelings but find better ways to handle them. Self-confidence returns; you feel less isolated and more comfortable. You can now look onward and upward.

Phase 4: At last you come to feel at home and to truly enjoy the country and culture. Your sense of humor returns, you have made friends, you "know the ropes." *You* are now the local expert who can give advice. Newcomers can now cry on *your* shoulder.

Phases may repeat. Bob Kohls, director of Washington International Center, says you can expect two low points during an overseas tour, and that the length and severity of culture shock vary with the individual and the assignment. Some people don't get to Phase 4, but suffer so severely in Phase 2 that they must return home, or worse, continue in the assignment without help. One study used in the State Department indicates that 5 percent of expatriates experience severe problems, including drug addiction, alcoholism and nervous breakdown, sometimes even suicide. Another 5 percent was described as "escapers, beachcombers, going native." These statistics should not frighten but make the point that culture shock is real and serious. If you think you need help, you should certainly get it, and know that you are not alone. Virtually every expatriate, all those seemingly well-adjusted folk you will see around you, have experienced it. Because the problem is real, more and more American communities abroad offer professional counseling.

Fortunately, culture shock is predictable, patterned and manageable. If you are prepared, you can control it. If you don't take steps to deal with it, it can be expensive in time, money and heartache.

The single expatriate can have a very lonely experience.

The single person abroad experiences many of the same difficulties as the family person—culture shock is the same for everyone. But a complaint unique to the single person is severe loneliness. The expatriate community is largely family-oriented; the married expatriate has a family to return to each evening after work. As a single person, it is important to find opportunities to be with other people. Do not go directly home each day. Friendships are very important—no one should have to deal with culture shock by themselves.

The spouse faces a much greater challenge than the employee.

The employee has the support of the organization, a defined role and often a familiar work routine. The employee has some continuity—contact with colleagues, corporate goals and so on. For the spouse, on the other hand, everything is likely to be new, and the assignment may well be much harder. Harold Sheets, of Mobil Oil, says: "The spouse has far more adjusting to do." Male or female, the expatriate spouse is often left in a vacuum, not allowed to work and isolated from friends. Transportation and telephones may be unavailable, so the spouse becomes housebound and cut off from the world. Career or other activities must be suspended, and even parenting may be put into the hands of servants or boarding schools. The spouse must accept a support role to the employee. In many countries this role is severely limited, especially if the spouse is a woman—as is usually the case. (Married women are virtually never offered international assignments; less than 3 percent of expatriate managers are women.) In Saudi Arabia, women are not allowed to drive, and in Belgium they must have their husband's written permission to have a checkbook. A wife overseas typically ends up with lots of responsibilities but little authority. She tends to suffer feelings of depersonalization, loneliness and boredom. As Jim Peterson, of 3M, says: "The wife will cry a bucket of tears."

While the spouse copes with a tremendous sense of loss and isolation, she must grapple with the new on all fronts: figuring out how to buy the right size bathtub stopper in a foreign language; spending hours at the bank or an entire day in customs; learning how to supervise a house full of servants. Often the help companies give wives misses the mark because the wives themselves have not been directly asked about their needs. Cross-cultural consultant George Renwick says: "I talk with the men often. They know me and talk very honestly. When I ask them about their wives, they answer, 'Oh, getting along quite well.' But when I talk with the wives, I get a very different picture. So my advice to the men is: Never assume that you understand what the women are going through. If any decisions are to be made that will affect them, it is the women who should make those decisions."

"What's in it for her?" is a very important question. Depending on the wife's age, career and personality, lack of motivation is a factor in her adjustment. Noel Slocum, president of International Relocation Resources in Chicago, says: "To do well abroad one must be highly motivated to succeed. The employee usually is, but the wife often does not see direct payoffs. It is important for her to have her *own* goals and objectives." Her attitude is critical; by far the greatest number of early returns result from family-related, not job-related problems. If the spouse is unhappy or unable to adapt, the employee may return before the tour is complete. Nessa Loewenthal, president of Trans Cultural Services in Orinda, California, says: "The employee can get another job, but he can't get another wife." The employee must involve his family in making the decision to go abroad and ensure that their needs are met overseas. The employer should treat the spouse as part of the overseas team and provide the necessary support.

Children mirror their parents' attitudes and reactions.

Children typically adjust very well abroad if the parents are good role models and support them in dealing with their fears, expectations and losses. Schooling, medical care and other basic family needs are real concerns and should be carefully researched before the family leaves home. However, children should not be an exaggerated concern: unless your requirements are unusual, you can expect to find whatever resources your children will need.

The overseas experience can be the time of your life.

Those who are prepared and who have good adaptive abilities say they wouldn't take back their travels for anything. Many say the experience brought the family closer together, a feeling that stayed with them even years after their return. Spouses often have more time to spend together and become better friends. Certainly travelers feel themselves enriched and their horizons expanded.

Nevertheless, change is always hard. There is always a sense of loss and perhaps trepidation mixed with the excitement. Proper preparation and the right attitudes are essential. If family commitment to the move is strong, the experience is likely to be a good one. Living overseas is a family experience—those "coming along for the ride" will be in trouble. All must want to go and be willing to pull together. A little hesitation is normal, but anyone who decides that "this really is not for me" should not go.

An American law student agreed to quit school and move with her husband to Jiddah, where he was going to work for a hospital corporation. She says: "I thought I would be the right kind of person to go into an environment like that. I had moved throughout the U.S.A. and always adjusted well. I found that was not a valid assumption.

"You don't believe it until you get there. You hear only what you want to hear, and the company paints a rosy picture. You feel deceived—you hate the company. It would have been better if they had told me about the smell, the dirt, the goats, the insects in the rice. I should have been told that the men are never home. I did know that women can't drive or use public transportation and that there would be no theaters, no TV, no library, no phone and few restaurants. I had read a number of books. I knew all about Saudi Arabia intellectually—reality, however, is something else. It took me nine months to find a job at the American school. If you are a person who gets satisfaction out of accomplishment, it is very hard to sit around the pool and sew. It was hard on us as a family."

Prepare for the move long before you go.

Every experienced traveler stresses one piece of advice: "Know before you go." People who go abroad with unrealistic expectations run the greatest risk of failure. Yet people have such innocent illusions about foreign countries that they fail to do the kind of reconnaissance they would do right at home. No one would think of moving across town without checking out the neighborhood, schools, property values, and so on. Certainly it is easier and cheaper to drive across town than it is to fly abroad, but it is vastly more important to know what you are getting into overseas. Even without an exploratory trip, there is much that can be learned about the country and the culture.

TEN WAYS TO PREPARE FOR AN OVERSEAS ASSIGNMENT

1. Gather as much information as you can on the host country, past and present. Read about politics and religion, art and literature, national heroes. Visit your host country's consulate or national tourist offices for information.

2. Learn the fundamentals of the language. At the minimum, master pleasantries, and essential questions and phrases you will need so as to function comfortably in your first few weeks. Try to get at least 20–30 hours of language lessons before you leave home, and listen to language tapes to become used to new inflections and cadences.

3. Study maps so as to get a feel for the layout of the city or country. Draw your own simplified map showing only the major roads and landmarks, such as office, shopping, clubs and sights, in the areas where you will be living and working.

4. Practice using the currency. You should feel comfortable making change and should be able to calculate quickly the approximate value. A money packet can be obtained at most currency exchanges or international banks.

5. Learn the measurement system so you can comfortably read signs, instructions and package descriptions.

6. Set up a meeting with someone from the host country through a consulate, university or airline. Ask about the differences between your two countries and peoples. What bothers foreigners in your country will give you reverse clues to what might be problem areas for you over there. Be sure to ask about words or behavior which are to be avoided. Don't be shy —people love to talk about their country.

7. Talk with others who have lived in the country recently. Try to find someone who had a good experience. What positive, constructive advice can they give you?

8. If your family is going with you, spend time together talking about the move. Everyone should be briefed on the country. Are they accepting the assignment and feeling positive about it? Have you considered and resolved those issues that affect each member? Do all family members see that they have a part to play in making the move and living abroad? Specifically, what will the role and goals of the spouse be?

9. Arrange ways to say goodbye and to let go of your life here, but plan ways to keep in touch with friends. Take steps to pave the way for your return home. (See below about re-entry.)

10. Think about what you need to take with you to make you feel at home. Advice on this varies. Some people choose to leave everything behind and start anew in a new home. Others feel it is important to bring as much as possible to maintain the familiar. Many take a few favorite things for continuity but not everything. Whichever—it is important to think about your needs. If you have children, each should be given a box for bringing private treasure.

How to get medical help.

If you are not fluent in the necessary foreign languages, you may want to carry with you a list of English-speaking doctors around the world. The International Association for Medical Assistance to Travelers (IAMAT) in Lewiston, New York, has a free list of about 450 physicians (most trained in the United States, Canada or Great Britain) in 120 countries. Call (716) 754-4883 eight weeks before your trip. Intermedic Inc. in New York City also provides a list of doctors in about 190 foreign cities, for a $10 family membership fee. Call (212) 486-8900. International SOS Assistance, based in Geneva and Philadelphia, extends a variety of 24-hour medical services to injured or ill corporate travelers, worldwide. For information, call (800) 523-8930.

TEN WAYS TO COPE WHEN THE GOING GETS ROUGH

What helps one person will not help the next. You are going to have to find your own solutions, but some prescriptions that have helped others include:

1. Review and review. Reread the information you read when you prepared for the overseas assignment, and keep learning about the country and the people. Experts say the best antidote to culture shock is a sense of mastery of and knowledge about where you are. Read more local history and literature. Learn more of the language. Understand the religion.

2. Look for the local logic. Explore the reasons for what is going on around you, from the point of view of the local people. Is your staff or the maid really lying to you or are they being polite? Were the neighbors laughing at you or just nervous? Are people always late or are you rushed?

3. Make a friend. Some experts think that the way to establish a feeling of home abroad is to develop just one close relationship with a local person. That friend can explain and help you understand many situations. Many travelers say that some of the most meaningful friendships in their lives have been with other overseas Americans or expatriates from other countries. Reach out for those friendships.

4. Avoid complainers who refuse to adapt, and don't get stuck in the American ghetto. Almost any location to which you may be assigned has an American community where expatriates cluster. Those who never venture out of the ghetto are less likely to succeed.

5. Don't neglect your partner. Work together as a family. Your spouse is a partner in a joint venture and must be given respect and support. This is a responsibility of both company and employee, but the spouse usually must ask for it.

6. Use the gift of time. Don't spend all your time at the office. Get out and make contacts—you need to meet people socially as well as for business. Single people particularly must work on ways to meet people—taking classes, volunteering, participating in sports, teaching at a local university. Many people abroad say they valued the opportunity to enjoy life outside the "rat race of home."

Expatriates stress the importance of exploring what the country offers. Do something, anything, but don't stay at home. The families in our films succeeded so well because they were doers. One joined a gourmet club in Hong Kong. Another joined the Audubon Society in Venezuela and camped all over the country. Another explored the German wine country and took in all the German festivals. One family living in Saudi Arabia decided to see much of the world, traveling from Arabia throughout the Far and Middle East. Bob Rix, after his years in Indonesia and Saudi Arabia, says that many families hoard their money, saving it for their return home —a bad idea, in his opinion. If you don't treat yourself to all the advantages of being overseas, "you will spend that money on the psychiatrist's couch when you get home."

7. Don't burden yourself by denying reality when things go wrong—you *do* have maid trouble, school problems, house trouble, difficulty with transportation, and it *is* hot. And no one cares, that's true too. It is important to allow yourself your emotions, but try not to let them get the best of you. Take time to look for solutions.

8. Don't make comparisons with home. Constant comparisons with how things are done in the United States can only increase the frustration and

alienate your hosts. Expatriates say it is essential to accept the local ways and work with them—people are not going to change for you. It is easier to move forward when you are not looking backward.

9. Don't get hung up on being liked. One Japanese executive says: "Americans are too concerned about being loved everywhere, but that is not going to happen." You may reach a good level of friendship or respect, but rarely if ever the kind of relationship that is reached between compatriots. Don't worry when people act as if they don't like you; don't take things so personally. If you are the kind of person who needs to be loved by everyone, don't go—you will cost your company a lot of money if you come back early.

10. Be careful about the culture-shock cures you choose. One American woman, lonely during her husband's long trips, heard she could sleep better if she smoked a little marijuana each night. She got some from a friend and all went well until she became ill one night and called a doctor. When it was discovered what she had done, the family was repatriated in great shame. Many expatriates say alcohol is a menace because of the more active social life abroad and the stress. Some major multinational corporations now have alcohol- and drug-abuse counseling for their overseas personnel. Again, if you need help, *get it.*

"My fondest memories of Tokyo are bike riding with another American. We would get on our bikes and put 13 miles on our bikes in a day, just riding anywhere. It was a lot less threatening than driving a car. We would stop and look at shops; we would find neighborhood parades going on; we would eat lunch. We had a small business together, using Japanese fabric to make Western goods: placemats, napkins, clothes. And that would take us all over Tokyo, into little shops, into people's homes. You can have a tremendous time there if you just jump right in. Do it!"
Laurie Dorman, Bank of America, Tokyo

RE-ENTRY

A senior executive at a major construction company became emotional when we told him about *Welcome Home, Stranger,* the fourth film in our series. He said he had never heard re-entry spoken of as a problem, but he had suffered painfully when he returned after years abroad. He thought something was wrong with him and kept it a secret.

Re-entry is such a problem that it keeps many people from accepting a second overseas assignment. "I could get through culture shock again," said one repatriated executive, "but I just couldn't face coming home again." He had just turned down an assignment to a country where he had always wanted to go. A study by Korn/Ferry International some years ago found that well over half the polled repatriated executives thought that knowledge of re-entry problems was a factor in discouraging others from taking assignments abroad. Employers, on the other hand, seemed unaware that it was a factor.[1] Just before we produced the re-entry film, several corporations told us they would not buy it, saying, "We don't want our people to know what they are in for, because if they did, they wouldn't go."

But now those companies and many others are facing up to the fact that ignoring the problem has not been an effective response. One reason may be the costly "brain drain" of the corporation's international expertise. An outstanding number of repatriated personnel leave their companies shortly upon return from abroad. And seeing that international assignments may be risky for one's long-term career, others in the company become unwilling to go.

Re-entry is a shock.

Most expatriates are not prepared for the terrific "comedown" they experience when they come home. Memories and myths of home—how it is cheaper, cleaner, better and more efficient—are shattered. Compared to Germany, America seems loud and dirty; after Brazil, people seem too rushed and impersonal. The bureaucracy here is slow too, waiters are rude, and crime a constant concern. You are not likely to have servants, a chauffeur and other perquisites. You are back to doing your own housekeeping and catching the 7:32 with all the other commuters. And if returning to the same community you left, you find it is not really the same place at all. The cost of living is much higher. The neighborhood has changed. Former neighbors have moved away. Home is not the home you expected it to be. The disappointment can be overwhelming.

Re-entry shock would be a lesser problem if it were only a matter of letdown, dashed expectations, and return to a previous lifestyle. People would readjust just as they adjusted to culture shock overseas. But there is a difference. There is an outstanding lack of psychic support and outlet for the returning expatriate. Overseas, travelers somewhat expect difficulties, and they get reassurance and moral support from the natural bonding that occurs among people who feel "we are all in this together." But when you come back to the United States, you and your family feel alone; you get little understanding or opportunity to share your feelings. Virtually everyone who returns is shocked by the lack of interest of people at home. Friends say, "I'm dying to hear all about Indonesia," but soon they switch the subject to last weekend's football game. Returnees need to talk about their experience—a major event in their lives—yet no one will listen. One executive says: "It's one thing to feel different from an Arab or Asian, but worse to feel alienated from your own people. If you talk about your overseas experience, people don't know how to relate to you—you don't fit in."

Children in particular have a hard time. They are different, more sophisticated, literally more worldly than children who have not left their home country. At the same time, they may feel odd not knowing the latest slang, rock and television stars, or ways to dress.

Re-entry is a problem at work too.

The expatriate typically has greater autonomy, authority, prestige, and salary. The heads of American company offices in remote locations are treated as dignitaries. They and their spouses have elevated social status— dinner with the Premier and Ambassador perhaps. At work the expatriate manager is like the corporate president. But back home, he or she becomes just another middle manager whose opinion is no longer sought, and who has fewer major decisions to make. Says HP's John Toppel: "Overseas you are used to being somebody. You get your way a lot. It's hard for Americans to come back and lose that feeling of importance and power." The Korn/ Ferry study showed that 93 percent of repatriated employees missed the "decision-making autonomy," and 80 percent missed the responsibility. Jobs at home were not nearly as satisfactory as their jobs abroad.

Loss of status and remuneration is also a problem. Take-home salary may be half what it was overseas, and with inflation even a promotion may feel like a demotion. 3M's Jim Peterson says: "You sell both cars when you go over but when you come back you can hardly afford to buy one car."

The greatest challenge of all facing the returning employee is how to use new skills and knowledge and find a meaningful place in the corporation. Repatriates often suffer the consequences of being "out of sight, out of mind" when job promotions are considered. (In the Korn/Ferry study, 69 percent of those surveyed felt they suffered from that problem.) Upon return they find that people either don't remember them at all, or worse, think of them as they were years earlier, like a younger sibling who never grows up. It is hard to demonstrate your new maturity and aptitudes in the home setting, especially in a typically less demanding job. Motorola is tackling the problem by providing re-entry workshops complete with videotapes to help employees better merchandise themselves when they come home. Jim McCarthy says the expectation that "If I do a good job overseas, I will have a good job coming back" is erroneous. A good performance and effective communication are what it takes.

Prepare for re-entry as seriously as you prepared to go abroad.

Preparing for re-entry is like preparing for old age—you don't begin when you are seventy. There are a number of steps you can take at various stages of an overseas assignment to prepare for the eventual return:

1. Before you go overseas, say goodbye to friends and the lifestyle you have in the United States. Plan ways to keep in touch with friends, but bear in mind that you and they will have changed before you meet again.

2. Find a sponsor at work who will look out for your interests while you are gone, to keep your name "alive" in the organization, and to keep others informed of your progress abroad. This may be easier said than done, but it's worth the effort.

3. While abroad, communicate often with family, friends and colleagues. Frequent short notes are better than infrequent voluminous letters. Send photographs. Keep in contact with the home office: describe your successes, what you are learning, and what new skills you will bring back with you. Make frequent trips home, and each time stop in to see as many colleagues and superiors as possible.

4. At the end of your tour of duty, before returning to the United States, do what you did before you went abroad: do your homework. Research the things you will need to know about schooling, real estate, your job back home. At the same time, begin opening doors at home: write and ask people what you should bring them. Create anticipation for your return.

5. Upon returning home, readjust your expectations and don't constantly compare the present with your life overseas. Forgive your country for not being what you had built it up to be. Think back to what worked for you when you first went abroad—those things may help you now in your return home.

6. Distill your experience into one or two significant things. Share those things with people close to you. Don't expect people to listen to much more than that.

7. Be sure to listen to people who stayed home. They too have grown. What has happened in their lives?

8. Find new friends who, like you, have lived in other cultures. Don't expect your old friends to fit your new needs.

9. Find ways to put your overseas experience to use at home, at work, at school or community group, perhaps with foreign students or refugees. At work, find ways to use your new talents and expertise—short- and long-term. Think about how you have grown professionally and what new skills you bring—you may have to point these out to your superiors, who may act as though you have been on ice the whole time you were gone and have come back at the same level as when you left.

10. Think about how you can preserve the experience. Consider keeping up with your former country, with its language, going to its restaurants,

cooking its dishes, maintaining contact with friends there, keeping photographs and souvenirs, and so on.

SUMMARY

The Frequent Traveler

Frequent travelers can experience tremendous difficulties sustaining a life outside of work. Try to create continuity and routine. Maintain contact.

The Expatriate

Culture shock is a part of the overseas passage. The phases of culture shock are predictable. The single expatriate can have a very lonely experience. The spouse may face a greater challenge than the employee. Children mirror their parents' attitudes and reactions. The overseas experience can be the time of your life. Prepare for the move long before you go.

Ten Ways to Prepare for the Overseas Assignment

1. Read and learn about the culture.
2. Learn the language.
3. Study maps.
4. Practice the currency.
5. Learn measurements.
6. Meet someone from the country.
7. Talk to someone who has been there.
8. Prepare as a family.
9. Arrange goodbyes.
10. Take what you need to make a home.

Ten Ways to Cope when the Going Gets Rough

1. Review and renew.
2. Look for the local logic.
3. Make a friend.
4. Avoid complaining Americans.
5. Don't neglect your partner.
6. Use the time.
7. Don't deny reality when things are bad.
8. Don't make comparisons with home.
9. Don't get hung up on being liked.
10. Be careful about the culture-shock cures you choose.

Re-entry

Re-entry is a shock at home. Re-entry is a problem at work too. Prepare for re-entry as seriously as you prepared to go abroad.

CHAPTER 12

THE ROAD TO SUCCESS

✦ ✦

*What does it take
to be a winner?*

"AT THE RISK OF STATING THE OBVIOUS," says Frank De Angeli, Johnson & Johnson's senior international executive, "the essential ingredient in conducting international business is people . . . having the right people in international assignments." Some people are just not cut out for international work, and some are effective and happy in some cultures but not in others. Before making or accepting an overseas assignment, careful selection and honest *self-selection* is a process warranting serious attention.

Are you internationable?

What are the characteristics of people who are successful overseas? When we analyze everything we have learned from international travelers, expatriates, heads of personnel, foreigners and diplomats, we can boil down to one word the difference between people who do especially well abroad and those who do not: *breadth.*

The person who does well abroad must know not only the job and company, as he or she does at home, but also the cultural patterns, business norms, and national character of the assigned country. This knowledge must be founded on an understanding of the country's history, arts, politics, economic conditions, and so on. Those who succeed show breadth of knowledge and intellectual curiosity, but also breadth of character—an open-arms and open-eyes personality. They are what one expert calls "geocentric" in attitude, thinking in world terms and seeing opportunities, not constraints, in the millions of differences they encounter abroad.

Looking closely at the personalities, attitudes and skills of people who perform at high levels of excellence abroad, we have settled on seven success traits that seem to define the person of "breadth," and which make the difference, wherever the assignment and whatever the job. Of course, in certain countries individuals will need qualities peculiarly adapted to the demands of the particular environments, and careful attention should be paid to those unique demands.

Success trait 1: hard like water.

Claus Halle, president of Coca-Cola's international soft-drink business sector, says: "The key to developing our international business lies not in the rigid application of a global strategy, but in a flexible planning system, heavily reliant on input from the market and able to respond quickly to shifts in local growth and competitive conditions."

Hans Becherer, senior vice president of Deere & Company's Overseas Division, says much the same: in a word, the key to international success is "flexibility." "A company needs all the attributes and qualities that make it successful in its home market," Becherer says. "In addition, it must take into account differences in culture and marketplace, as well as international realities such as shifting currencies and political relationships." The international individual, like the international company, needs to be adaptable to succeed abroad.

Words such as "flexible" and "adaptable" should not suggest an individual who is weak, malleable, compliant, a pushover. Our successful people abroad are not pushovers. They do not bend to every wind, nor adapt like chameleons to each circumstance—quite the contrary. But neither are they rigid, immovable or unimpressionable. They are what the Japanese would call "hard like water." Water goes with the flow, bending with the turns in the riverbed, but it's water that carved out the Grand Canyon. Water is soft and takes the shape of its container, but water can carry the load of a thousand-ton ship. The internationable person and water have another trait in common: if you watch the river, you will see that it is always the same while it is always changing.

Don't take a romantic view of "hard like water," however. People who have that trait are still people—engineers, consultants, marketers and lawyers. They are people who get where they want to go by hitching a ride on the local form of transportation. When necessary, they leave their task orientation aside in cultures where personal rapport is more important in business, and they concentrate on reaching their goals through relationships instead. They can relax and ride with events, and they are able to accept failure without despair. Everybody fails at something overseas.

People who make the best out of a situation seem to share another trait: a lively sense of humor. Many experts say an ability to laugh at oneself or a situation is one of the most important success traits, and we believe it. During the filming of *Going International,* we were impressed by the cheerful dispositions of our "stars"—all international travelers and expatriates —who were amused rather than dismayed when our crews totally took over their homes, rearranging furniture and turning off telephones and refrigerators. They had a "ready for anything" attitude. While we were creating havoc with her home, Laurie Dorman interviewed us about filmmaking. We suspect that truly internationable people are "experience collectors"—people who love the moment and then love it again in telling about it later. These were people who could tell us about the fun times they had, the wonderful things they did and saw, and laugh about the bad times. With few exceptions, those who had not done well overseas were full of complaints, bitterness, resentment—and had no funny tales to tell.

People who are hard like water are also patient, and patience is a requirement everywhere. No one flies into Beijing or Cairo or Rome one day, works out a deal the next day and returns home on the third day with the job complete. Most foreigners will not be hurried by the traveler's schedule. The American can be frustrated by weeks of delays, repetitious and microscopic attention to seemingly trivial details, and unexplained postponements. It took ARCO three and a half years to negotiate an offshore drilling contract with China. Rolm Corporation's first contract with the Japanese telephone company took two years and more than twenty trips to Japan, plus an investment of $1 million. Only those who can persist over the long term stand a chance of developing a strong foothold in the global market.

Success trait 2: resourceful independence through people.

People who do well internationally are resourceful, meaning that they have both plenty of internal resources and a comfortable willingness and ability to call upon the help of others. They are self-reliant, self-motivated and full of creative solutions to problems where others might be stuck. They are not afraid of taking responsibility alone, but they are not John Waynes. They are much more likely to enjoy and succeed by working with other people. In fact, they have a demonstrated ability to get results with limited resources by winning the cooperation of others.

Practically every chapter of this book stresses the importance of social and personal rapport and relationships in international business: to do business effectively in a foreign culture you must be accepted by the people. Individuals who are loners at home or who are unskilled in relating to their own people are not likely to be any better with people abroad, and should not be considered good candidates. "People skills" does not necessarily mean popularity, but rather the ability to establish communication, trust and respect.

Success trait 3: curiosity.

Curiosity never killed the international cat. To succeed abroad, one needs to be like an inquisitive child. The person of "breadth" is willing to try new things, to learn a language at age forty, to experiment with new ways of relating to people. Most important of all is the skill of listening. Foreign executives often say the greatest obstacle preventing most Americans from succeeding in business everywhere is their noticeably poor listening ability.

Mike Copeland, personnel services manager of Procter & Gamble's International Division, says his Japanese instructor told him "I'll teach you only one third of the words *you* think you will need. I'll train you to understand the other two thirds, but you will not need them to speak." The instructor's reason: "Americans talk too much and don't listen well enough."

Success trait 4: positive regard for others.

The foundation for successful interaction with people anywhere in the world is sincere respect for and interest in others. You are likely to do well abroad if you can show, through your words, body language and actions that you have empathy, are considerate of people's needs and feelings, are interested in their point of view, and are respectful of their ways. Moran, Stahl & Boyer's research shows that "acceptance of the foreign culture as a valid set of beliefs and customs" by the expatriate is essential to the foreigner's acceptance of the expatriate in his country.

The person of breadth is not only tolerant but appreciative of differences, and when confronted with things he or she cannot accept, shows diplomacy and tact. Foreigners from around the world can forgive the traveler's *faux pas* if they sense the traveler's sincere good will. Our person of breadth has an open and warm heart, and others know it.

Success trait 5: emotional stability.

International work inflicts stress. People who are emotionally insecure or unbalanced cannot hope to do well in foreign assignments of any duration. The emotional health of your family too may affect your performance abroad if you travel frequently, and especially if you move overseas. Expatriates whose spouses are unhappy with the move must often return home prematurely, at great cost to the company. International assignments are never viable solutions to family problems—invariably they only cause greater turmoil.

You must be emotionally secure enough to tolerate ambiguity. You must be able to face the unpredictable without great frustration and hostility; you must manage with dignity your anxiety or confusion when your situation is unclear. Price Cobbs, author of *Black Rage,* and president of Pacific Management Systems in San Francisco, suggests that the traveler ask, "Can I accept not knowing everything that is going on around me, not knowing what people are laughing at, not understanding the different ways they are doing things, not being in control?"

Success trait 6: technical competence.

International expertise is no substitute for business ability and professional competence. You will not be able to get help from the specialized talent you might be able to call upon at home. Your credibility depends on your professionalism and know-how.

Success trait 7: motivation.

If you really don't want to go abroad, don't. You will not do well if you or your family resist a move, or your frequent travel. Nor will you do well if you are going for the wrong reasons, such as escape from problems at home, or money. It may be difficult to say no and maintain your status in a large corporation, but you will be a bigger loser if you take the wrong job. There is no shame in being better suited to Chicago than to Karachi.

LET THE FACTS SPEAK FOR THEMSELVES.

It is hard to define precisely what makes one person very successful and another a failure overseas, so the success factors described above should be used only as guidelines. They are not hard and fast rules meant to exclude people who might be able to do well abroad in spite of handicaps.

TEN RULES OF THUMB FOR ALL OCCASIONS, ANYWHERE IN THE WORLD

Rule 1: Be a good guest.

When you travel abroad, you are a guest in every foreign country you visit. Just as when visiting a home in your own country, you must respect the host and the rules of the household. Learn to live with the way things are—it is not your role to change a culture.

Always remember whose country you are in. An Arab executive complained to us: "Americans in foreign countries have the tendency to treat the natives as foreigners, and they forget that actually it is they who are the foreigners themselves."

Rule 2: Do not be a freeloader.

More companies are realizing that their future abroad depends on the degree to which their presence in any country is perceived as contributing to the real welfare of the country. George Keller, Chevron Corporation's chief executive officer, recently stated: "To maintain a long-term relationship, it is essential to make sure that your role in a country reflects the needs and economic objectives of the host government and the people it represents." He emphasizes that benefits must accrue to both nations.

Rule 3: Slow down, take time to establish rapport.

Trust and relationships cannot be rushed. Wherever your business, don't neglect the preliminaries. Reaffirm the friendship first, and don't rush out at the end of a meeting. Before leaving, reaffirm friendship again.

Rule 4: Listen, watch, learn, assimilate.

Some people ask, "Why should I do the adapting? Why don't they adapt to me?" One thing to remember, whether you are working in France, India or Singapore, is that the foreigner has gone more than halfway to adapt to you. As consultant Nessa Loewenthal says, "He speaks your language. He watches American television shows and American movies. He reads American books and magazines. He knows about you, but you need to know more about him."

Get in the information flow. This will take sensitivity and trust building —most people will tell you only those things they feel will be received well. But you must listen intently to what others are saying. You learn a lot when you are not talking.

Some people believe they can do their job without ever going outside the American community or their office, avoiding contact with all but the local social elite. They are fooling themselves. You have to be close to the customer and work with your suppliers and agents, or you will be headed for failure.

Rule 5: Accept that there are some things you will never understand.

It is impossible to understand everything but don't be discouraged. You don't need to understand every little thing. The anthropologist Tom Rohlen states: "What is important is not your expertise but your ability to use what you do know to get results." A positive attitude will open many doors.

Rule 6: Don't be parochial.

Considering the demands and stresses of the international assignment, it is no surprise that some people are swept into the local drama, especially in crisis areas. Try not to become so immersed in the local scene that you lose sight of responsibilities that extend beyond your immediate personnel and local objectives.

Expatriates and travelers also risk being overly impressed by the high-level people with whom they have contact: royalty and other foreign heads of state, and diplomats. Consequently they may shy away from anything that might displease the local power holders. It is possible to be respectful without being obsequious, and to preserve relations with foreign dignitaries while making sound, if sometimes unpleasant business decisions.

Rule 7: Take care of yourself.

Get plenty of sleep, exercise and healthy food. Get out and get fresh air. Take walks. If you get sick, stop pushing; get a doctor and stay in bed.

Rule 8: Be yourself.

Be yourself. You cannot be anyone else. Be respectful of the culture, but assimilate in ways that are comfortable for you. People generally like and are interested in Americans. And if you want a hamburger and a milkshake to make yourself feel better, go ahead. Go to the All American Club if there is one in town. You need a breather from all that cross-cultural effort. It's okay to admit that it *is* an effort.

Rule 9: Treat the generalities in this book as hypotheses.

Every individual with whom you work is unique, and every situation will demand its own solutions. Use this book as a guide, not a book of law.

Rule 10: Choose to succeed.

When you prepare to go international, decide whether you want results—or reasons for not getting results. There are hundreds of excuses available for explaining failures abroad; many of them are quite credible. But instead of rationalizing away mistakes and disappointments, try to learn from every misstep—and move forward. Don't settle for excuses. Choose to succeed.

Now It's Up to You

In addition to reading this book, there are a lot of things you must do to prepare for your travels. After putting this book down, we suggest you proceed as follows:

Do your homework.

This book has not given you enough information about individual countries. You need to learn as much as possible about *where you are going.* You also must make sure you understand your *own culture,* and are thoroughly familiar with the history, values, and dynamics of your *own company.* Review the preparation recommended in Chapter 11 and pursue the resources described in the appendices.

To prepare for an international assignment, study the following subjects:

1. Social and business etiquette
2. History and folklore
3. Current affairs, including relations between the country and the USA
4. The culture's values and priorities
5. Geography, especially the cities
6. Sources of pride: artists, musicians, novelists, sports, great achievements of the culture, including things to see and do
7. Religion and the role of religion in daily life
8. Political structure and current players
9. Practical matters such as currency, transportation, time zones, hours of business
10. The language

Plan an entrance strategy.

Before leaving for a new country, set up realistic objectives, with limited expectations for short-term accomplishments. Priorities must be clear, and you should concentrate on only a selected few of those priorities. It will be impossible to succeed in all of the activities you might at home, and it is important that you and your employer recognize that.

Accountability should be well defined and agreed upon when you accept an assignment, making clear exactly what authority you, as expatriate or traveler, have while away, and to whom reports should be made. Develop a work plan so that misunderstandings will be avoided down the road.

Get a good mentor.

Every successful expatriate and traveler stresses the importance of a mentor —a cultural informant in the country who knows your country and company. Many people find it most reassuring to have two mentors. One is the local national, ideally someone on your own staff who is expert on local matters, up to date on company affairs, and who also understands Americans. You need someone who will call you off to the side and explain when you have done something the wrong way, and gently steer you toward greater understanding and skill in handling situations. The other ideal mentor is the American who has been in your job or a similar situation, and has performed well. You can learn from those who have gone before if they have no ax to grind. Even if they do have an ax to grind they may be useful if you use them not for advice about what to do but for historical information—what did they do and what were the results?

Whether the mentor is a native of the country or an American, it is important to have someone you can trust to coach you through the intricacies of giving a talk to the employees, or selling the product, or just finding a place to live. It may be hard to find such a coach, but they do exist. One executive recommends participating in local activities as a good way to find a mentor, as well as the standard business outlets, like the chambers of commerce and trade clubs.

Practice.

Before you face your first foreign client, employee, customer or government official, you must practice your new international style until you no longer feel like a total idiot. All your reading, all your academic knowledge, will be of little use if you do not develop ease in dealing with people of another culture. Growing up, we learn the nuances of our own culture so profoundly that we must be shaken loose from our old habits before we can hope to become comfortable with other ways of thinking and behaving. Like the natural talent of the musician or artist, cross-cultural skills must be developed. Just as we must practice when we are learning to play the piano, so we must work to become skilled in the ways of another culture. Not everyone can become a cross-cultural Beethoven, but most people should be able to attain passable competence in a foreign culture.

The Chinese say the journey of a thousand miles begins at the ground beneath our feet. It may seem forbidding to try to learn about another people, but every step you take toward learning is a step in the right direction. No matter where you are going, your performance and your personal pleasure will be in direct proportion to the amount of effort you devote to learning about the people and the culture of your destination.

SUMMARY

The internationable person is characterized in a word: *breadth.*

Success Traits That Define the Internationable Person

1. Hard like water.
2. Resourceful independence through people.
3. Curiosity.
4. Positive regard for others.
5. Emotional stability.
6. Technical competence.
7. Motivation.

Let the Facts Speak for Themselves

Ten Rules of Thumb for All Occasions, Anywhere in the World

1. Be a good guest.
2. Do not be a freeloader.
3. Slow down, take time to establish rapport.
4. Listen, watch, learn, assimilate.
5. Accept that there are some things you will never understand.
6. Don't be parochial.
7. Take care of yourself.
8. Be yourself.
9. Treat the generalities of this book as hypotheses.
10. Choose to succeed.

Now It's Up to You

Do your homework.
Plan an entrance strategy.
Get a good mentor.
Practice.

WOMEN IN INTERNATIONAL BUSINESS

The astronaut Sally Ride tells the story of a little boy who watched the hours of television coverage of her first space flight. When it was all over, the child turned to his mother and said, "Mommy, can boys grow up to be astronauts too?"

The ratio of women to men in space is greater than the ratio of women to men involved in international business. Women represent less than 3 percent of American expatriate managers. One study of 686 North American firms found *no* firm that sent a woman abroad alone, and when asked about women managers overseas, affirmative-action–conscious firms tended to inflate figures by including women who were not overseas managers—women who had taken brief business trips or women in secretarial positions.[1] Banks prove to be way ahead of other industries: one third of women expatriates are sent by banks. Nancy Carter of Chase Manhattan says, "There is no country where we could not send a woman." Women make up 10 percent of Chase's expatriate work force, and they participate in all functions of banking: client service, marketing, government relations and institutional banking.

In her ground-breaking research, McGill professor Nancy Adler found that American employers present three reasons to explain why women are not sent abroad: (1) women don't want to go, (2) companies won't send them (even if one manager wanted to make the assignment), and (3) foreigners are prejudiced against women and it would be bad for the company to send them. Research has shown that two of these three arguments are without foundation in fact. Surveys of men and women graduating MBAs found no difference in their international aspirations —if anything, women were *more* interested in international assignments.[2] Surveys of managers in multinational corporations have found that the majority would be inclined to send women to head an overseas subsidiary if they did not fear the resistance of foreign superiors, subordinates, colleagues and clients.[3] Others suggest that corporate executives fear that women could not master the international "game," but most company managers have not known any women employed abroad. They have known only expatriate wives who have had difficulties adjusting, and may be assuming the *wife's* problem to be a *woman's* problem. Experience shows that the role of the spouse is much more difficult than the role of the manager, male or female, but there is no evidence that women perform less well than men. Quite the contrary.

It certainly is true that women are treated differently than men in some countries. However, cross-cultural consultants, executives who have supervised women in international management, and internationally experienced women generally agree that foreign prejudice has been exaggerated. The real problem is in the mind of U.S. decision makers, not the foreigners who must work with women assigned overseas.

In some places, such as the Philippines, Thailand, USSR, Eastern Europe and China, women are much more visible in the work force. Until recently the Foreign Trade Minister in China was a woman; Madame Chen is now president of the People's Bank of China. And elsewhere women are making gains, as they are in the United States. Edith Cresson is France's Foreign Trade Minister, and a woman chairs the board of a major Swiss company. In Kuwait a woman heads one of the largest contracting companies, and Ms. Wanda Ale created no ripples when appointed U.S. Commercial Attaché to Kuwait in 1983. Saudi Arabia and some other Gulf countries have the strongest restrictions on women working, yet even here there are dichotomies. American women are treated differently than local women. Moreover, Islamic law permits women to conduct their own business affairs, consequently many Arab women have sizable personal funds. All-women banking centers are growing. The Saudi government supports education for women and child-care programs. In this country of contrasts, where women wear the latest French fashions under their abayas, a woman can work if she is needed. Japanese women, too, are changing roles. JETRO recently dispatched its first all-woman buyers' mission to America to represent Japanese companies interested in importing U.S. products. The women met with business leaders to discuss Japan's market and to conduct trade negotiations with U.S. companies.

How local women are treated in a country is not necessarily an indication of how American business women will be treated. A better measure would be how Americans are treated. Experienced travelers say that foreigners respond to a woman first as an American and second as a representative of the company, and only third as a woman. And when it comes to gender, being female may even be an advantage. One trader, after a year in the United Arab Emirates, complained that women managed to get meetings with people who could not find time to meet with him, and when women got in, they had the benefit of longer meetings and were remembered afterward. "The women were visible and unusual," he said. "I was just some other guy trying to get business." Chase Mannattan's Nancy Carter agrees: "In banking, being a woman is an asset, not a liability, because an educated woman is considered special. An aura sets her apart." Others say that some of the socializing influences on girls and women in the U. S. give them skills that are success requirements abroad: listening ability, concern for harmonious relations, adaptability, and so on. When a woman is given the backing of a large firm, barriers either do not materialize or are less formidable than expected.

With increasing competitiveness in the international arena, American organizations must become more sophisticated in using male and female human resources abroad. Even the small percentage of women in international management represents a significant increase from the past; Nancy Adler says that "only five years ago almost no women existed in international management in expatriate status and very few in professional travel status."

Women travelers must be prepared for all the cross-cultural difficulties that their American male colleagues experience. In addition, they certainly will encounter foreign men who, like some American men, will not take them seriously. In Latin America an especially attractive woman may trigger the macho response. In Saudi Arabia, women generally cannot work in the same environment as men, except in an American company, in nursing and some newer fields where roles have not been established. In Australia, a woman may violate protocol by joining the men after dinner, when they prefer to go off with their male "mates," leaving the women to chat among themselves. It is particularly hard for the foreign woman returning to her own country if local women are not accepted at work; one Japanese woman, for example, returned to Tokyo with her Ph.D. in computer science and could find work only in tea service until an American firm hired her in personnel.

The solution to these cultural quirks is the same for women and men: adapt. The woman who understands the culture and can finesse her way through the local customs, and who is bringing a product, project or expertise that the foreign country needs, can succeed. Colombe Nicholas, president of Christian Dior U.S.A., says: "The most important thing is the image you project. Don't talk about being a woman—just do a good job. Show confidence. Be professional. Don't have a chip on your shoulder."

There are countless stories that seem to prove the point that women are bad for overseas business, but often there is more to the story than is told. Take, for example, the story of a woman vice president of an American firm who headed a delegation to Saudi Arabia. When invited to one of the Saudis' homes for dinner, the American woman, even though she was head of the delegation, was rather quickly escorted into a separate room for the women. Realizing what was taking place, and feeling that she was not being accorded due respect, she joined the men. "Needless to say" remarks the storyteller, "the dinner ended quickly and discussions were broken off." The story did not have to end this way. If the woman had understood the culture, she could have headed trouble off when she first got the invitation. She should have very courteously declined the dinner, showing utmost respect for the Saudi culture by not forcing her presence upon the men. Then she should have called her male subordinates together and given them clear instructions on how to behave themselves (if necessary), and strict admonishment against making any decisions or commitments. Business discussions would proceed the next day. Says Apple Computer's Ron Boring: "In all such awkward situations, the woman must take the high road."

A similar story is told about a World Bank delegation, which included two women, that was sent to South Korea to negotiate with the Central Bank and other major commercial bank personnel. The American telling the story concludes: "The Koreans wondered what they had done wrong and why women were sent. It upset the entire protocol and manner in which the delegation was received." Koreans, like most Asians, hate surprises, and the arrival of two women was astonishing to them.

Of course the meeting was disastrous. Advance communications should have presented the names and credentials of the negotiation team, emphasizing the women's expertise, authority and status. Time is needed to cultivate business relationships and establish professional credibility. And most important, symbols of authority and proper endorsement from the home office are necessary.

The most irksome problem facing women overseas is sexual harassment, not at work but *outside* work. Women professionals as well as expatriate wives and daughters complain that their greatest aggravation abroad is men touching, staring, making obscene noises or following them. Part of the behavior can be attributed to the foreign male's confusion, misinterpreting the American woman's dress or behavior as a "come on." Particularly in Islamic countries, women must dress to avoid exposure of arms and legs or shape. Even girls as young as eleven or twelve wear the veil in many countries—a Western woman in her business suit or running around in shorts and T-shirts is violating rules meant to protect women in that culture. Janet Wells, director of the international division of Insta-Graphics, says she wears her business clothes even in "social" business settings. Evening dress in a dimly lit restaurant may make it even harder to maintain professional decorum. Generally speaking it is best to wear conservative clothes, with high-buttoned fronts, long sleeves and long skirts.

> When Linda Platts was traveling in Tibet, she wore throughly practical, albeit unattractive hiking clothes. She looked more like a young boy than a woman journalist. Her two traveling companions were less practical and wore cool summer dresses. One evening the three women were walking in a village just after sunset; Linda was lingering behind when she noticed ahead that a crowd of men were gathering around and following her two friends. As she watched, the mood of the men seemed to be turning ugly—they were closing in and hissing. She ran into the crowd and grabbed the arms of the two women, yelling at them to hurry up. The men backed off immediately. Linda understood later that they mistook her for a man and concluded that these American women were Linda's wives. They did not want to mess with a husband, even one as apparently young and frail as this one.

In some cultures males may be extremely embarrassed if forced to talk with a woman outside the family. The uneducated or "un-citified" Moslem male, for example, must ignore her out of politeness and to avoid her irate husband. He has learned a limited repertoire of interaction with females, and when women don't behave the way he expects them to, he can be thoroughly confused. Most likely, the traveler will only have to deal with this problem outside the corporate setting. When two American women archaeologists went digging in the desert outside Amman, the Jordanian Department of Antiquities assigned them a chaperon, presumably to make sure they didn't steal anything. The poor man did not know what to make of these women traveling without their husbands to protect them. He did what he thought was expected of him—he moved in for the seduction. When his efforts were thwarted, he sulked for days, until a *modus vivendi* was established. Judith Miller, the first woman *New York Times* bureau chief in Egypt, found that men didn't know how to deal with her until she invented a family back in the States. Many women working in countries where the role of women is different from that in the United States have found that they can do their job without difficulty once they give the local people, men and women, a "handle" for understanding and accepting them.

Five rules for the manager:

Rule 1: When considering human-resources allocations in overseas assignments, consider women as well as men. Do not make assumptions; ask the *women* themselves if they are willing and able to go. Be ready to solve relocation problems just as you might with a male employee. Be willing to innovate: this is new terrain for everyone.[4]

Rule 2: Give your international business women the authority, status and perquisites that they need to do their job. Make the proper introductions to pave the way for a new woman manager, same as you would for a new male manager. Certainly don't present the assignment as an "experiment." If you do, she may be finished. During the transition, if the foreign customer or employee continues to turn to the departing male or the woman's male boss, it is entirely appropriate to say, for instance, "Ms. Jones is the best person to answer your question. She has studied this issue in depth and will be responsible for this area." The American supervisor must help modify old habits.

Rule 3: Give women thorough cross-cultural orientation, as you do for all your traveling and expatriate personnel. A woman's orientation should also include information on what to expect from her male superiors, peers and subordinates, as well as male customers or suppliers. Furthermore, as Margie Winder Goldman, a manager at Baxter Travenol, says: "Male managers should also gain insight into the situations their female colleagues might be facing."

Rule 4: Don't interpret foreigners' surprise as disappointment or offense. Their surprise may be nothing more than surprise. Don't assume the foreigner will be prejudiced against a woman or that she will be treated in the ways local women are treated.

Rule 5: Recognize that your women managers abroad will suffer the same culture shock or culture fatigue as men. Keep expectations reasonable and remember that she too will need the support of the home office.

Five rules for women in international business:

Rule 1: Know that you are crossing traditional barriers in many countries, adding to the confusion the foreigner may already be feeling working with an American. Many foreigners, when confused, begin to feel that *you* are unreliable. Greta McKinney, a woman who sells computers and related equipment in the Middle East and Asia, says: "Remember, business abroad is always based on trust and on knowing who you are dealing with." It is your job to create the professional trust necessary for you to accomplish your goals.

Rule 2: Consider asking the foreign man whether he has done business with a woman before. Sometimes it helps to bring up the subject, not immediately, but soon enough to put him at ease and to establish ground rules. The foreigner may admit he doesn't know quite how to work with a woman. You can tell him to approach it as he would approach business with a man. In some situations a woman can use the foreigner's discomfort and confusion to her advantage. One woman in Korea found the men there so insecure working with her that she had the upper hand. They gave her whatever she wanted. Another woman working with Westinghouse in Brussels found that when she learned to tolerate the patronizing attitude of traditional European men, she could use it to her advantage.

Rule 3: Be prepared to handle sexual overtures with the same composure you would in the United States. You must be in control. Never let the situation get out of hand. Remind your foreign colleague or customer that you are there for business, but avoid any emotional outburst or anger. One woman, caught by surprise when a South American interrupted their negotiation to comment on the beauty of her legs, was so stunned she couldn't think what to do. She said, "I'll be right back," and walked out of the room to think. When she came back she picked up the negotiation where they had left off. He didn't stray again.

Rule 4: Have faith in yourself. Don't let your American colleagues project their prejudices on you, or let their attitudes get in the way of your performance abroad. When you hear "Women can't do business in . . . ," try to find out what the obstacles, and the opportunities, really are. Analyze stories of women's failures abroad; don't accept them at face value, but learn from them. Andrea Shah, of Digital Equipment Corporation, says: "The woman who has successfully dealt with the male corporate culture in the U.S.A. probably has developed the right instincts to help her deal with the barriers of a foreign culture. She has already experienced working in a foreign environment and brings special skills to the international assignment."

Rule 5: You are a pioneer and a model. It will be up to you to educate your organization. Practically nobody is *looking* for women to send abroad; you will have to skillfully demonstrate a readiness to travel or move, and if married, you will have to answer the company's concerns about your husband's willingness to relocate. As Nancy Adler points out, few organizations have any history of expatriate or traveling women managers: when your colleagues have problems with you in this role, go about the task of altering perceptions and behavior patterns. Your behavior and performance will set a precedent for other women to follow you in international business.

COUNTRY SUMMARIES

TOP 25 U.S. MARKETS

**U.S. Domestic and Foreign Merchandise
Exports, 1985
f.a.s. Value**

		$ BILLIONS
	WORLD TOTAL	$213.1
1.	Canada	47.3
2.	Japan	22.6
3.	Mexico	13.6
4.	United Kingdom	11.3
5.	West Germany	9.0
6.	Netherlands	7.3
7.	France	6.1
8.	South Korea	6.0
9.	Australia	5.4
10.	Belgium & Luxembourg	4.9
11.	Taiwan	4.7
12.	Italy	4.6
13.	Saudi Arabia	4.5
14.	China	3.9
15.	Singapore	3.5
16.	Venezuela	3.4
17.	Brazil	3.1
18.	Hong Kong	2.8
19.	Israel	2.6
20.	Spain	2.5
21.	U.S.S.R.	2.4
22.	Egypt	2.3
23.	Switzerland	2.3
24.	Sweden	1.9
25.	India	1.6

SOURCE: Department of Commerce

LEADING U.S. SUPPLIERS

U.S. General Merchandise Imports, 1985
c.i.f. Value

		$ BILLIONS
	WORLD TOTAL	$361.6
1.	Japan	72.4
2.	Canada	69.4
3.	West Germany	21.2
4.	Mexico	19.4
5.	Taiwan	17.8
6.	United Kingdom	15.6
7.	South Korea	10.7
8.	Italy	10.4
9.	France	10.0
10.	Hong Kong	9.0
11.	Brazil	8.1
12.	Venezuela	6.8
13.	Indonesia	4.9
14.	Singapore	4.4
15.	Netherlands	4.4
16.	Sweden	4.3
17.	China	4.2
18.	Switzerland	3.6
19.	Belgium & Luxembourg	3.6
20.	Nigeria	3.1
21.	Australia	3.1
22.	Spain	2.8
23.	India	2.5
24.	Algeria	2.4
25.	Malaysia	2.4

SOURCE: Department of Commerce

AUSTRALIA AT A GLANCE

U.S. Foreign Commercial Service Post: U.S. Embassy, Moonah Place, Canberra, A.C.T. 2600. There are commercial officers also in Melbourne, Perth and Sydney.
Fundamentals in Business: Despite British origins, Australia is very different from Great Britain. Australians are proud of the uniqueness and prosperity of their country. In business, they are pragmatic, efficient and profit-oriented.
Sensitivities: Avoid any comparisons between the United States and Australia; avoid any affectation of "airs." Don't give unsolicited advice or comment.
Forms of Address: First names are widely and quickly used, but generally wait to use first names until invited to do so.
Courtesies: Shake hands at the beginning and end of meetings. Generally, people are more informal—don't be too stiff or overly tactful.
Business Do's: Because of the great distances, it is important to have representation within Australia. There is an Australian version of the Old Boy network among senior industrial executives, and it does help to have connections and introductions from one of these key people. At meetings, make brief preliminary comments (sports, cultural events, Australian sights), then get quickly down to business. Presentations should be complete, not concealing problem areas. Communicate directly and respond to Australian pointedness with confidence and good humor.
Business Don'ts: Do not use social occasions to talk business; recreation and eating are for relaxation, not work. Don't be obsequious or condescending. Don't waste time.
Negotiations: Negotiations proceed crisply. Australians are concerned with goals, productivity and profits. Stress the pragmatic. The opening proposals should be very close to the acceptable settlement; bargaining is not the local style, but there will be some give-and-take as details are worked out. Contracts will be defined and firm.
Entertainment: Dinner is usually about six o'clock. Come a half-hour early or be on time, but never late. Guests sometimes bring flowers, wine or beer, not usually gifts. A "Thank you" upon leaving is all that is expected.
Language: English
Religion: 80 percent Christian (about evenly Anglican, Roman Catholic and Protestant); 15 percent uncommitted.

BELGIUM AT A GLANCE

U.S. Foreign Commercial Service Post: U.S. Embassy, 27 Boulevard du Regent, B-1000 Brussels. There is also a consulate general in Antwerp.

Fundamentals in Business: Belgium is culturally divided between two groups: the French Walloons, who speak French, and the Flemings, who speak Flemish, a derivation of Dutch, and are more oriented toward Holland. Marketing and operations materials should be in both languages. When traveling, it helps to know both the Flemish and French names for roads and cities.

Sensitivities: Avoid discussing the cultural dichotomy in the country, and try not to confuse the two groups.

Forms of Address: First names are only used with old friends; address French-speaking people as Monsieur, Madame or Mademoiselle; Dutch-speaking people will expect you to use Mr., Mrs. or Miss.

Courtesies: Shake hands each time you meet someone and each time you leave, including each morning and at the end of every day, and do not forget anyone, including your staff or secretary in a faraway corner of the office. Introduce yourself to anyone in the office whom you don't know. During meals, keep your hands on the table. You may discuss business during a meal, but wait for the Belgian host to initiate work-related conversation.

Business Do's: Be punctual. Come straight to the point of your business. Generally, social relations are cultivated only after a good relationship has been established.

Business Don'ts: Don't flaunt wealth; don't be casual or neglect formalities.

Negotiations: Belgians are shrewd businessmen and tough negotiators. Be prepared with facts and figures. Proceedings will be formal and efficient.

Entertainment: Bring a small gift for the hostess: flowers (not chrysanthemums), chocolates or the local "pralines." During the meal, pay a discreet compliment on the cuisine and choice of wine.

Language: French and Flemish (Dutch). In Flemish regions, speak English if you can't speak Dutch.

Religion: Roman Catholic, especially in Flemish Belgium.

BRAZIL AT A GLANCE

U.S. Foreign Commercial Service Post: U.S. Embassy, Lote No. 3, Avenida das Noces, Brasília. Commercial officers are also in the consulates in Rio de Janeiro and São Paulo.

Fundamentals in Business: Families are very strong, and their obligations affect many areas of business. State enterprise plays a vital role in the economy, many firms being totally or partially controlled by the government.

Sensitivities: Brazil is very different and proudly independent from the rest of South America. Use Portuguese (not Spanish) and do not refer to Brazilians as Latin Americans. Some Brazilians might be offended by North Americans claiming "America" for the United States. Do not make negative comments about people that might get back to them, as damaged egos can cause much trouble.

Forms of Address: More casual than other South American countries, Brazilians are quick to use first names, but wait to be asked. Last names are confusing, often a combination of both the mother's and father's last names. Most commonly, people are addressed by their first name with a title, as in Senhor Paulo or Dona Maria.

Courtesies: Shake hands when meeting and leaving; at a party, go around to each person and say the appropriate "Good evening" or "Goodbye." The broad "Hi, everybody" insults the *dignidad* of each individual. Brazil is a very free and relaxed country—people are warm and friendly, and not very formal.

Business Do's: Conduct business in person as much as possible, and try to maintain a continuous working relationship. It is good to use business cards. Hire a *despachante* to help you maneuver through bureaucracies. Be expressive in your speech.

Business Don'ts: Don't speak Spanish; use English or an interpreter if you don't speak Portuguese. Do not rush your visits, and do not get directly down to business.

Negotiations: Brazilians like to bargain. Proceedings will be formal, but presentations should be made with flair: data with salsa.

Entertainment: Some invitations will tell you to come "American" or "airport" time, which means on time; otherwise try to be a bit late so as not to embarrass your hosts by arriving before they are ready. Gifts are not necessary, but candy, champagne or a basket of fruit will be appreciated. Send flowers the next day.

Language: Portuguese, not Spanish.

Religion: Predominantly Roman Catholic.

CANADA AT A GLANCE

U.S. Foreign Commercial Service Post: U.S. Embassy, 100 Wellington Street, Ottawa. Commercial officers are also in the consulates in Calgary, Montreal, Toronto and Vancouver.

Fundamentals in Business: Because of strong cultural ties to Europe, particularly France and England, traditional European styles prevail. However, most Canadians live within a few hundred miles of the U.S. border, and American ways are well known.

Sensitivities: There are strong feelings about French-English relations, particularly in Quebec. In addition, many Canadians feel snubbed by Americans; they hate being "talked down to" by Americans. Recognition that Canada is one of our major trading partners as well as a good neighbor will be appreciated.

Forms of Address: Use first names after invited to do so. Among Francophones, use the polite *vous* pronoun, not *tu,* which is reserved for family and very close friends.

Courtesies: Canadians are generally more reserved and attentive to etiquette than most Americans.

Business Do's: Business communications are direct and to the point; aim for clarity and thoroughness in information exchange. In general, be conservative in presentations and behavior. Indicate that you are familiar with Canadian geography, political system and current events.

Business Don'ts: Don't come on too strong or slick.

Entertainment: Dinner may be served as early as five o'clock, or after seven. Plan to stay two or three hours. A "Thank you" at the door is sufficient.

Language: Canada is officially bilingual (English and French) except in Quebec, where the official language is French.

Religion: Christian. United Church predominates in Western Canada, the Roman Catholic Church in French Canada, and Catholics, Anglicans and Baptists in Atlantic Canada.

PEOPLE'S REPUBLIC OF CHINA AT A GLANCE

U.S. Foreign Commercial Service Post: American Embassy, Beijing

Fundamentals in Business: You must be invited to trade with China and must work through the appropriate state trading corporation. The bureaucratic machinery is extremely cumbersome, and delays are interminable in all phases of business; only the organization with long-term interest and resources to spare should approach the China market.

Sensitivities: Avoid remarks about politics or Chinese leaders, Taiwan, or other nonrecognized countries (South Korea, Israel).

Forms of Address: The family name is always mentioned first, so that Lin Wu is Mr. Lin, or Li Paio is Madame Li. (The use of "Madame" is a diplomatic legacy. Usages are fast changing in China now; for instance, it's not always advisable to use "Comrade" anymore).

Courtesies: A nod or slight bow from the shoulders (not the Japanese bow) is customary, but shaking of hands is acceptable. Introductions are formal. Learn the intricacies of banquet etiquette.

Business Do's: Business cards in Chinese and English are essential. Pay strict attention to rank and hierarchy. Demonstrate long-term commitment: perseverance will go further than one quick impressive presentation. Go to meetings thoroughly prepared and bring a team of experts; the Chinese expect you to know every detail about your own (and competitors') products, markets and organization.

Business Don'ts: Business is generally not discussed during meals, although this is an important vehicle for indirect business references and "hot tips." Don't try to rush. Do not give gifts except ceremoniously at banquets; avoid any suggestion of a bribe.

Negotiations: The Chinese practice soft sell and hard buy. Discussions will be endless, repetitive and detailed. Give consistent answers. No formal agreement exists without a written contract. Until that time, visibly keep notes as negotiations progress.

Entertainment: Most entertaining will be at restaurants or banquets. Each guest may be seated and served by the host; do not serve yourself. Eat sparingly, as there are many courses. Don't drink alone—make a toast so that others will join you. The host will signal the end of the meal, and you should depart promptly.

Language: Chinese, principally Mandarin, but there are hundreds of local dialects. Interpreters are essential.

Religion: Communist; officially, atheism is endorsed.

Forbidden: Foreign currency. Gifts are risky and tipping is officially discouraged, for anything. Customs officials are particularly meticulous in their search for contraband, including weapons, drugs, or literature and films of questionable or controversial content. Keep a record of every transaction, and bring out of the country everything you take in with you, or you will be suspected of bribery.

EGYPT AT A GLANCE

U.S. Foreign Commercial Post: U.S. Embassy, 5 Sharia Latin America, Cairo.

Fundamentals in Business: Egyptians will be put off by the hurried American style of business; plan a more leisurely, personable approach.

Sensitivities: Politics and religion are sensitive subjects, best avoided.

Forms of Address: Use the first name, but with (Mr. Mrs. Dr., etc.). Titles are important. Forms are changing—it is quite acceptable to use the last name with a title, particularly for a government official.

Courtesies: Egyptians are very courtesy-conscious. Shake hands with everyone present, upon arriving and leaving. Use business cards. It is not unusual to interrupt a meeting with frequent telephone calls, visitors and unending cups of tea; do not become impatient. Do not eat, drink or smoke in front of a Muslim during the daytime Ramadan fast.

Business Do's: Find an Egyptian who has the right connections. Warm personal relations are important; confidence must be established before business can proceed. Always take time to socialize before getting to the purpose of your visit.

Business Don'ts: Don't try to go it alone. It is best to do business through a local representative or agent.

Entertainment: Lunch is the main meal rather than dinner, usually from two to four o'clock, and you may be invited for the day. You should arrive around eleven or twelve. Bring candy or cake for the children, but not flowers, unless someone is sick or getting married. Wash your hands before the meal and after.

Language: Arabic, but English and French are spoken widely.

Religion: Islam or Christianity.

FRANCE AT A GLANCE

U.S. Foreign Commercial Service Post: U.S. Embassy, 2 Avenue Gabriel, 75382 Paris Cedex 08. Consulates general are also located in Bordeaux, Lyon, Marseille, Nice and Strasbourg.

Fundamentals in Business: France is extraordinarily bureaucratic; be prepared for paperwork and procedures to complicate your efforts. The government plays a major role in business affairs.

Sensitivities: Avoid talking about politics, money and personal matters.

Forms of Address: First names are rarely used, even among colleagues. Always wait until the superior or elder person invites you to use their first name. Address everyone as either Monsieur, Madame or Mademoiselle without adding the surname. When introducing one's wife, it is incorrect to refer to Madame Smith, but rather "my wife."

Courtesies: The proper handshake is a single, quick jerk of the hand, with light pressure in the grip—the American firm pumping is considered boorish. During meals, good, cultured conversation is as important as fine food. Present a business card whenever making a call.

Business Do's: Decisions are made only after much deliberation, so allow plenty of time. Hard selling will lose you a customer. Generally, a local representative or agent is advised; joint ventures or branch offices, or even a network of distributors throughout France may be needed for success.

Business Don'ts: Avoid personal questions—the French are very offended by our prying. Don't be ostentatious. Don't talk business over lunch.

Negotiations: The French apply reason and logic to negotiations. Presentations should be formal, informative, rational and subdued. The French team is likely to be argumentative, disagreeing for the sake of discussion. Expect negotiations to take a long time, a matter of French prudence. An agreement may be reached orally and written contracts will follow later if approved by top management.

Entertainment: The dinner hour begins around eight or later; you can comfortably arrive ten minutes late. Guests often bring flowers, pastries, wine, candies or even a plant. Unless you know your wines, bring something else. A "Thank you" note is expected.

Religion: The majority are Catholic.

GERMANY (FEDERAL REPUBLIC OF GERMANY) AT A GLANCE

U.S. Foreign Commercial Service Post: U.S. Embassy, Delchmannsaue, 5300 Bonn 2.

Fundamentals in Business: German society and business is paternalistic—many decisions that we might consider routine must be referred to top management. Secrecy is also a fundamental fact of business life—cards are held close to the chest, making it hard to get information and slowing down negotiations. Germans are strongly loyal to their employer—most people stay with their company their entire career.

Sensitivities: Politics and World War II may be sensitive subjects. Refer to the country as the Federal Republic of Germany, not West Germany; the people are Germans. In literature do not talk of German products but specify products of the Federal Republic or German Democratic Republic.

Forms of Address: Never use a first name unless specifically invited to do so. Always address a person as Herr, Frau or Fräulein with the last name; anyone with a doctorate degree (such as a lawyer) is addressed Herr Doktor X, and a professor is Herr Professor X. It is important to know a person's proper title.

Courtesies: Germans are formal and reserved in first meetings, and may seem unfriendly. Most people shake hands when meeting and leaving—a firm handshake. Be punctual.

Business Do's: Germans conduct business with great attention to order and planning. Make appointments well in advance at the highest possible level. Participate in German trade fairs and contact the chambers of commerce; both are prestigious institutions in Germany. Always dress neatly, maintain formal decorum and practice restraint.

Business Don'ts: Avoid surprises and hard sell. Do not give spontaneous presentations.

Negotiations: Germans are technical and factual in negotiations. Your proposals should be concrete and realistic, presented in an orderly and authoritative manner. Beyond normal courtesies, do not bother with efforts to establish personal relationships—Germans remain aloof until business is complete. German contracts are detailed. There are two kinds of signing authority, which both mean "by proxy": the marks "p.p." or "ppa" *(per procura)* indicates a manager with restricted authority, and "i.V." *(in Vertretung)* indicates an executive with full authority.

Entertainment: The evening meal is generally simple. Hands are kept above the table. Candy, wine or flowers may be brought or sent afterward. A "Thank you" note is expected.

Religion: About evenly Protestant and Catholic, but Germany is a secular society.

NOTE: The U.S. does significant trade with the German Democratic Republic (East Germany), mostly through West European countries. Do not call the people East Germans or the country East Germany. The economy is mostly state-owned and centrally planned. Fortitude is necessary.

HONG KONG AT A GLANCE

U.S. Foreign Commercial Service Post: U.S. Consulate General, 26 Garden Road, Hong Kong.

Fundamentals in Business: Hong Kong is a British colony, but on July 1, 1997, it will become part of the People's Republic of China. The transition has already begun; British power and prestige is on the ebb, and economic and political power has started to shift to Communist-owned companies and banks. The colony has long operated relatively free of government interference but will increasingly feel state control. The right contacts have always been important in Hong Kong—now a different group of players are becoming the "right contacts."

Sensitivities: Saving face is important. Always show respect. Some Chinese may resent the British caretaker government, but generally this is not a sore subject.

Forms of Address: Same as in China.

Courtesies: Same as in China.

Business Do's: Hong Kong Chinese are vastly more experienced in working with Westerners than PRC Chinese, so in some regards, business is easier. Still, it is wise to work through an agent or commissioned importer.

Business Don'ts: Never embarrass a Chinese, thus causing loss of face.

Negotiations: Same as in China but without the cumbersome bureaucracy. Moreover, because of a history of legal contracts and trading with the West, many terminology problems have long been worked out. Hong Kong Chinese, like PRC Chinese, discuss all issues affecting the deal, saving compromises ("discounts") for the end.

Entertainment: Chinese businessmen generally entertain in restaurants; eight- to twelve-course meals are common. In the European community, dinner parties are most often held in the home. Guests are expected to arrive on time. Gifts are brought for the children, or fruit in a basket. At a restaurant the guest of honor usually ends the meal by rising and thanking the host on everyone's behalf.

Language: English and Chinese.

Religion: Confucianism is predominant. Many also practice Buddhism, Taoism or Christianity.

INDIA AT A GLANCE

U.S. Foreign Commercial Service Post: U.S. Embassy, Shanti Path, Chanakyapuri 21, New Delhi.

Fundamentals in Business: Religion has a strong influence in social and business activities. Fatalism affects work attitudes, and a concern for social harmony affects the conduct of business.

Sensitivities: Religion is taken very seriously. Never say anything disparaging about any religious practices. Don't ask personal questions except with very close friends.

Forms of Address: First names are used only among very close friends; always use Mr., Mrs. or Miss.

Courtesies: Men shake hands. When greeting a woman, do not shake hands but make a *namaste,* placing palms together (as if in prayer) and bowing slightly. If meeting a man and woman together, make a *namaste.* Men should avoid touching women or talking alone with a woman. Apologize if your foot or shoe touches someone—feet are considered dirty.

Business Do's: India is a paternalistic society and decisions are made at the top. Connections with the right families are very helpful. Try to make contact at the highest levels and provide incentives for middle managers and assistants to help nudge your concerns or proposals upward. Do not rush business. Several visits will be necessary to get business moving. Permits are essential for virtually all transactions—make sure you have the necessary papers, or you will be penalized. It is wise to have an Indian agent. Telex is more reliable than mail.

Business Don'ts: Don't neglect formalities and social rituals. Don't behave impulsively—self-control is valued.

Negotiations: Negotiations are usually constrained by the middle manager's limited authority to make decisions. A little flair will help get people interested, but facts and realism in proposals will enable the Indians to gain acceptance of ideas. Prices should be fairly firm—there will be little haggling.

Entertainment: Most entertaining is done in hotels or restaurants, and wives are generally invited. Some food may be eaten by hand—the right hand. Devout Hindus do not eat beef; Moslems do not eat pork, ham or bacon, nor do they drink alcohol. Many people do not eat meat, fish or eggs. Wash your hands and rinse your mouth before eating.

Language: Hindi, English; fourteen languages are recognized in the constitution.

Forbidden: Alcohol is prohibited in some areas—find out what the local rules are or get a special license for liquor from your travel agent or at the airport upon arrival.

Religion: Hinduism, Islam, Jainis and Sikhism.

INDONESIA AT A GLANCE

U.S. Foreign Commercial Service Post: U.S. Embassy, Medan Merdeka Selatan 5, Jakarta.

Fundamentals in Business: Indonesia is incredibly diverse; its archipelago of 13,000 islands is the home of numerous distinct cultures, each with their own personality, languages, religions and modes of business.

Sensitivities: The Chinese in Indonesia remain a distinct and somewhat suspect ethnic group—be sensitive to the fact that everyone in Indonesia knows who is and who isn't Chinese, and that Chinese are not fully accepted as full Indonesians. Indonesians tend to be xenophobic—Western influence is not entirely welcomed. Respect the food-and-drink restrictions of Ramadan—do not eat in front of Moslems during the day.

Forms of Address: Address a man of status or age as *bapak* (father) and woman as *ibu* (mother).

Courtesies: Shake hands and bow the head slightly when first being introduced or when saying goodbye before a long absence; otherwise, handshaking is not customary. The social kiss is in vogue in Jakarta—a touching of first the right then the left cheek as one shakes hands. Remove your shoes before entering a mosque or other sacred place, and in a home if the host is not wearing shoes. Do not touch a person's head—not even a child's.

Business Do's: It is essential to have a local agent. Generally be restrained physically (good posture is important) and expressively. Accept hospitalities, and maintain a friendly, casual approach to business. Business cards are essential.

Business Don'ts: Never embarrass anyone publicly. Avoid conflict. Never express emotion in public.

Negotiations: Negotiations with an Indonesian firm should occur on several levels, senior executives meeting at the top and technical people at the operating level. The pace of negotiations is slow. Quick concessions are seen as stupidity. Avoid disagreement and argument; tread softly around sensitivities. Indonesians deal in probabilities, not facts; they will be concerned about the terms of a deal but also the credibility of the foreigner and agent. A contract will provide the gist of an agreement but little more. Focus on relationship.

Entertainment: Normally a family will dine at seven or seven-thirty. A guest usually asks *"Permisi?"* (May I be permitted?) before entering a home. Guests wait to be invited to eat, drink, go through doors, and so forth. Spoons are held in the right hand, forks in the left. Keep both hands on the table. "Thanks" at the door is sufficient.

Language: Bahasa Indonesian, also Dutch, English, Chinese.

Religion: Islam (80 percent), also Hindu, Confucian, Buddhist or Christian, as well as mystic veneration of ancestors.

ISRAEL AT A GLANCE

U.S. Foreign Commercial Service Post: U.S. Embassy, 71 Hayarkon Street, Tel Aviv.

Fundamentals in Business: Business procedures in general are quite similar to our own, and the pace is like New York City. However, business is strongly affected by religious laws—this is a theocratic society, with no separation between church and state. Get local business, legal and accounting help, as differences are subtle but can create great problems. Laws change rapidly, and in an inflationary environment, things change quickly. Israelis generally like Americans.

Sensitivities: The Arab-Israeli conflict: even if they don't admit it, people live on the edge; their lives are endangered and they feel defensive—they do not appreciate "objective" discussion. Religious observances are important too. People may be angry if you drive or smoke on the Sabbath. Obviously, anti-Semitic jokes will offend.

Forms of Address: Somewhat more formal than in the United States, but not as formal as in Europe, depending on the Israeli's ethnic origins. Titles, however, are even less important than in America—even military officers and enlisted men use first names or nicknames.

Courtesies: *Shalom* is used for "Hello" or "Goodbye." Shake hands when meeting and leaving. Greetings are casual and friendly.

Business Do's: Learn the history of Zionism. Remember that most businesses are closed Friday afternoon, and Saturday is the Sabbath. Know if your business associates are religious and respect their religious observances. Soft sell will go unnoticed: you must hard-sell in Israel. Be tough.

Business Don'ts: Never criticize the government, even to an Israeli who is violently anti-government.

Entertainment: Evening meals are light, and an invitation to lunch is more usual. Typically, arrive around twelve-thirty for a one-o'clock lunch. Books, candy or flowers are good gifts. Either the oldest person or the host will begin eating first. Thank the host upon leaving, and again with a card or flowers later. Many observe dietary restrictions: pork, ham and shellfish.

Language: Hebrew and Arabic are the official languages; English is commonly spoken.

Religion: Judaism among the majority; Islam and Christianity.

ITALY AT A GLANCE

U.S. Foreign Commercial Service Post: U.S. Embassy, Via Veneto 119/A, 00187 Rome.

Fundamentals in Business: The Italian market is highly competitive, and business law is quite different from ours. Milan is the leading business city. Many businessmen do not speak English—most speak French.

Sensitivities: Avoid Italian politics or discussion of taxes.

Forms of Address: Only close friends use first names. Use titles, and when in doubt, address someone as "Dottore."

Courtesies: Shake hands on meeting and leaving.

Business Do's: Get an Italian agent; you may also need a local attorney. Business cards are a routine part of business. Get right down to business after a few minutes of general conversation. Be well prepared for your presentation—you must have a solid knowledge of your products, local applications, track record elsewhere, and so on.

Business Don'ts: Don't talk business at a social event (instead, talk about family, sports, international events); don't joke at a purely business meeting. Do not mistake courtesy for interest in your products or proposals.

Entertainment: Except in Milan, business entertaining is not popular. Dinner may be from eight to ten, sometimes earlier in smaller towns. You may bring a gift or send flowers afterward, but not chrysanthemums which are used for funerals and grave sites. Usually entertainment is in a restaurant. Hands are kept above the table. Compliments on the meal and home are appreciated.

Religion: Catholic.

JAPAN AT A GLANCE

U.S. Foreign Commercial Service Post: U.S. Embassy, 10-1, Akasaka 1-chome, Minato-ku (107), Tokyo. Commercial offices or consulates are also in Nagoya, Osaka-Kobe and Sapporo.

Fundamentals in Business: The Japanese are practical and hard-working; group orientation and loyalty to the company are top values. The process of business may appear to be slow because many people are involved in the decision-making process, but once a decision is made, implementation occurs quickly. Many Japanese are well educated about the West. However, never assume that your Japanese associates understand your actions or your business. In importing and exporting, it is often advisable to work through one of the large Japanese trading companies.

Sensitivities: The Japanese are highly status-conscious. Always show respect, give face, and preserve harmony. Loudness of any kind is offensive. Never single an individual out of a group, either for criticism or praise. Avoid any hint of excessive pride.

Forms of Address: People are addressed by their surname and the suffix *san,* as in Jones-san. Never use first names.

Courtesies: Japanese usually bow to each other, but handshaking is common in business. If you bow to a peer, bow as low and long as the Japanese. If you're visiting a Japanese-style home, remove your shoes before stepping inside. All etiquette is aimed toward creating *wa,* good feeling and harmony. The Japanese are formal but warm.

Business Do's: Travel with hundreds of business cards and use them whenever you must give your name; give them to everyone present. Connections and introductions are essential. Always allow time for the Japanese to get to know and trust you. Be prepared to give gifts in a number of situations. Do participate in evening entertainment—a time to communicate freely with your Japanese associates over sake.

Business Don'ts: Don't rush. Avoid conflict or any embarrassment that would cause loss of face. Don't always assume that "yes" means agreement or understanding.

Negotiations: Japanese typically negotiate in teams made up of experts in relevant fields. Interpreters are often necessary. Negotiations begin with gentle probing of fundamental issues such as the motives of the parties and the potential for long-term, mutually beneficial relationships. Negotiations will continue over a period of time with several meetings, or information will flow by correspondence. Expect some bargaining, but do not greatly inflate your proposals. Throughout, it is important to maintain a posture of integrity, courtesy and interest. When problems arise, involve an intermediary.

Entertainment: Most entertaining is done in restaurants. If you are invited to someone's home, bring a small gift and present it with both hands to the host. Sake is served before dinner, and it is polite to fill each other's cups. Try to use chopsticks. Send a note of thanks.

Religion: Buddhism and Shinto.

KOREA (SOUTH) AT A GLANCE

U.S. Foreign Commercial Service Post: U.S. Embassy, Sejong-Ro, Seoul.

Fundamentals in Business: It is virtually essential to work with one of the government-approved agents, who will represent you in this complicated market. Korean business is characterized by youthful entrepreneurial spirit, Confucian principles and Japanese management practices.

Sensitivities: Korean society is highly structured; great respect is paid to age and position. Rituals of courtesy are important, and modesty is the rule. Always preserve face and harmony. Avoid discussions of socialism, Communism or Korean politics.

Forms of Address: Address business associates by their title and the one-syllable family name; the family name comes first. Hence Lee Song-Hyon is Mr. Lee.

Courtesies: Korean men bow slightly and shake hands; women do not shake hands. As in other Asian countries, business cards are expected whenever introductions are made. A sweet coffee, tea or soft drink is usually offered at meetings; drink it without comment.

Business Do's: Keep interactions formal until a relationship has been established. Travel with plenty of business cards. Acknowledgment of the country's tremendous economic growth over the past two decades will be appreciated.

Business Don'ts: Never criticize, openly disagree or behave abruptly with Koreans. Never appear to be excessively proud of accomplishments.

Negotiations: Koreans are much more direct than, for example, the Japanese. Relationship and trust are very important—always be diplomatic. They will want detailed information, and may be repetitive in questions. Negotiations will be protracted, and the Koreans play tough. Repeated answers are likely to do more for your credibility than fresh answers—maintain consistency. Be firm but avoid conflict. Do not sign the contract with a red pen.

Entertainment: Entertainment plays a major role in business—social contacts foster understanding and rapport. When entering a Korean home, remove your shoes and wait to be invited inside. Bring a small gift or flowers. Conversation takes place after, not during, the meal. Wives are rarely included in invitations to a restaurant or bar.

Language: Korean.

Religion: Buddhist, with strong Confucian tradition.

MALAYSIA AT A GLANCE

U.S. Foreign Commercial Service Post: U.S. Embassy, A.I.A. Building, Jalan Ampang, Post Office Box No. 35, Kuala Lumpur.

Fundamentals in Business: Malaysia is a multiethnic country. The Chinese are the majority in urban areas and predominant in business; the Malays are mostly Moslem, living in rural areas. Many people believe in animism, and business activities will be affected by folk beliefs and customs. Attitudes toward work are affected by belief in fate.

Sensitivities: Among Moslems, avoid discussing the Israel-Palestine situation, and generally do not discuss religion. Comparison of local standards to the West may arouse hostilities.

Forms of Address: Address a Moslem man with "Encik" followed by his name, and the women as "Cik" followed by her name. Use titles to show respect. Among Chinese and others, Mr. and Mrs. are adequate.

Courtesies: Men shake hands; close friends grasp with both hands.

Business Do's: Use business cards. Expect to have to provide a lot of information —the Malaysian is likely to be punctilious. Entertaining is an important part of business; follow important meetings with a dinner or lunch, and invite a number of people from the organization. Status is important.

Business Don'ts: Never underestimate your Malaysian associate's knowledge or act condescendingly.

Negotiations: Chinese negotiation styles prevail.

Entertainment: Dinner is around seven or eight; it is acceptable to be half an hour late. You may bring a gift, but not alcoholic beverages. Malays and Indians eat with their hands and spoons, the Chinese with chopsticks and spoons. Moslems do not eat pork; Buddhists and Hindus do not eat beef. Send a "Thank you" note or flowers.

Language: Bahasa Malaysia.

Religion: Islam is the official religion. The Chinese are mostly Buddhist. Indians are mostly Hindu.

MEXICO AT A GLANCE

U.S. Foreign Commercial Service Post: U.S. Embassy, Paseo de la Reforma 305, Mexico 5, D.F.

Fundamentals in Business: Personal relationships are essential to business. Be prepared to make frequent direct contact and have representation in Mexico. Much business is done through unofficial channels and one's connections.

Sensitivities: Mexicans have strong feelings about their neighbor on the other side, *"en el otro lado,"* and will be sensitive to any hints of condescension or comparison. Mexicans are proud of their independence from the United States. Some object to the use of the word "American" as referring to people from the United States.

Forms of Address: First names are not used unless you know a person very well and are on friendly terms. For Mr., Mrs. and Miss, say "Señor," "Señora" or "Señorita." When in doubt about a woman's marital status, refer to her as "Señorita."

Courtesies: Shake hands each time you meet someone and when introduced for the first time. When meeting a Mexican woman, bow slightly; shake hands only if she offers hers.

Business Do's: Always be warm and personable in approach. Take time to establish rapport. Demonstration of knowledge of Mexican culture will impress. Always maintain dignity, courtesy and diplomacy. Get agreements confirmed in writing, since verbal agreement may be reached out of politeness, only to be reversed later by mail.

Business Don'ts: Don't rush; don't push. Don't injure an individual's pride or dignity. Even an honest "no" to a request may be taken as rude.

Negotiations: Much of Mexican negotiations will center on personal aspects of the business relationship: trust and compatibility. Proposals should not be highly inflated, or the Mexican may feel exploited, though a good margin for bargaining should be allowed. Deliberations will be cautious, and presentations must overcome initial suspicion. Graphs, charts, computer printouts, samples and models are appreciated.

Entertainment: The main meal is in the afternoon between two and five o'clock. If you're invited to the home, flowers for the hostess are usual for the first visit. A spouse is customarily invited too when business colleagues have a personal relationship. Dinner is around eight-thirty or nine. Never come early. "Thanks" at the door and a telephone call later are sufficient.

Language: Spanish.

Religion: Mainly Roman Catholic.

NETHERLANDS AT A GLANCE

U.S. Foreign Commercial Service Post: U.S. Embassy, Lange Voorhout 102, The Hague; consulates general also in Amsterdam and Rotterdam.

Fundamentals in Business: The Netherlands economy is one of the strongest in the world. The Dutch are experienced traders, open to new ideas, welcoming foreigners, and efficient in business.

Sensitivities: Holland originally designated its two western provinces North and South Holland, but people from other provinces may object to these terms. The people are referred to as Netherlanders or the Dutch.

Forms of Address: Address people as Mr., Mrs. or Miss until invited to do otherwise. Many will quickly switch to first names.

Courtesies: Shake hands with all present (even children) when meeting and when leaving. If not introduced, introduce yourself. Say "Pleased to meet you" rather than "How do you do?" Do not stand with your hands in your pockets.

Business Do's: The Dutch are pragmatic and down-to-earth, so your presentations must be factual and full of figures. Track record is what counts, not boasts or plans. Be punctual and straightforward. Fulfill all promises; if you say you will have something in the mail tomorrow, make sure it is in the mail or your credibility will suffer.

Business Don'ts: Don't exaggerate or present fluff. Don't treat business casually—lateness will be very bad for beginning relationships and sloppy preparation will damage your chances of establishing a business relationship.

Negotiations: The Dutch do not like haggling. Calculate as fair and exact a price as possible, and stick to it. A good proposal will make a better impression than concessions. Negotiations will proceed quickly, much as in the United States.

Entertainment: Guests come on time and may bring flowers. Do not make personal compliments when visiting unless you know your hosts well. Do not sip your drink until all the guests have assembled and the host has made a toast. Generally keep both hands on the table and elbows off the table. The fork is held in the left hand. Leave after coffee is served, before ten P.M. If coffee is served a second time, it is a hint that you should be going.

Language: Dutch.

Religion: About evenly Protestant and Catholic.

NIGERIA AT A GLANCE

U.S. Foreign Commercial Service Post: U.S. Embassy, 2 Eleke Cresent, Post Office Box 554, Lagos; there is also a consulate in Kaduna.

Fundamentals in Business: You must have a Nigerian partner, and it is important to have reputable connections. Investigate those with whom you do business. The Nigerian bureaucracy is very complicated; patience will be necessary. News travels fast: anything you say or do is likely to become widely known very quickly. The colonial history leaves some resentment and distrust of whites.

Sensitivities: African politics and ethnicity are sensitive subjects. Nigeria is striving to be a modern African country, and references to past colonial status or tribes may make people defensive. Hostilities exist between different racial groups.

Forms of Address: Many forms exist because of the great cultural diversity. Generally use titles, especially the honorific titles of traditional leaders.

Courtesies: Nigerians expect open friendliness—do not hesitate to smile and start a conversation.

Business Do's: Informal dress may be taken as disrespect: maintain proper professional appearances. Learn to tolerate the relaxed pace of business and be prepared to wait endlessly. Listen more than you talk.

Business Don'ts: Don't lose patience or show irritation. Don't interrupt a speaker even to acknowledge agreement ("I know.") Don't go overboard in currying favor, but also don't neglect to tip the numerous people who serve you directly or indirectly: usually these payments or tips are made before the service, not afterward. Personal space is very close; try not to back away.

Negotiations: Be prepared to bargain creatively. Maintain respectful manners, especially with government officials. Be precise, brief and direct. Be careful about any exaggerations or promises or you will trigger the Nigerian's distrust. Try to demonstrate the mutuality of your interests and your appreciation for the country's long-term interests. Negotiators should be mature—middle-aged or able to demonstrate advanced education—in order to win confidence. A company's track record will be an important basis for future business dealings.

Entertainment: It is unusual for a Westerner to be invited into a Nigerian's home. Most entertaining takes place in restaurants or clubs. Social occasions are characteristically festive—dress elegantly, be prepared to eat a lot and enjoy the open hospitality.

Language: English is the official government language. Hausa is spoken in the north, Yoruba in the south.

Religion: Primarily Moslem in the north, Moslems and Christians in the east and west, but many integrate traditional African beliefs into their worship.

PHILIPPINES AT A GLANCE

U.S. Foreign Commercial Service Post: U.S. Embassy, 1201 Roxas Boulevard, Manila.

Fundamentals in Business: Business practices are substantially patterned after U.S. practices; the Philippines became a U.S. commonwealth in 1935. Filipino culture has been influenced by the Chinese, Malays, Moslems, Spanish and Americans. Most business leaders have been to the U.S. (many are graduates of U.S. universities) and know about our industries and corporations.

Sensitivities: Filipinos are easily offended by criticism or disagreement. Be careful not to injure a person's self-esteem. Older relatives demand particular respect. Try to maintain smooth and harmonious relations.

Forms of Address: Use Mr., Mrs. and Miss or the professional title unless you are very close colleagues or friends. Address superiors as "sir" or "ma'am," or use their title.

Courtesies: Handshaking is usual for men and women. Greetings should be friendly and informal. Gifts are not generally opened in front of the giver.

Business Do's: Provide proper accreditations: if your company is not well known, you will need referrals from mutual friends and papers of introduction. When dealing with the government, try to see the top official. Make sure you know the background of any potential business partner before making any commitments.

Business Don'ts: Don't expect to do business right away—allow for a period of socializing first. Don't misunderstand the Filipino's hospitality or let your business judgment be misled by the Filipino's extreme helpfulness.

Negotiations: Know the background of your opponent. Negotiations are tough. Do not be too open.

Entertainment: The hotel is the center of social gatherings. Etiquette is the same as in the United States. Hospitality is important and guests should always be solicitous and tactful. People who have not been invited may turn up at a dinner.

Language: Tagalog (mainly Malay, with Spanish and Hindi influences).

Religion: Predominantly Roman Catholic.

SAUDI ARABIA AT A GLANCE

U.S. Foreign Commercial Service Post: U.S. Embassy, Sulalmania District, P.O. Box 9041, Riyadh.

Fundamentals in Business: Religion and family are extremely important. In business, Saudis are tough, shrewd and cautious. Saudis typically are meticulous in manners and hospitality. Islamic law is the basis of all commercial and social law.

Sensitivities: Do not eat or smoke in public in the daytime during Ramadan; alcohol is against the law. Women's dress must not expose arms, legs, or shape. Do not call a Moslem a Mohammedan. Refer to the Gulf as the Arab Gulf, not the Persian Gulf. Avoid discussions about women, politics or religion.

Forms of Address: Use the titles Mr., Sheik, Excellency (for ministers) or Your Highness (for members of the royal family) with the first name until you are accepted as a friend or business colleague. For example, Sheik Ahmed Abdel Wahab is Sheik Ahmed (pronounced "shake," *not* "sheek"). Prince Turki Ibn Feisal is Your Highness Prince Turki.

Courtesies: Do not inquire about the women in a man's family. Accept endless cups of coffee or tea. Shake hands with everyone present when meeting or leaving; use business cards. Sit without exposing the soles of your shoes and avoid using your left hand. It is polite to accompany a visitor to the street. Do not admire an object or the Saudi will feel obligated to give it to you.

Business Do's: Work with a Saudi agent. Once contact is established, the Saudi may prefer to work directly with you, avoiding middlemen. Make frequent visits to cement the business relationships. Begin each meeting with social conversation and tolerate frequent diversions and waiting.

Business Don'ts: Don't press for immediate answers or direct "yes" or "no"; allow time for deliberation. Do not try to conduct your business via telephone or the mail. It is not improper, just futile. Don't say "no religion" on your passport.

Negotiations: Traditionally, bargaining starts with inflated proposals and proceeds through a series of ritualistic concessions. Hard sell will not be appropriate and price should be discussed as a matter between friends. Be prepared to deal with a number of unresolved issues at once. Try not to rush. Despite the Arab's outstanding courtesy, assume you are starting from a position of distrust: you must build confidence. Eye contact and gestures of openness will be important. Do not confuse polite agreeableness with agreement; get a written contract and even then expect the deal to be renegotiated later.

Entertainment: Entertaining is usually done in restaurants and hotels. Women are generally not included; in the home they will dine in a separate room. Be prepared to eat with your hand—the right one. Leave soon after eating.

Language: Arabic.

Religion: Islam.

SINGAPORE AT A GLANCE

U.S. Foreign Commercial Service Post: U.S. Embassy, 30 Hill Street, Singapore 0617.

Fundamentals in Business: Singapore offers the second highest standard of living in Asia, after Japan, and is routinely rated politically and economically as safe as Switzerland. Singaporeans profit from a sharp sense of national purpose and entrepreneurial dynamism. Many Western business practices have been adopted, but the Chinese ways are still predominant.

Sensitivities: Face is very important. There is some hostility between Malays and Chinese. The society is very disciplined, with stiff penalities for minor offenses (such as littering or jaywalking) or antisocial behavior (wearing hair too long or chewing gum). Don't discuss religion or politics.

Forms of Address: Use Mr., Mrs. or Miss until invited to do otherwise. Chinese put their surname first, middle name next and given name last. Malays do not have surnames—their father's name is attached to their own with *bin*, meaning "son of." Most Indians do not have surnames but may use the initial of their father's name. Thus, a Chinese man, Lee Kuan Hock is Mr. Lee. A Malay, Hassan bin Ahmed, is Mr. Hassan.

Courtesies: Shake hands when meeting or leaving. Business cards are essential. Always show great respect for the elderly. Remove your shoes in mosques or temples. Don't touch people on the head.

Business Do's: Always be punctual. Business is generally straightforward: the Chinese will want good prices and fast results. You can be very direct in money matters. More traditional Chinese will do business on the basis of trust—work on relationship and keep legal documentation simple.

Business Don'ts: Don't give any indications of bribery; even gifts are risky, and tipping in restaurants is discouraged. Don't dress too formally—it's too hot—but have a jacket to put on in air-conditioned offices. Avoid jokes until you know someone well.

Negotiations: Negotiations will be quick, but Singaporeans will drive a hard bargain, particularly on prices and schedules.

Entertainment: Business can be discussed over a meal. Don't invite a recent acquaintance to dinner; wait until after several meetings. Public officials are not allowed to accept invitations. Try to use chopsticks. Malays or Indians may use their hands—don't use the left hand. Most entertaining is in restaurants. If invited to the home, bring a small gift (candy or flowers). It will not be opened in front of you.

Language: Malay, Tamil, Mandarin and English.

Religion: About 40 percent Buddhist, 15 percent Moslem, 10 percent Christian, 7 percent Hindu.

SOUTH AFRICA AT A GLANCE

U.S. Foreign Commercial Service Post: U.S. Embassy, Thibault House, 225 Pretorious Street, Pretoria.

Fundamentals in Business: Business is conducted much the same as in the United Kingdom, with the outstanding exception of the role of blacks and whites. Most international business dealings will be with people of British descent.

Sensitivities: Racial tensions are simmering. You may be distrusted both by whites who tire of the outsider's disapproval and by blacks who think you are not doing enough to change the status quo. Black Americans face even harsher scrutiny and expectation. There are some animosities between the Afrikaners and the whites of British descent.

Forms of Address: Address people at Mr., Mrs. and Miss until invited to do otherwise. First names are increasingly the custom.

Courtesies: Shake hands on meeting and leaving. Greetings should be somewhat extended—your asking about family or making other social conversation—not a mere "Hello." In some parts of the country, or among good friends, blacks may shake hands, clench thumbs and shake hands again.

Business Do's: Be punctual and somewhat more formal than in the United States. Be prepared for bureaucratic complexities and delays. Be self-motivating: some expatriates say the country's economic gravy train has caused management to be relaxed; people do not get much direction.

Business Don'ts: Don't be loud or boisterous—both British and Afrikaners are more reserved.

Entertainment: Dinner may be as early as five o'clock. Arrive on time, and bring a gift. The fork is used in the left hand. Guests do not ask for anything to be passed at the table. Stay for several hours after the meal.

Language: Afrikaans (derivative of Dutch) and English are official. There are nine widely spoken African languages.

Religion: Christian. White Afrikaans-speaking people are predominantly members of the Dutch Reformed Church.

NOTE: There is widespread debate about the political and social consequences of dealing with South Africa, and it is certainly advisable to consider your views on apartheid before doing business there, since most industries use black labor. There is an organization of American businesses, the International Council for Equality of Opportunity Principles, which has laid down guidelines, called the Sullivan Code, for U.S. businesses' involvement with South Africa.

SPAIN AT A GLANCE

U.S. Foreign Commercial Service Post: U.S. Embassy, Serrano 75, Madrid. Consulate general in Barcelona, and consulate in Bilbao.

Fundamentals in Business: Religion is an important part of daily life. Family relationships are important in business. Pace is relaxed. Regional differences are strong: Madrid, Barcelona and Bilbao have very different characters.

Sensitivities: If you don't care for bullfighting and it comes up in conversation, remember the Spanish consider it an art and are offended by criticism.

Forms of Address: Use Señor and Señora with the surname until invited to use first names. An unmarried woman is addressed as Señorita with her first name; married women do not change their names. A person senior to you may address you by your first name, but you should not do likewise unless specifically invited. In business cards, documents and letters, the mother's family name will be attached to a person's name, Juan Paiz De Leon, for example.

Courtesies: Shake hands when first meeting but not at subsequent meetings, and at the final departure. Wait for a woman to offer her hand first. Embraces are reserved for close friends.

Business Do's: Take time to establish rapport and connections. Use business cards. Appearances are important: dress well and give the impression of accomplishment and position. Demonstrate an interest in the country's history and culture. Be eloquent in presentations.

Business Don'ts: Never injure pride or honor; treat everyone with great respect. Don't try to do business during the afternoon siesta, from one-thirty to four-thirty.

Negotiations: Be prepared to bargain, leaving room for concessions, but do not haggle so hard that you jeopardize the relationship. Keep in mind that trust and compatibility will secure the business relationship. Pay attention to detail. Don't "think big"; think on the level of your associate's business. Don't push.

Entertainment: If invited to the home, a gift is not expected, but you may bring a box of candy. Do not send flowers except for special occasions. Dinner is usually after nine or ten o'clock.

Language: Castilian Spanish.

Religion: Roman Catholicism.

SWEDEN AT A GLANCE

U.S. Foreign Commercial Service Post: U.S. Embassy, Strandvägen 101, Stockholm. Consulate general also in Göteborg.

Fundamentals in Business: Scandinavia consists of Sweden, Norway and Denmark, each country with similar business practices but with a distinct history and cultural pride. Do not treat them as one nation. Business is conducted pretty much according to U.S. practices. Personal relationships in business are less important here than in most parts of the world.

Sensitivities: Compliments are vociferously denied by Swedes—one must never blow one's own horn. Intrusion into one's personal affairs will offend.

Forms of Address: First names are commonly used shortly after acquaintance, but to be safe, use Mr. or Mrs. with the family name, until invited to do otherwise.

Courtesies: Handshakes and "Goddag" are the common greeting, or "Hej" to friends. Men remove their hats when talking to a woman, even in cold weather. Don't say "How are you" or "How do you do" unless you want a recital on the state of the Swede's health.

Business Do's: Be punctual, prepared, direct, technically correct and formal. Try to have complete answers and details ready. Be conservative and find ways to reduce risk.

Business Don'ts: Don't be overly friendly, as you will seem insincere or pushy. Avoid physical contact, such as pats on the back. Do not give appearances of bragging, exaggeration or overenthusiasm in your presentation. Be sober, not flamboyant. Do not waste time. Do not talk or laugh loudly in public places.

Negotiations: Negotiators will want to know the facts and the direct benefits of a proposal. Grandiose claims or exuberance may stall proceedings. Negotiations will move crisply, but the Swedes tend to be inflexible. To them, the act of bargaining is embarrassing, though they will insist on squeezing margins. Agreements will be followed with written contracts, perhaps with interim memoranda of understandings.

Entertainment: Business may be conducted over lunch. Entertainment does not play a large role in business. Punctuality is crucial. If you are invited to someone's home, bring a gift of flowers or candy. The host traditionally helps the guest off with his topcoat. Try to eat everything on your plate and express appreciation for the meal.

Language: Swedish.

Religion: The majority belong to the Evangelical Lutheran Church.

SWITZERLAND AT A GLANCE

U.S. Foreign Commercial Service Post: U.S. Embassy, Jubilaeumstrasse 93, 3005 Bern.

Fundamentals in Business: Swiss business practices are very similar to those in the United States. Generally the people are more formal, and business proceeds in an orderly, planned fashion. Organizations are more paternalistic, and decision making is centralized. The country is 65 percent German-speaking, 18 percent French-speaking, and 12 percent Italian-speaking.

Sensitivities: The Swiss are very conscientious about courtesy to others. Noise at night is frowned upon.

Forms of Address: Use Herr and Frau to address German-speaking Swiss, Monsieur and Madame to French-speaking, and Signor and Signora to Italian-speaking Swiss. It is very rude to use first names, even after some acquaintance, unless specifically invited.

Courtesies: A handshake is customary when first meeting someone and when leaving, but not each time if you see someone regularly. When visiting a firm, give your business card to the receptionist.

Business Do's: Business proceeds efficiently. People have tight schedules, so always be punctual and do not waste time chatting. You are expected to know your industry well. Formalities matter: try to be conservatively dressed, well-mannered and reserved.

Business Don'ts: Don't approach business casually. Avoid surprises and spontaneity. Presentations must not look hurriedly prepared. Errors will reflect badly on your attention to detail.

Negotiations: Negotiations should proceed in an orderly way, beginning with factual and authoritative presentation of a competitive proposal well backed up with documentation. Proposed price structure should be close to the final version. Do not waste time trying to cultivate personal relationships—that must come after completion of negotiations. The contract will be thorough.

Entertainment: Dinner is around seven o'clock. It is customary to bring a small gift or flowers (not red roses or carnations, chrysanthemums or white asters). If it is a grand occasion, send flowers beforehand. The guest begins eating first after prompting by the host. Do not discuss dieting during the meal; it is a compliment to finish everything on your plate. Keep your hands (not elbows) on the table. When leaving, shake hands with every family member. Send a "Thank you" note the next day. Wives are normally included in evening entertainment in restaurants.

Language: German, French, Italian.

Religion: 50% Catholic.

TAIWAN AT A GLANCE

Fundamentals in Business: Chinese cultural traditions are very strong. Since 1979, official diplomatic relations between the United States and Taiwan have been severed. However, unofficial trade relations continue through the American Institute in Taiwan, a nonprofit corporation headquartered in Arlington, Virginia, with subsidiary offices in Taipei and Kaohsiung.

Sensitivities: Taiwan is The Republic of China. Do not refer to "mainland China" or bring up the subject of the People's Republic of China. Photography of aircraft or military installations is forbidden. Do not push a door, chair or other objects with your feet—they are considered dirty.

Forms of Address: Always use the one-syllable family name, which usually comes first, with a title or Mr., Mrs. or Miss. (Sometimes the names are reversed or even reduced to initials.)

Courtesies: A nod of the head when meeting someone is appropriate, but the handshake is common among acquaintances. Always acknowledge and greet elderly persons first. A slight bow shows special respect.

Business Do's: Travel with plenty of business cards. Maintain friendliness with reserve and refinement. Make connections, and work on cultivating relationships. Give face. Have patience. Be thoroughly prepared, and maintain consistency in your presentations.

Business Don'ts: Avoid being abrupt or direct; frankness is not appreciated. Do not be loud or boisterous. Business is generally not overtly discussed during social events.

Negotiations: Like Chinese in the PRC, the Taiwanese are characterized by soft sell and hard buy, but negotiations are not so burdened by bureaucratic constraints. The Chinese are very competitive bargainers—but haggle in the spirit of harmony and respect.

Entertainment: Entertainment is usually in restaurants, and is part of the Chinese hospitality. The visitor is not expected to entertain, but should reciprocate with small gifts, which will not be opened in front of the giver. If invited to the home, arrive on time and bring candy, fruit or cookies "for the children." Be prepared for dozens of courses—eat sparingly. The host will serve the guests. Try to use chopsticks. Thank your hosts, and when they apologize that the food was not very good, argue that it was indeed very good.

Language: Mandarin Chinese and Taiwanese.

Religion: Buddhist, Confucian, Taoist.

UNITED KINGDOM AT A GLANCE

U.S. Foreign Commercial Service Post: U.S. Embassy, 24/31 Grosvenor Square, London W1A 1AE.

Fundamentals in Business: The United Kingdom consists of England, Scotland, Wales and Northern Ireland. Business practices are fairly uniform, but local differences in business style vary. The old class system still lives; business is tradition-bound. Although there is a changing of the guard, making connections with the Old Boy network helps.

Sensitivities: Do not ridicule the royal family, the British affection for their dogs, or the lack of "work ethic." The British themselves may refer to the "British disease" but you had better not. Avoid personal questions; many British find Americans to be pushy and intrusive. Avoid demonstrative touching. Do not refer to the Scots, Welsh or Irish as "English."

Forms of Address: First names are increasingly used, but rushing too fast may offend. Play it safe with Mr. and Mrs. A knight is addressed Sir, followed by his first name.

Courtesies: Men shake hands when meeting, but not aggressively. It is not necessary for a woman to shake hands; wait for her to extend her hand. Both people being introduced say "How do you do," rather than "Pleased to meet you." The words "Please" and "Thank you" are used constantly for any small request or service. Never rush to the bus, ticket office, shop counter or other vendor without taking your place in line. Be conspicuously polite to older people.

Business Do's: Always be punctual for business meetings. Presentations should be matter-of-fact, complete in technical or marketing detail, and understated. Conversation should be completely impersonal except with close friends.

Business Don'ts: Do not be overly demonstrative, enthusiastic or emotional. Avoid any comparisons to the United States. Do not push for agreements or appear to be in a hurry. Try not to do most of the talking. Some humor helps. Be conservative in gifts and entertainment, avoiding any suggestion of intentions to bribe.

Negotiations: British negotiators often operate under a burden of conflicting political and economic demands as well as a plethora of restrictions and union pressures. Emphasize the practical implications of your proposal within the long-term picture. A disciplined approach will be more persuasive than bombast. Bargaining is not the norm, but some concessions will satisfy the British negotiator's interest in economy.

Entertainment: If invited to the home (and you may be the only guest), bring a small gift (flowers or chocolates). The fork is held in the left hand. Thank the hosts for their hospitality and send a "Thank you" note the next day.

Language: English; Welsh in Wales.

Religion: Christian.

USSR AT A GLANCE

U.S. Foreign Commercial Service Post: U.S. Embassy, Ulitsa Chaykovskogo, 19/21/23 Moscow.

Fundamentals in Business: The people are Soviets, not Russians; Russians make up no more than 50 percent of the population. The USSR is a centrally controlled economy: all business dealings must go through the appropriate ministry. The machinery moves slowly. Virtually all contracts are signed in the USSR, and a trip there is without doubt essential to establishing a business. It is likely to take several years to get a business going.

Sensitivities: It is a crime to exchange currency with or to sell anything to a Soviet citizen. Dissident literature and exporting of art objects are also forbidden.

Forms of Address: Address people as Mr., Mrs. or Miss with the last name, or with a title.

Courtesies: Shake hands when first meeting people and leaving. Introductions tend to be direct and informal. The Soviets are very status-conscious: use titles and show respect.

Business Do's: Try to abandon your distrust of the Soviets, who see themselves as totally honest and trustworthy. Always allow plenty of time to get your visas, make appointments and conduct any business. You will not be able to budge the bureaucratic routine. Presentations should be strictly factual and full of technical detail.

Business Don'ts: Don't threaten the Soviets' pride. Avoid promotional fluff and be careful not to spill too much information.

Negotiations: Soviet negotiators plan and prepare thoroughly. The only wild card is the potential for sudden change in political priorities. Proposals must be competitive, and the negotiation team made up of experts. Negotiations will be protracted due to greater attention to detail and the cumbersome decision-making process. By their own admission, Soviet negotiators are likely to be "sentimental, sullen, suspicious, and servile." No agreement is final until signed.

Entertainment: Dinner is eaten about six o'clock. It is rare to be invited to a Soviet's home for dinner, but if you are, it is customary to bring flowers or liquor, vodka or wine. Compliment the host on the food and sit at the table a long time after the meal. You may send flowers afterward. Invitations are more likely to include a ballet, circus or concert, and dinner in a restaurant. Toasts are common, and the guest must be prepared to return toasts.

Language: Russian, and about 130 different languages.

Religion: Despite government efforts to eliminate religion, the Russian Orthodox Church thrives.

VENEZUELA AT A GLANCE

U.S. Foreign Commercial Service Post: U.S. Embassy, Avenida Francisco de Miranda & Avenida Principal de la Floresta, Caracas.

Fundamentals in Business: Venezuela is the most urban and the richest of the countries of Latin America. Venezuelans tend to be less religious than other Latins, but family continues to be a dominant factor in business life. The pace of business is relaxed.

Sensitivities: People stand closer together than is customary in the United States. Backing away may suggest dislike or aloofness. Be respectful of historical and religious figures.

Forms of Address: First names are not used until you know someone well.

Courtesies: Shake hands upon first meetings and among friends. Use business cards. Close friends greet with the *abrazo,* a full embrace and hearty pat on the back. When served coffee in an office, accept it graciously or you will offend your host.

Business Do's: Be punctual, even though the Venezuelan is likely to be late. Be demonstrative and gracious. Always converse socially before discussing business. Maintain eye contact and try to establish friendly rapport. Dress fashionably and give the appearance of business success and social position.

Business Don'ts: Don't injure pride. Don't rush. Don't forget to give gifts to service people (garbage collectors, mailmen, etc.) at Christmas or you may lose the service.

Negotiations: The personal relationship must be nurtured while bargaining. Expressiveness and eloquent presentation of materials impress. Leave margins for concession but avoid appearing to have too much fat in your proposal or you will arouse distrust.

Entertainment: Dinner is usually after nine o'clock. Afterward, send a "Thank you" note, call or send flowers.

Language: Spanish.

Religion: Roman Catholic.

RECOMMENDED RESOURCES

FILMS

Going International, the film series we produced to prepare Americans (and others) for their international assignments, is the only audio-visual program currently available covering the wide range of issues that the international business person will confront anywhere in the world. The films have won eight prestigious film-festival awards and are being used in over 75 percent of America's top multinational companies. We believe that a complete orientation program for international businesspeople should include the expertise of consultants and trainers and literature, as well as audio-visual materials. The *Going International* films are available for purchase or rental, in film or any video format, from Copeland Griggs Productions, 411 Fifteenth Avenue, San Francisco, California 94118 (415) 668-4200. The series includes:

Bridging the Culture Gap is for anyone involved in international activity, whether managers, marketers, engineers, teachers or students. Colorful film from around the world powerfully illustrates and explains the complexities involved in interacting with people from different cultures. The impact of cultural differences on the conduct of business is demonstrated, as well as how to become more effective in foreign situations. (28 minutes)

Managing the Overseas Assignment dramatically shows specific problems Americans have doing business in such countries as Japan, Mexico, Saudi Arabia, England and India. Cultural taboos and accepted standards of business behavior are explained by foreign nationals of the host countries, and strategies for improving personal performance in foreign situations are described by experienced corporate travelers. (29 minutes)

Beyond Culture Shock is specifically for the family or the individual moving abroad. Experts explain the psychological phases of the process of adjustment. Expatriate families discuss their tactics for overcoming culture shock; overseas footage shows their experience. Spouses' and children's needs during relocation are given particular attention. The film offers practical suggestions on how to make living abroad an enriching adventure. (28 minutes)

Welcome Home, Stranger focuses on the unexpected problems of returning home. Families describe how they overcame the difficulties of re-entry into both the workplace and the community. Re-entry is often the hardest part of the assignment, and cannot be overlooked. (14 minutes)

Newly added to the *Going International* series are two films which do the reverse of the first *Going International* films. Foreign personnel working for American firms, whether abroad or in the United States, are often confused by their American employers and fail to meet the expectations of management. When they move to the States, their families suffer the same difficulties that Americans experience living abroad. With the financial support and expertise of a number of American companies, we produced two half-hour films specifically for foreigners:

Working In The USA orients the foreigner to the American workplace, value system and work habits. Differences in boss-subordinate relations, communication styles, negotiation patterns, selling, and so forth, are illustrated. Corporate culture in America is shown in its tremendous diversity. Business people from around the world will learn much about the Americans with whom they currently, or would like to, do business.

Living in the USA orients the foreign family to the practical issues involved in making a home here. The American way of life is explained, particularly differences in pace, lifestyles and social customs. Tips are presented for a range of family concerns: housing, schooling, medical care, shopping, safety, and so forth.

All of the *Going International* films are accompanied by user's guides.

BOOKS AND REPORTS

There are very few good books written on the cultural aspects of doing business in specific countries, with the exception of Japan and China. However, the sources below are a good place to start your search for written materials. The list is not exhaustive; for a comprehensive compilation of virtually all the resources and literature relevant to foreign business and foreign countries, see the *Global Guide to International Business,* edited by David Hoopes and published by Facts on File Publications, 460 Park Avenue South, New York, New York 10016.

Publishers

The Intercultural Press, P.O. Box 768, Yarmouth, Maine 04096, is an organization that specializes in publications on international and cross-cultural subjects. Its staff is able to steer you toward materials that are most appropriate to your needs. The Intercultural Press publishes two particularly valuable series, *Interacts* and *Updates,* which provide the kind of practical country-specific business and cultural information that will help a traveler interact more effectively with the people.

International Society for Intercultural Education, Training and Research, 1414 22nd Street, N.W., Washington, D.C. 20037, is a professional association of cross-cultural trainers, personnel administrators, academics, and others interested in intercultural education. The organization sponsors an annual conference and other events, and publishes books in this field.

David M. Kennedy International Center, Brigham Young University, Box 61 FOB, Provo, Utah 84602, offers academic courses to aid intercultural understanding. Its publications include a set of 81 *Culturegrams*, which, in four pages each, describe a country's customs, manners, lifestyles and travel information. Other publications include *Infograms* on various subjects, such as "Questions Asked about America," "Coming Home Again," "Keeping the Law Internationally," "Jet Lag," and so on.

U.S. Department of Commerce, International Trade Administration, 14th and Constitution, Washington, D.C. 20230, publishes vast amounts of statistical data and descriptive market analysis, available in a number of reports, including Export Statistics Profiles, TOP Bulletin, International Market Research Reports, Country Market Surveys, Annual Worldwide Industry Review, World Traders Data Reports, Overseas Export Promotion Calendar, and more. The Department's biweekly magazine, *Business America,* includes news and opportunities in international business.

U.S. Department of State, Foreign Service Institute, Overseas Briefing Center, 1400 Key Boulevard, Arlington, Virginia 22209, prepares State Department personnel for overseas assignments. It maintains a library, which is not open to the public. However, if you are trying to establish a cross-cultural training or expatriate service program for your organization, the Center staff will be happy to share its knowledge. It is a resource worth using. The State Department also produces in-depth country *Area Studies* and briefer *Post Reports* on virtually every country where there is a U.S. embassy. These are available at government bookstores throughout the country.

General Reference for the Business Traveler

Business Customs and Protocol Series, SRI International, Menlo Park, California. A collection of passport-sized books, covering the basics of business protocol in sixteen countries.

Business Traveler's Handbook, Jane Walker *et.al.,* editors, Facts on File, New York. A series of books covering Africa, Asia, Australia, the Pacific, Europe, Latin America, the Middle East, U.S.A. and Canada. Each gives detailed country-by-country economic, business and travel information; useful data, but very little on the cultural aspects of doing business.

International Yearbooks from the World of Information: Middle East Review, Africa Guide, Asia & Pacific, Latin America & Caribbean, from the World Almanac

Education Division, Cleveland, Ohio. Annual editions analyze the economic, political and marketplace dynamics in each region and country, with concise assembly of basic business facts.

Multinational Executive Travel Companion, published annually by Multinational Executive, Inc., in Cambridge, Massachusetts, provides travel information and business data on 160 countries—it is a mini-encyclopedia.

Newsletters

The International American, 201 East 36th Street, New York 10016. A monthly publication addressing the interests and concerns of frequent business travelers and the expatriate community.

FOREIGN TRADE OFFICES

Many countries have foreign trade offices whose job it is to help importers and exporters. Some publish excellent booklets, such as "How to Approach the German Market," produced by the German Foreign Trade Information Office. The Japan External Trade Organization (JETRO) is the most impressive, providing a complete library of publications and films on Japanese business. JETRO's "Now in Japan" reports are particularly instructive. JETRO has offices in New York, Los Angeles, Chicago, San Francisco and Houston.

The embassies of foreign countries should be able to provide you with valuable information on doing business in their countries—they too offer excellent booklets, or they can guide you to the relevant trade organization. All embassies are in Washington, D.C., but if there is a consulate in your city, it would be more efficient to check there first.

EDUCATIONAL INSTITUTIONS

Many universities and community colleges have or are currently establishing programs incorporating international business, including Brigham Young, Columbia, George Washington—it would be impossible to list them all. The only graduate school specifically dedicated to international business training is:

American Graduate School of International Business (Thunderbird)

Thunderbird Campus, Glendale, Arizona 85306. The graduate program offers a

Master of International Management as well as research services and in-service training for business executives.

How to Find and Use Consultants

Every field has its experts, and international business is no exception. In fact, there are so many people available to consult that you should be able to find someone who has the particular knowledge and skills that relate to your specific situation, i.e., your industry or profession, your geographical area and your objectives. Be selective. A relocation consultant who is expert at moving employees and families abroad will probably not be the best choice for consulting on your foreign advertising or structuring of joint ventures. An export trade specialist might have little to offer the company needing help in designing training programs for international personnel.

Few consultants advertise. They generally become known through word of mouth, and can be found by asking others in your line of work. But always consider several consultants, compare their abilities and select the one that best fits your needs. Never hire a consultant without checking references; a client recommendation is your safest assurance of capability. Do all you would do if you were hiring personnel at home, and more.

Consulting agreements should define expectations, including description of the task and territory, schedule for work, plans for payment, performance measures, protections for confidentiality and proprietary information, limitations of liability, grounds for termination of contract, and any limits on expenditures or authority. In addition to specifying the end results, in some cases you might want to specify how a job is to be accomplished.

U.S. Government Services

Although foreign trade information and services are concentrated in the Commerce Department, described below, almost every American government agency has some international activity. One excellent guide through the maze of government agencies is *Washington's Best Kept Secrets—A U.S. Guide to International Business,* edited by William A. Delphos and published by John Wiley & Sons, Inc., 605 Third Avenue, New York, N.Y. 10158.

U.S. Department of Commerce, International Trade Administration

14th Street and Constitution Avenue, N.W., Washington, D.C. 20230.
The ITA operates four major programs, including:

U.S. and Foreign Commercial Service (US&FCS), through its domestic and foreign operations, maintains current and comprehensive market-related information and provides direct assistance to new and experienced American exporters.

The most important service of the US&FCS is the direct and professional counseling provided by trade specialists in 47 District Offices throughout the country. The prospective or already active exporter can receive counseling on overseas opportunities, information about the foreign market, shipping, documentation requirements, financing, tax advantages, and trade exhibitions, as well as advice about how to find an international banker, insurance, freight forwarder, and so on. Recently, free legal counseling has been added to the services. The US&FCS District Offices also coordinate 51 District Export Councils, a cadre of experienced American exporters who conduct seminars and who counsel prospective exporters in the "how-to's" of international trade.

Overseas, the US&FCS maintains offices in 120 major foreign cities in the 63 countries that are our principal trading partners. Commercial officers provide a full range of business, investment and financial counseling services, including political and credit-risk analysis, advice on market-entry strategy, sources of financing, and major-project identification. They also can help make introductions to local business and government leaders, assist in trade disputes, and identify or evaluate potential importers, buyers, agents or joint-venture partners for American firms.

International Economic Policy (IEP) is the ITA's own "State Department." When you want country-specific expertise, this is the place to go; IEP country specialists can provide information on foreign market conditions, commercial policies, business practices, economic and political developments, tariffs and trade regulations, as well as statistical data on imports and exports, production, and third-country competition. Working with the US&FCS, they also assist in identifying agents or distributors for the exporter. IEP's Office of Multilateral Affairs handles questions that U.S. firms may have regarding their rights and benefits under various trade agreements.

Trade Development (TD) provides industry-specific analysis and assistance for major export sectors including aerospace, automotive and consumer goods, basic industries (forest products, metals, energy, chemicals), science and electronics, textiles and apparel, services, and capital goods/international construction (e.g. industrial machinery). When you want expertise in your particular industry, this is an important stop.

Trade Administration is the ITA's policeman, responsible for licensing and export controls. The Office of Export Administration (OEA) handles export licenses and provides counseling on licensing matters.

Subscription services of the ITA

In addition to the free government services provided by the four major arms of the ITA, a number of specialized services are available on a subscription basis. New programs are formed from time to time, so you should ask your District Office trade specialist for current information. To give you an idea of the range of services, a few are described below:

Agent Distributor Service—US&FCS officers in over 200 embassies and consulates abroad conduct a customized search for interested and qualified foreign representatives for your product or service. Armed with your own literature, the commercial officer works to identify and screen potential foreign agents or distributors who are interested in your product or service. The US&FCS officer returns to you a list of up to six potential foreign representatives. The fee is $90 per country.

Export Mailing List Service—a mailing list containing information on about 140,-000 foreign firms, including name and title of key officials, telephone and Telex numbers, product or service interests, and indicators of size. Lists can be provided by country, product, or both. Prices vary with information requested.

New Product Information Service (NPIS)—disseminates information of a product you want to test in a new market, via the *Commercial News USA* bimonthly publication, which is distributed to about 200,000 foreign buyers, agents and distributors. The price is $40. Your product may also be selected for mention on the weekly Voice of America broadcast.

Trade Opportunities Program (TOP)—notifies exporters of foreign business leads, including information on product specifications, quantities, end-use, delivery and bid deadlines and other requirements for the product or services wanted by the foreign customer. The weekly TOP Bulletin costs $175; the more selective TOP Notice Service costs more, depending on the leads.

World Traders Data Report (WTDR)—commercial profiles of individual foreign firms. Each report includes product and company data as well as credit rating, payment history, trade references and the US&FCS evaluation of the company's suitability as a trade contact. The fee for each WTDR is $75.

Experienced traders complain that the Commerce Department programs are helpful only when you do careful market research on your own, because the Department's information may be too old and not well enough researched. "Hot leads" may be long gone by the time you hear of them via the Department, and of course the trade specialists or commercial officers can be expected to know about only a portion of the business opportunities. If leads are not well qualified, you can spend a lot of time and money spinning wheels with organizations inappropriate for your business. The services of the ITA are not a substitute for your own careful exploration and analysis, but used appropriately and intelligently, the ITA services can be extremely valuable.

U.S. & FOREIGN COMMERCIAL SERVICE
DISTRICT OFFICES

NORTHEASTERN REGION I

CONNECTICUT
★ *Hartford,* 06103, Room 610-B, Fed. Bldg., 450 Main St. (203) 722-3530.

MAINE
Serviced by the Boston District Office

MASSACHUSETTS
Boston, 02116, 10th Floor, 441 Stuart St. (617) 223-2312.

NEW HAMPSHIRE
Serviced by the Boston District Office

NEW YORK
Buffalo, 14202, 1312 Federal Bldg., 111 W. Huron St. (716) 846-4191.
New York, 10278, Rm. 3718, Federal Office Bldg., 26 Federal Plaza, Foley Sq. (212) 264-0634.

RHODE ISLAND
Serviced by the Boston District Office

VERMONT
Serviced by the Boston District Office

MID-ATLANTIC REGION II

DELAWARE
Serviced by the Philadelphia District Office

DISTRICT OF COLUMBIA
Serviced by the Baltimore District Office

MARYLAND
Baltimore, 21202, 415 U.S. Customhouse, Gay and Lombard Sts. (301) 962-3560.

NEW JERSEY
★ *Trenton,* 08608, 240 West State St., 8th Fl. (609) 989-2100.

PENNSYLVANIA
Philadelphia, 19106, 9448 Federal Bldg., 600 Arch St. (215) 597-2866.
Pittsburgh, 15222, 2002 Fed. Bldg., 1000 Liberty Ave. (412) 644-2850.

APPALACHIAN REGION III

KENTUCKY
Louisville, 40202, Rm. 636B, U.S. Post Office and Courthouse Bldg. (502) 582-5066.

NORTH CAROLINA
★ *Greensboro,* 27402, 203 Federal Bldg., 324 W. Market St., P.O. Box 1950. (919) 378-5345.

SOUTH CAROLINA
Columbia, 29201, Strom Thurmond Fed. Bldg., Suite 172, 1835 Assembly St. (803) 765-5345.

TENNESSEE
Nashville, 37239, Suite 1427, 1 Commerce Pl. (615) 251-5161.

VIRGINIA
Richmond, 23240, 8010 Federal Bldg., 400 N. 8th St. (804) 771-2246.

WEST VIRGINIA
Charleston, 25301, 3000 New Federal Office Bldg., 500 Quarrier St. (304) 347-5123.

SOUTHEASTERN REGION IV

ALABAMA
★ *Birmingham,* 35205, Suite 200-201, 908 S. 20th St. (205) 254-1331.

FLORIDA
Miami, 33130, Suite 224, Federal Bldg., 51 S.W. First Ave. (305) 350-5267.

GEORGIA
Atlanta, 30309, Suite 600, 1365
Peachtree St., NE.
(404) 881-7000.
Savannah, 31401, 27 East Bay St.,
P.O. Box 9746. (912) 944-4204.

MISSISSIPPI
Jackson, 39213, Suite 3230, 300
Woodrow Wilson Blvd. (601)
960-4388.

PUERTO RICO
San Juan (Hato Rey), 00918, Room
659 Federal Bldg., Chardon Ave.
(809) 753-4555, Ext. 555.

GREAT LAKES REGION V

ILLINOIS
Chicago, 60603, Room 1406,
Mid-Continental Plaza Bldg., 55 E.
Monroe St. (312) 353-4450.

INDIANA
Indianapolis, 46204, 357 U.S.
Courthouse & Federal Office Bldg.,
46 E. Ohio St. (317) 269-6214.

MICHIGAN
Detroit, 48226, 445 Federal Bldg.,
231 W. Lafayette (313) 226-3650.

MINNESOTA
Minneapolis, 55401, 218 Federal
Bldg., 110 S. 4th St. (612) 349-3338.

OHIO
★ *Cincinnati,* 45202, 9504 Fed.
Bldg., 550 Main St. (513) 684-2944.
Cleveland, 44114, Room 600, 666
Euclid Ave. (216) 522-4750.

WISCONSIN
Milwaukee, 53202, 605 Federal
Bldg., 517 E. Wisconsin Ave. (414)
291-3473.

PLAINS REGION VI

IOWA
Des Moines, 50309, 817 Federal
Bldg., 210 Walnut St. (515) 284-4222.

KANSAS
Serviced by the Kansas City,
Missouri, District Office

MISSOURI
Kansas City, 64106, Rm. 1840, 601 E.
12th St. (816) 374-3142.
★ *St. Louis,* 63105, 120 S. Central
Ave. (314) 425-3302.

NEBRASKA
Omaha, 68102, Empire State Bldg., 1st
Floor, 300 S. 19th St. (402) 221-3664.

NORTH DAKOTA
Serviced by the Omaha District Office

SOUTH DAKOTA
Serviced by the Omaha District
Office

CENTRAL REGION VII

ARKANSAS
Little Rock, 72201, Rm. 635, 320 W.
Capitol Ave. (501) 378-5794.

LOUISIANA
New Orleans, 70130, 432
International Trade Mart, 2 Canal
St. (504) 589-6546.

NEW MEXICO
Albuquerque, 87102, 505 Marquette
Ave. N.W., Rm. 1015. (505)
766-2386.

OKLAHOMA
Oklahoma City, 73105, 4024 Lincoln
Blvd. (405) 231-5302.

TEXAS
★ *Dallas,* 75242, Room 7A5, 1100
Commerce St. (214) 767-0542.
Houston, 77002, 2625 Federal Bldg.,
Courthouse, 515 Rusk St. (713)
229-2578.

ROCKY MT. REGION VIII

ARIZONA
Phoenix, 85073, 2950 Valley Bank
Center, 201 N. Central Ave. (602)
261-3285.

COLORADO
★ *Denver,* 80202, Room 119, U.S.
Customhouse, 721 19th St. (303)
837-3246.

IDAHO
Serviced by the Salt Lake City
District Office

MONTANA
Serviced by the Denver District
Office

NEVADA
Reno, 89502, 1755 East Plumb Lane,
Rm. 152. (702) 784-5203.

UTAH
Salt Lake City, 84101, Rm. 340, U.S.
Post Office Bldg., 350 S. Main St.
(801) 524-5116.

WYOMING
Serviced by the Denver District
Office

PACIFIC REGION IX

ALASKA
Anchorage, 99513, P.O. Box 32, 701
C St. (907) 271-5041.

CALIFORNIA
Los Angeles, 90049, Rm. 800, 11777
San Vicente Blvd. (213) 209-6707.
★ *San Francisco,* 94102, Rm. 15205
Federal Bldg., Box 36013, 450
Golden Gate Ave. (415) 556-5860.

HAWAII
Honolulu, 96850, 4106 Federal Bldg.,
300 Ala Moana Blvd., P.O. Box
50026. (808) 546-8694.

OREGON
Portland, 97204, Room 618, 1220
S.W. 3rd Ave. (503) 221-3001.

WASHINGTON
Seattle, 98109, 706 Lake Union
Bldg., 1700 Westlake Ave. North.
(206) 442-5616.

★ Denotes Regional Managing Director's Office

NOTES

INTRODUCTION

1. "Trying to Turn a Rival into a Partner," *Business Week,* October 15, 1984, p. 56.
2. John F. Naisbitt, *Megatrends,* New York, Warner Books, 1982, p. 76.

CHAPTER I

1. Beatrice K. Reynolds, "A Cross-Cultural Study of Values of Germans and Americans," *International Journal of Intercultural Relations,* Vol. 8, # 3, 1984, p. 269.
2. G. Hofstede, *Culture's Consequences: International Differences in Work-Related Values.* Beverly Hills, Sage, 1980.

CHAPTER 3

1. "The Ad Biz Gloms Onto Global," *Fortune,* November 12, 1984, p. 77.
2. "Media Notes and Quotes," *Advertising World,* July 1984, p. 34.

3. Edward T. Hall, *The Silent Language,* Garden City, N.Y., Anchor Books, 1973.

4. "Media Notes and Quotes," *loc. cit.*

5. Michael Hook, "London Eye-view of Ad Placement Skills," *Advertising World,* April-May 1984, p. 56.

Other excellent sources of marketing information include:

Franklin Root, *Foreign Market Entry Strategies,* New York, American Management Association, 1982.

Robert F. Roth, *International Marketing Communications,* Chicago, Crain Books, 1982.

Philip Cateora, *International Marketing,* Illinois, Irwin Press, 1983.

Dean Peebles and John Ryans, *Management of International Advertising,* Rockleigh, N.J., Allyn and Bacon, 1984.

CHAPTER 4

1. Richard Pascale, in his negotiation class at Stanford's Graduate School of Business, stresses this concept of negotiations creating "new values." The authors are indebted to him for this concept and several other negotiation concepts which we have adopted or modified for the international arena, based on material in his working paper "Negotiation and Intervention," Spring 1980.

2. Christopher Wren, "US-China Trade," *New York Times Magazine,* April 10, 1983.

3. "Behavior of Successful Negotiators," Huthwaite Research Group Report 1982, as reported by Robert T. Moran, *Getting Your Yen's Worth,* Houston, Texas, Gulf Publishing, 1983, p. 93.

4. Glen Fisher, *International Negotiation: A Cross-Cultural Perspective,* Yarmouth, Maine, Intercultural Press, 1980. This is one of the few books dealing with cultural differences in negotiation, comparing Mexican, Japanese and French styles.

Additional sources:

The best source for information on negotiation in China is: Lucian Pye, *Chinese Commercial Negotiating Style,* Boston, Mass., Oelgeschlager, Gunn & Hain, 1982.

CHAPTER 5

1. "Back-patting Clapping," *Forbes,* June 18, 1984, p. 20.

2. Alison Lanier, *Nigeria Update,* Yarmouth, Maine, Intercultural Press, 1982.

3. Jan Carol Bemis, "The Art of Interpreting," in *Communicating with China,* Robert Kapp, ed., Yarmouth, Maine, Intercultural Press, 1983.

CHAPTER 6

1. John Condon, *Interact: Guidelines for Mexicans and North Americans,* Yarmouth, Maine, Intercultural Press, 1980.
2. Richard Pascale and William Ouchi, "Made in America (Under Japanese Management)," *Harvard Business Review,* September-October, 1974.
3. "The Japanese Manager Meets the American Worker," *Business Week,* August 20, 1984, pp. 128–129.
4. Peter Wright, "Doing Business in Islamic Markets," *Harvard Business Review,* January-February, 1981.

Additional sources:

Phillip Grub, ed., *The Multinational Enterprise in Transition,* Princeton, N.J., Darwin Press, 1983.

CHAPTER 7

1. Silvere Seurat, *Technology Transfer,* Houston, Texas, Gulf Publishing, 1979. This is one of the few books that deals systematically with the training aspects of technology transfer—it was most helpful to us in structuring this chapter.
2. James Lee, "Developing Managers in Developing Countries," *Harvard Business Review,* November-December 1968, p. 134.
3. *Ibid.*
4. Nancy Adler and M. Kiggundu, "Awareness at the Crossroads: Designing Translator-Based Training Programs," to be published in *Handbook of Intercultural Training: Issues for Training Methodology,* D. Landis and R. Brislin, Elmsford, N.Y., Pergamon Press.
5. Alison Lanier, *Living in the USA,* Yarmouth, Maine, Intercultural Press, 1981.

CHAPTER 8

1. Dudly Miller, "The Honorable Picnic," *Harvard Business Review,* November-December 1961.

CHAPTER 9

1. Boye De Mente, *The Japanese Way of Doing Business,* Englewood Cliffs, N.J., Prentice-Hall, 1981, p. 59.
2. Ibid., p.88.

CHAPTER 11

1. Korn/Ferry International, "The Repatriation of the American International Executive," New York, December, 1981.

Additional sources:

Virginia McKay, *Moving Abroad—A Guide to International Living,* Wilmington, Del., VLM Enterprises, 1982.

Robert Kohls, *Survival Kit for Overseas Living,* Yarmouth, Maine, Intercultural Press, 1979.

GOING INTERNATIONAL: THE FILMS

Copeland Griggs Productions, 411 Fifteenth Avenue, San Francisco, California 94118

Film is a powerful way to expose people to the overseas experience before they ever leave home.

Whether your organization is new to the global marketplace or a well-established multinational enterprise, your personnel who are involved in international business will benefit from the *Going International* films. Even the most experienced traveler knows there is always more to learn.

Going International is designed to assist all those who have contact with people of other cultures, whether employees or students, in the public or private sector, and anywhere in the world.

Going International is the winner of eleven awards from America's most pretigious film festivals. The films are informative, entertaining and fast-paced; they respect the intelligence of the viewer.

Going International costs less than the airfare for a typical international business trip. The cost of *Going International* is only 1% of the average cost of failure when a family returns prematurely.

For more information about each film, see p. 258 or call (415) 668-4200.

Cut here) -

ORDER FORM   Please send *Going International* as indicated below:
____16mm film   ____¼"Umatic   ____½"VHS   ____½"Beta I   ____½"Beta II

Indicate quantity on the lines below. Prices subject to change. *Educational discount 30% in video.* Call us for rentals, previews, and volume discounts.

Going International films	ONE-PART PRICE	TWO-PART PRICE	USER'S GUIDES	TOTAL
For international travelers:				
Bridging the Culture Gap	____ $495		____ $5	$ _____
Managing the Overseas Assignment	____ $495	____ $895	____ $5	$ _____
For those relocating abroad:				
Beyond Culture Shock	____ $495		____ $5	$ _____
Welcome Home, Stranger	____ $395	____ $795	____ $5	$ _____
For new or non-U.S. citizens:				
Working in the USA	____ $495		____ $5	$ _____
Living in the USA	____ $495	____ $895	____ $5	$ _____
			SUB-TOTAL	$ _____

Less 30% for educational/non-profit purchase in video $(_____)
Plus sales tax for California orders $ _____
Plus $5.00 per film/tape for shipping (unless check enclosed) $ _____
Mail check and/or order form to Copeland Griggs Productions.   TOTAL: $ _____

Name _____ Street Address _____
Title _____ City _____ State _____ Zip _____
Organization _____ Phone (___)_____ Purchase Order #_____

Just a few things buyers say about the **Going International** *films:*

"A vital message." *AMOCO*
"On target." *PepsiCo*
"Outstanding." *Federal Express*
"Excellent . . . all the basic tools for any culture." *Hewlett-Packard*
"Should be viewed by anyone going overseas." *Raymond Kaiser Engineers*
"Addresses all levels of traveler, seasoned as well as novice." *3M*
"Everyone I've shown them to has been impressed." *Bethlehem International*
"Fascinating, and so important." *CBS Morning News*

And a few of the organizations using the films:

Aetna Life & Casualty, Alcoa, Allied Bendix, Amdahl, American Cyanamid, American Motors, American Standard, AMF, AMOCO, ARCO, Arthur Anderson, Arthur D. Little, Arthur Young, AT&T, Bank of Boston, Baxter Travenol, Beatrice, Bechtel, Bell Helicopter, Bently Nevada, Bethlehem International, Betz, Boeing, Booz Allen & Hamilton, Bristol-Myers, Brown & Root, Burger King, Burlington Northern, Leo Burnett, Cargill, Caterpillar, CHP International, Chase Manhattan, Chesebrough-Pond's, Chevron, Chrysler, Chubb & Son, CIGNA, Citibank, Coca-Cola, Colgate-Palmolive, Continental Illinois Bank, Control Data, Coopers & Lybrand, Corning Glass, Cray Research, Cummins Engine, Dart & Kraft, Del Monte, Deloitte Haskins & Sells, Digital Equipment, Disneyland, Dow Chemical, Dow Corning, Dresser Industries, Dun & Bradstreet, Eastman Kodak, Eli Lilly, Ernst & Whinney, Federal Express, Exxon, Firestone, First Interstate Bank, FMC, Ford, Foster Wheeler, General Dynamics, General Electric, General Mills, General Motors, General Tire, Gillette, Goodyear, Grey Advertising, GTE, Gulf Oil, Harris, Hewlett-Packard, Honeywell, Hospital Corporation of America, Hughes Aircraft, Humana, IBM, Intel, International Flavors & Fragrances, International Multifoods, Irving Trust, Johnson Wax, Kaiser Aluminum & Chemical, Kendall, Kentucky Fried Chicken, Lear Siegler, Levi Strauss, Lockheed, Manufacturers Hanover Trust, Marathon Oil, Marine Midland Bank, Mattel, McDermott, McDonald's, McDonnell-Douglas, McGraw Hill, Merck, 3M, Mitre, Mobil, Monsanto, Motorola, Nabisco, NCR, Northrop, Occidental Petroleum, Olin, PAN AM, Parsons, Peat Marwick Mitchell & Co., PepsiCo, Phibro Salomon, Philip Morris, Pillsbury, Pratt & Whitney, Price Waterhouse, Procter & Gamble, Ralston Purina, Raychem, R.J. Reynolds, Rockwell, Rohm & Haas, Rolm, Safeway, Scott Paper, Scovill, Seagram & Sons, Searle, Security Pacific, Shell Oil, Singer, SmithKline, Sperry, SRI, Stauffer Chemical, Tenneco, Texaco, Texas Instruments, TRW, Union Carbide, Uniroyal, UPS, Walgreens, Wang Labs, Westin Hotels, Westinghouse, Weyerhaeuser, The World Bank, Xerox, Young & Rubicam and numerous universities, community colleges, high schools, government agencies, military organizations, church groups, cities, states, and foreign companies and organizations.